W9-ARA-688

ZEMKE'S
WOLF PACK

ZEMKE'S WOLF PACK

The Story of
Hub Zemke
and
the 56th
Fighter Group
in
the skies
over Europe

AS TOLD TO
ROGER A. FREEMAN

Orion Books • New York

Copyright © 1988 by Roger A. Freeman

All rights reserved. No part of this book may be reproduced or transmitted
in any form or by any means, electronic or mechanical, including photocopying,
recording, or by any information storage and retrieval system, without
permission in writing from the publisher.

Published in the United States in 1989 by Crown Publishers, Inc.,
201 East 50th Street, New York, New York 10022

Originally published in 1988 in Great Britain as *The Hub: Fighter Leader*
by Airlife Publishing Ltd.

ORION and colophon are trademarks of Crown Publishers, Inc.

Manufactured in the United States of America

Library of Congress Cataloging-in-Publication Data

Zemke, Hub, 1914–
    Zemke's wolf pack / Hub Zemke with Roger Freeman.
        p.   cm.
    1. Zemke, Hub, 1914– .   2. World War, 1939–1945—Aerial operations,
American.   3. World War, 1939–1945—Personal narratives, American.
4. World War, 1939–1945—Campaigns—Western.   5. United States.   Army
Air Forces—Biography.   6. Fighter pilots—United States—Biography.
I. Freeman, Roger Anthony.   II. Title.
D790.Z44   1989
940.54'4973—dc20   89-3396

ISBN 0-517-57330-X

10 9 8 7 6 5 4 3 2 1

First American Edition

CONTENTS

Acknowledgements

In the course of the extensive research backing this narrative many individuals provided information or material. Several are retired officers but I hope no offence is given if rank is omitted here. To David Annand, John R. Alison, Mrs. Nell Bloor, Cliff Bishop, James R. Carter, Harold E. Comstock, Johnny Deetjen, Gotz Diehm, Peter M. Elliott, Garry Fry, Francis S. Gabreski, Werner Girbig, David Hubler, Curtis C. Houston, Professor John W. Huston, Damon Itza, Gerald W. Johnson, Robert S. Johnson, Witold Lanowski, Harlan Leachman, Leo Lester, Lord Martonmere, Melvin McNickle, James Parton, Robin Olds, David W. Robinson, Henry Selib, Christopher Shores, David Smith, Marty Stanton, Alex Vanags-Beginskis and Sylvester Walker I offer my sincere thanks.

My gratitude is also expressed to Patricia Keen for delving into dusty archives, to George Pennick and Ian Mactaggart for photographic expertise, to Bruce Robertson and Bruce Quarrie for editorial guidance and Jean Freeman for mastering the dreaded 'Alice'.

Roger A. Freeman

INTRODUCTION

In the summer of 1944 my father obtained permission to cut grass on the flying field at Boxted aerodrome. The grass was free and he needed extra hay for winter feed. This was a heaven-sent opportunity for me, then a sixteen-year-old aeroplane obsessed youth, to indulge my fancy. Whenever possible I became part of the haymaking team despatched to the airfield. Issued with passes, we were allowed to work close to the aircraft dispersals on which were parked the red-nosed Thunderbolt fighters of the resident unit, the United States 8th Air Force's 56th Fighter Group. Early one July evening we were told by military police on motor cycles to keep well back from the perimeter track, a warning that usually meant a mission was going out. But first a staff car, indicative of someone of import, arrived at the Thunderbolt close to our activities. Out stepped a young man in pilot's gear, smiling as he chatted with a mechanic, before climbing up into the cockpit of the fighter.

After the aircraft had departed on their mission the haymakers struck up conversation with some of the mechanics nearby. I ventured the question: "Who was that in the staff car?" 'That was our Colonel. He's one hell of a guy,' was the reply.

When, some weeks earlier, I had learned from another soldier on the airfield that the commander was a Colonel Zemke (pronounced Zem-key), I had visions of a very senior man. All the retired British Colonels in our neighbourhood seemed old men — at sixteen anyone over fifty could only be viewed as old. Thus, it was hard to accept that the youthful man I had just seen was the Colonel commanding the Group. For that reason I was to remember this evening, although, perhaps given the passage of time, it was not quite as described. Nevertheless, when early the following year I read a paperback called *Fighters Up* in which Hub Zemke featured prominently, the image brought to mind was that of the smiling young man beside a Thunderbolt.

In later years, while writing the history of the 8th Air Force, the name Zemke became very familiar. It was frequently to be found in the records of fighter operations and often mentioned in correspondence with former fighter pilots and commanders. As a result, over the years, I gained a good knowledge of this man's career and an objective appreciation of his contribution to fighter operations conducted by the US air forces from the United Kingdom.

Prior to a visit to California in October 1981, I wrote to Hub Zemke, relating the story of my first sight of him and asked if I might briefly call and say hello. The response was in the affirmative and, with typical wry Hub humour, I was invited to stay over — there being some dry bales of hay in the barn. The best part of forty years had, naturally, transformed the young Colonel seen that summer's evening in 1944 but it did not take long to discover that the qualities which had made Hub Zemke the premier fighter leader of his day were still evident.

The story that follows is mostly as told to me by Hub. To circumnavigate his modesty and give other viewpoints, the account is embellished with anecdotes recounted by others. While I acknowledge my admiration of the man, every effort has been made to portray him in an unbiased light; I know he would not want it any other way.

Roger A. Freeman
Dedham
England

PROLOGUE

Two days later, 6 March 1944, the heavies made their first really successful strike on the enemy capital and, as we had anticipated, the Luftwaffe rose to give battle as probably never before. The air battles over the Continent were of epic proportions, resulting in the 8th Air Force's heaviest loss of the war, 69 B-17s and B-24s and eleven fighters. Claims against the enemy were 97 by bombers and 81 by fighters. His true losses were later established at around seventy and our fighter claims were not far from the mark.

I led A group off from Halesworth at 10:13 hours and Gerry Johnson, who had taken command of the 63rd when Burke left, headed the B group which departed twenty minutes later. Our job was to shepherd the bombers through the Happy Hunting Ground until relieved by P-51s. The route was more or less straight and climbing out we made landfall over Egmond while at around 22,000 feet. We passed one formation after another of the Big Friends until we established our rendezvous with the leading box near Lingen at 11:28 hours. So far the enemy had not shown his hand. The familiar shape of Dummer Lake passed below, a landmark we knew the Luftwaffe used to assemble its formations for attacking the bombers. 'Tackline', our fighter wing ground control, gave me the coded warning that a large formation of enemy aircraft was somewhere ahead to our north. Shortly afterwards Jim Stewart called that he was engaging a large enemy formation, an estimated 75 to 100 planes! The 61st Squadron was about fifteen miles north-west of the 63rd which I was leading. 'Yardstick here: Postgate Squadron follow me.' Throttle and boost to maximum we cut through the icy air with the tense commands of men in combat coming over the radio. All eyes in my squadron scanned the horizon for sight of combats. But where were they? After five minutes the radio calls ceased and it was evident that the battle was over. We finally saw parachutes and burning aircraft further to the west; we had arrived too late.

Then I caught sight of a lone FW 190 around 3,000 feet below diving towards one of the Fortress formations. Calling my flight to follow, I did a fast wing over and went down. The '190 was lining up to attack one of the trailing B-17s so I gave the engine water injection, but my rate of closure was still not fast enough to catch the Focke Wulf before he opened up on the Fort. After strafing the bomber he immediately banked left, enabling me to cut across behind his tail. When he filled the 300 yard graticule marks on my sight I gave him a burst of about fifty rounds before a quick evasive manoeuvre had to be made to avoid a collision. As I glanced back I saw the '190 going down in a steep dive trailing flame and smoke.

While starting to regain altitude an Me 109 was glimpsed to the south. Turning towards it in a shallow dive, speed was increased to catch him. Again when about 300 yards behind my quarry, but being slightly to one side twenty degrees deflection was allowed, I fingered the fire trigger. At first no hits were seen, then many strikes on his right wing, whereupon the pilot put the '109 into a dive. My superior speed quickly carried me into close range and another burst brought hits all over my victim causing it to burst into flames and go into a spin.

I called Postgate White flight to circle up to 20,000 feet and reform. As we climbed, yet another lone enemy fighter was seen, soon identified as an Me 109. 'Postgate White Flight: follow me.' Power was increased to bring him into range but the pilot saw us coming in time and pulled the old familiar escape routine of split-S and dive. An advance of boost and rpm and a wing over to follow him. He was diving vertically. Then suddenly the '109 burst into flames and went tumbling and spinning down. My immediate reaction was that some eager beaver in my flight had got there first, but no, they were all to my rear with no other fighters in the vicinity. The dying Messerschmitt continued its fiery descent and was almost consumed with flame when it finally hit the ground. Its demise was to remain a mystery, for back at Halesworth it was confirmed no other member of my flight had fired a shot. Other members of the A group had seen action and with red lights blinking many touched down on home plate after near three hours forty minutes in the air. B group also returned with a few victories and our standing for the day was ten in the air for one missing. Not until many years after the war did I learn that the Me 109 that so mysteriously ignited had been badly damaged in a fight with 78th Group P-47s and as we attacked its pilot baled out, unseen by us, opening his parachute at lower altitude.

1

THE MOULDING OF A FIGHTER

The best anniversary present in Anna Zemke's life arrived on her 25th birthday, 14 March 1914. Just before half past six in the morning her only child, a seven and a half pound boy, was delivered by Doctor Pease at the Missoula, Montana, Maternity Hospital. Thus entered into this world Hubert Zemke. His mother preferred the name Wolfgang, that of her favourite composer Mozart; but her husband Benno decreed that the boy should be named in honour of his deceased uncle. Many years later the son was to ask his mother why he had been given only one first name; her reply was to the effect that with Hubert and Zemke who needed a middle name?

Hubert Zemke's parents were both German immigrants to the United States, unhappy family situations playing a major part in decisions to depart the country of their birth. Benno Zemke, an eldest son, chose to run away to sea to escape an oppressive father, a Pomeranian forester. As a seaman on Hamburg/American Steamship Line vessels plying the North Atlantic, he saw better opportunities in the United States and decided to jump ship. In Philadelphia he gained employment in a butcher's shop until his illegal immigrant status was discovered and he was turned over to the German Consulate.

Returned to Germany in 1902, the authorities ordered two years conscription in the Imperial Army or, alternatively, a prison sentence. He chose the former, serving as a gunner. However, he was determined to return to America, attracted by the greater opportunities and freer society afforded to a working class man than in his native Germany. Following the release from his military service he obtained the necessary papers and was successful in passing through United States Immigration at Ellis Island, New York. Benno had heard that there were several small communities in the north-central states, largely settled by people from Germany. He therefore made his way to Mankato, Minnesota, where he took a job with a farmer from his native land

Although at first happy with this appointment, it began to dawn on him that his employer had other plans. The farmer had two daughters and intimated that a healthy, good looking young man like Benno would be a favourable match for one of these young ladies. Not wishing to jeopardise his recently acquired freedom, Benno quickly moved further west into Montana, where work was said to be available.

At that time — 1906 — Montana was a very sparsely populated state with large tracts of country completely devoid of human inhabitants. Three railroads had penetrated through Montana to Seattle and Portland, linking the Pacific coast to Chicago. The railroads, then the main arteries of America, were thriving organisations offering employment to men willing to work hard and long. Benno was taken on as a locomotive fireman at Livingston, a small town north of the famous Yellowstone Park, but soon moved on to a similar job at Missoula, a larger town set between the Rocky and the Bitterfoot mountain ranges. Although the work was hard, he liked the camaraderie of the railroads. Being a frugal batchelor, he had by 1910 accumulated the then considerable sum of $4,000, making him a man of relative affluence compared to his relations back in Germany. His desire to show them how he had made good was a prime motive to obtaining three months leave of absence for return to his fatherland. It was while aboard the vessel returning him to the United States from this visit that Benno met Anna Maria Kutter.

Anna was born at Fussen, a town on the edge of the Bavarian Alps, not far from the fairytale castle of Neu Schwansteiu. Like Benno, she was the eldest child of a family where the mother had died. Her father, with five youngsters and a guesthouse to run, soon married again but proceeded to procreate more children, eventually doubling the size of the family. Anna and the elder children were found employment but were called upon to contribute from their earnings to support their father's new family. Estranged from father and stepmother, Anna borrowed the equivalent of $100 in gold from her eldest brother and, having secured the promise of employment as a housemaid to a Chicago family, sailed for the United States. This was a bold step for a young woman of 21 in the days before the general emancipation of women. Anna Kutter was undoubtedly a person of strong character, yet susceptible to the charm of the man "in the little green hat" who befriended her on the ocean liner, took her through the immigration procedures at Ellis Island with apparent ease, and escorted her to Chicago.

Correspondence ensuing between the Missoula railroad fireman and the Chicago housemaid resulted in a proposal of marriage and its acceptance. The wedding took place in Chicago in 1911. An intelligent woman with a love of music and an interest in literature, Anna aspired to more intellectual pursuits than her husband. Benno's life was the railroad and his friends mostly the rough tough men who worked with him. A strong labour man, he became the grievance official for his union. His relaxations were hunting and fishing with his friends.

Home for the newlyweds was 509 North Fifth Street, a rough neighbourhood 'on the other side of the tracks' in Missoula, and it was here young Hubert spent his early years. Although there were to be no more children — Benno's wish — another young boy lived with the Zemke family for some years. A railroad friend of Benno's involved in divorce had his six-year-old son taken in by Anna and brought up as her own until he was twelve. Rod Howard Clarke was the nearest Hubert had to a brother although the six year age difference tended to limit their association. The experience must have come hard for Rod as father Zemke saw no reason why somebody else's boy living under his roof should not be subject to the same discipline that he expected of his own child. Thus Rod quickly learned to accept a direct order and never to question. As the Zemkes usually conversed in German he was soon adept at communicating in this tongue. Misdemeanours for Rod, and later Hubert, were dealt with by the razor strap from the washroom, smartly administered to 'the butt'.

The United States' entry into the First World War brought a certain amount of hostility and, to some extent, isolated the Zemke family who were the only people of German origin in the immediate neighbourhood. There were instances of cabbages and manure being thrown over into the yard. Benno always insisted that he was of Swiss origin, in fact his wish to ignore his true origins must have stemmed from an earlier date as his naturalisation papers showed him as Swiss. In the First World War, Eberhart, one of his two brothers, became an early military pilot and was shot down and killed. The other brother, Hubert's namesake, had died of a heart attack prior to the conflict.

The anti-German attitude persisted among some people in the neighbourhood for a time after the Armistice and young Hubert was soon made aware of this when entering grade school. Taunts of 'square head' and 'kraut' were not uncommon from the more loutish boys. Aggravating the situation was Hubert's difficulty in speaking fluent English, simply because until starting school at the age of six, German had been the predominant language used at home. His mother, becoming sensitive to the situation, made an effort to converse regularly in English. The anti-German feeling from the war was a useful excuse for school bullies, notably an eleven-year-old named Elton Love who lived in the same block as Hubert. This boy seemed to delight in finding an opportunity to punch little Zemke who, after a few encounters, began to worry as to how he would overcome this unpleasantness. When Rod Clarke was not around to afford protection, fear of Elton Love led to Hubert running the three quarters of a mile to and from school as fast as his legs would carry him, dodging down different alleys to avoid the tyrant.

After the comparative sheltered upbringing and the loving attention bestowed by Anna on her 'little Hoobart', the early days at school came as a rude awakening to the hard outside world. True, at home the benevolence of the mother had been countered by the harsh discipline of father, Benno being intent on making a man of his son. To further this he was now taken on winter hunting trips into the forest where temperatures were often as low as minus 20 degrees. The outings most disliked by Hubert were the deer hunting treks up into the mountains. Benno was a fast walker and it was difficult to keep up with him, particularly in deepish snow. On these expeditions young Hubert was sometimes instructed to take a different route to a certain point and left alone to struggle through the alien landscape. In later years Hubert came to recognise all this as a deliberate policy of testing his abilities, and that father was all the time looking out to see that he didn't get into real trouble.

Benno's salary from the Northern Pacific Railway was not large — about $170 a month — but by frugal living he and three other employees had accumulated sufficient funds to purchase part of a block of land close by the University of Montana in a better part of Missoula. Here they each built a house and in 1925 the Zemke family moved from their rented accommodation across the tracks to the new home. Prior to the move, Rod Clarke was moved by his father to lodgings in another part of the town. Rod was later to have a distinguished career, for as a talented engineer he served at the US Army's Aberdeen Proving Grounds near Washington and was responsible for much of the development work on the Jeep and other Second World War vehicles. Ultimately he became Vice-President of White Trucks Company.

The Zemke family was generally much happier in their new home, 740 Eddy

Avenue. For Benno, as before, his railroad job took him away for several days at a time, but now he had been promoted Locomotive Engineer with a bit more salary and prestige. He still chose the company of those he worked with, a boisterous, hardworking, hard drinking crowd, mostly of Scots, Irish, Scandinavian and German extraction. The move offered a new environment to Anna, always one to better her knowledge and understanding. Living in close proximity to the university she was eventually able to make the acquaintance of many lecturers and professors. One of the latter, a Professor Weisberg, was enlisted to teach her seven-year-old son the violin. It was not the sort of activity that Benno would have encouraged his son to take up but he was tolerant of his wife's desires. To pay for the music lessons, acquire a good instrument, and generally enhance the family budget, Mrs Zemke commenced a catering service which eventually became well patronised, particularly by the University fraternity. A comely woman of attractive personality, she gathered a wide circle of friends and there always seemed to be some caller at the Zemke home.

Hubert persevered with the violin and eventually Anna considered him worthy of an imported European violin, an Anton Osteler, for which she paid the then not insignificant sum of $100. However, by this time his musical interest was beginning to clash with more physical and enjoyable activities.

From playing softball with the scout troop a delight in field sports developed, particularly catch. By the time Hubert moved from grade school to high school at fourteen he was above average weight and height for a boy of his years. In his junior year at high school, when aged sixteen, he was, like many other boys, attracted to the month's soldiering experience offered by the Civilian Military Training Corps during summer vacation. The lone battalion of regular army infantry at Fort Missoula, an old Indian fort, provided this facility, setting up tented accommodation for the youngsters, staging an athletic programme, conducting physical training, range shooting and instilling some appreciation of military discipline. Hubert liked this; discipline was easy to accept after his father's harsh regime. One of the instructors, Eddie Krause, encouraged him to take up boxing. Hitherto Hubert had learned to use his fists in alley fights for self-defence but the technique of boxing was something quite new. Krause coached him and quickly realised he had someone with potential. Contests of three two-minute rounds were set up in the open air ring and Hubert was the victor in half a dozen fights, emerging as the middleweight champion but not without receiving 'a real shiner' of a black eye.

Surprised at his success, Hubert was intent on exploiting it. He studied other boxers' form, picking up tips whenever he could. Missoula was a lumber centre with three big mills processing the timbers floated down the Black Foot river from the forests each spring. With the timber came the many foresters ready to spend money earned during the winter's felling, and there were people in the town only too willing to help them do so. At one saloon fights were staged as an attraction for clients. The man who ran this place, 'Packy' MacPharlan, offered Hubert $5 a fight, a lot of money to the teenager. But as he did not want to lose his amateur status Hubert ostensibly fought free of charge and was paid $5 for helping to take down the ring and stack chairs after the event. His expertise in the ring was such that he won his first three fights by knock-outs and MacPharlan, realising he had 'a champ', then upped the remuneration to $10 a go. Fight promoters and coaches viewed Hubert as a 'natural'. He had the hard punch essential to success in boxing allied to excellent ring tactics.

I soon learned that a straight jab and a right cross were the most effective means of shaking my opponents and that the sooner you got in some hard hitting the sooner things would start to go your way. You didn't wait for him to start the hitting. But you learned to first feel the other guy out; especially if he was a big gorilla who looked as if he could throw you out of the ring. You found out where his weaknesses were and then worked on these. Tenacity was essential if you were going to win. Even if your nose was bleeding like mad you didn't let up, you didn't lose the initiative. That doesn't mean it had to be a slogging match, if the opposition was tough then you aimed to win on points. The main points were: to use your wits, size up the opposition, keep hitting him where it hurt and always keep the initiative.

The same attributes would reassert themselves in later years under more deadly circumstances. Mrs Zemke did not particularly favour her son's pugilistic activities or, for that matter, know the extent of them. In deference Hubert kept a secret tally of his fights pencilled on the underside of the breakfast nook table.

For his second High School summer vacation Hubert took a job on a dude ranch, a cattle ranch were the owner augmented his income by taking in tourists plus arranging horse trekking, hunting and fishing activities for them. The dollar a day earned chopping wood, shovelling manure, grooming horses and performing other odd jobs around the ranch was not sufficient attraction to return the following summer. Instead Hubert and a friend journied into the wild country around the head waters of the Salomon River in Idaho to seek placer gold. Parents grub-staked them — provided food and other essentials — and accommodation was a tent. Every day the two boys shovelled stream bedrock into a 'rocker' to wash out the gravel, panning any gold dust from the residue in the evening. It was exhausting and not very fruitful for the inexperienced youngsters.

When the next summer came round he arranged, through a friend of his parents, to join an old miner who lived in a remote area of the Rocky Mountains near Superior on the Idaho-Montana state line. This man, John McDowell, kept himself in the style of the old pioneers, and taught Hubert more about basic living than anyone else he would ever meet. The boy also experienced some of the less pleasant problems of primitive living. His first night's sleep in McDowell's cabin was interrupted by painful bites in the groin. Hubert tried splashing water on himself to alleviate the smarting and returned to bed. Further assaults on his person by mites caused him to spend the remainder of the night outside, thereafter sleeping in the woodshed. McDowell, either untroubled or immune to the attentions of bed bugs, continued slumbering in his hut.

Hubert learned how to drill rock by hand for blasting and to use dynamite, how to sharpen picks with a hand forge, saw timber by hand to supply all needs for lumber, how to make and cook sour dough bread, hot cakes and biscuits, which were the basic part of the diet during his stay; how to preserve elk meat by salting it down, or to turn it into Indian jerky; preserve wild huckleberries and many other things necessary to existence in the wild. Together they panned gold and at the end of that long hot summer the old man split their finds. Hubert brought five ounces of gold out of the hills — which at that time had a value of $33 an ounce — and presented it to his mother.

While appreciative of her son's enterprise, Anna was more interested in his progress through high school and the intention that he should go to university. Hubert had come to enjoy hunting and fishing and other outdoor pursuits and, through parental guidance, was to train for a career in forestry. Benno was influential in this matter and undoubtedly warmed to the thought of his son carrying on the family tradition. His sporting prowess resulted in athletic scholarships which partly funded the university place. The close proximity of the Zemke house to the campus enabled Hubert to live at home and thus mitigate any financial strain on the family, albeit that at this time Mrs Zemke's catering business was flourishing and she was employing girls, part-time, to help her. This and her social activities often meant that Hubert was alone in the family home, left to his own devices.

Some years earlier his father had acquired a used car which he maintained in good order, annually grinding in engine valves and performing other overhaul requirements. Hubert, at fourteen, with father's tutelage had learned to drive. Benno, however, laid down the law that Hubert was not to have the car without permission, and that was rarely given. To ensure there was no temptation to disobey his orders while he was absent on the railroad, the car ignition key was taken. His son was not so easily outwitted and when the opportunity arose Hubert had a duplicate key cut. Mother's compliance was not difficult to obtain, beside which she often provided the cash for the gasoline. Anna was not easily manipulated into doing or agreeing to something she did not approve of, but if she viewed one of Benno's dictates as unreasonable she was not amiss to circumnavigating it. Thus Hubert availed himself of this occcasional transport during his late high school and university years without his father ever becoming aware of what was going on. After each clandestine trip the car was cleaned and put back in the garage. There was the occasional crisis. Once, while returning with a party of friends from a joy ride to Lolo Hot Springs, some forty miles north of Missoula, Hubert veered off the road on a bend and swiped a tree. The large dent in the fender was knocked out, filled and painted by the time Benno returned later next day.

If Benno was generally the staunch disciplinarian towards his son, he was nonetheless capable of surprising acts of kindness. The culmination of the senior year at high school was the 'Senior Prom', a graduation dance and formal occasion at which boys were expected to wear tuxedos (dinner jacket suit). Acquainted with the facts, Benno volunteered to be the provider and invited his son to accompany him 'down town'. To Hubert's amazement he was bought, not rented, a complete suit, shirt, bow tie and studs for this one occasion. It was one of the few indications of pride in his son's achievements that he would occasionally make.

In his university years Hubert developed his boxing ventures. He held the Montana state middleweight championship for two years, together with other regional championships. His boxing prowess became well known. It was the sports writer, Ray Roscene who, feeling Hubert was not the right tag for a pugilist, dubbed him 'The Hub'. The name Hub stuck and soon he was Hub Zemke to everyone outside his immediate family. Donations received from participating in fights staged at clubs, saloons and county fairs were a welcome source of income; on one occasion there was an additional compensation. Hub had agreed to appear at the Elk Club Smoker in a staged main event of six rounds. To his surprise — and inner delight — his opponent was a '180 pound, pudgy dissipated type' named Elton Love, the very same who had terrorised young Hubert when first starting grade school. In those six rounds, using six ounce gloves, Hub made up for all the beatings and frights of his childhood. Love was knocked to the floor several times but in the true tradition of sportsmanship, Zemke helped his opponent to his feet, even if the man became a little reluctant to get up. In later years, when recalling this occasion, Hub would insist that it was not a case of revenge, rather that justice prevailed!

To take his boxing further, Hub had to fight as a semi-professional which brought him more into contact with the real fight promoters and the commercialised side of the sport. He realised that whereas he had pretty well ruled the roost in the Montana area, going further afield would bring him against tougher opposition and one day he was going to get really hurt. He had met enough cauliflower ear and punch-drunk boxers to know the risks and not want to turn professional. Boxing had been a sport he enjoyed, it helped build his self-confidence and had given him a place where he excelled. The score under the home table finally ran to 59 fights of which 56 were wins, and 27 of these by knock-outs. Of the three lost, two were by decisions and the third a knock-out when he had foolishly entered the ring while suffering from 'flu. Overall, a creditable record by any standard.

During his last year at University, Hub obtained a job as night switchboard operator at the local hospital, with bed provided. Apart from the money, his father's work and mother's activities often meant the family home was empty in the evenings or alternatively it was filled with university girls his mother had befriended. In his teens Hub was usually uneasy in the company of girls, probably stemming from his isolated home life in earlier years. Dating girls all seemed rather fearful; boxing, hunting and other manly activities were in any case then more attractive.

For practical experience, during the summer recess Hub took forestry work. Missoula was the regional headquarters of the US Forestry Service and forestry students were regularly employed to aid the normal workforce with the seasonal workload. Early in the season the tasks were mostly clearing mountain trails, stringing telephone wires to look-out stations, building wooden bridges over streams and handling pack horse trains — wrangling. The last two summer months were spent on peak lookout posts observing weather conditions and reporting outbreaks of fire caused by lightning or careless campers. Hub's lookout was a small cabin with glass sides some 5,000 feet up in the Bitterroot Mountains. On a clear day one could see from 75 to 100 miles. The great thundering cumulus storms that swept through the western mountains at that time of year were often frightening, particularly at night. Lightning sometimes struck the earthing arresters on the cabin roof but occasionally hit the cast iron cooking stove and jumped to the telephone or metal bed frame. Hub took to sleeping on the wood floor when there were storms around.

There was also time for conjecture as to the prospects for a young fellow with a degree. They did not seem all that great, particularly in a time of economic depression, besides which one could possibly end up behind a desk, something Hub definitely did not want.

Like other state universities at that time, Montana had a Reserve Officer

Training Corps. Unless debarred by physical or other special reasons, all boys in the university were required to do two years service in the ROTC. Administered by the Army, the programme mostly involved physical exercise and the basic rudiments of military training, with the main object of finding suitable candidates for further training and promotion to Second Lieutenants in the Army Reserve. Hub quite enjoyed this ROTC commitment and with two of his football buddies, Roger Graton and Leo Maclain from the university football team, decided to take the advanced course. One of the options open to them was to try for selection in the Army Air Corps flying training programme. A university professor had advised that it was a worthwhile exercise for if accepted for training they would get a free trip to San Antonio, Texas, and each receive $75 a month pay. While the chances of completing the course were slim, there was nothing to lose as if they 'washed out', they could return to the University of Montana and take up studies where they had left off.

Hitherto Hub had little interest in anything to do with aviation. Few aircraft were seen around Missoula and then mostly 'barnstormers' who flew into the fields alongside fairgrounds in the summer, or a Ford Trimotor giving joy rides at $5 a time. As his two friends were keen Hub agreed to enrol.

The first step was a 'physical' at Fort Missoula. Hub passed with ease but surprisingly both his friends failed. In view of this Hub seriously considered withdrawing himself but finally decided to report for further more exhaustive medical examinations at Vancouver Barracks, near Portland, Oregon. He spent two days at this Army post in December 1935, again passing all tests. His acceptance for flying cadet training was now fairly certain. Taking the same examinations were a dozen students from the Washington, Idaho and Oregon state universities. Of these Ross Greening, Del Wilson and Loren MaCollom would be met with again in later years.

The attitude of Hub's parents to this venture was not negative, although they did not seriously think anything would come of it. However, a letter received by Hub early in the new year ordering him to report to Randolph Field, Texas on 17 February 1936 brought confirmation. But the senior Zemkes were still inclined to look on the forthcoming flying instruction as just a passing phase and that their Hubert would eventually obtain his degree in forestry. Hub, however, became even more convinced that forestry did not offer good prospects for advancement. Employment vacancies were advertised on the university notice board and the only position of note in forestry during summer 1935 was a job in a rubber plantation for the Firestone Company. Degree or not, it looked as if the only type of job available in conventional forestry was going to be that of an ordinary worker leading horse pack trains, straining telephone wires or fighting fires. Much as he loved the forest life, Hub aspired to better remuneration and chances of advancement.

That fall, feeling that he should get to know something about aircraft, Hub borrowed books from the university library and studied the basic principles of powered flight and learned how ailerons, elevators and other aeroplane components functioned. Further, he made himself and his future commitment known to the Johnson Flying Service. Mr Johnson had a Stinson biplane down on a field strip serving as a local airport, from which he ran a charter service. Hub paid for a ride with Mr Johnson which, apart from the thrill of a first flight, left him completely confused when trying to relate the experience to the functioning of an aircraft as gleaned from books. When February 1936 finally came round and Hub departed from blizzard shrouded Missoula by train for Texas, it was more for adventure than any great desire to fly.

2
A GENTLEMAN'S CAREER

Primary and basic flying training for the US Army Air Corps was conducted at Randolph Field while the advanced course took place at Kelly Field. Randolph was situated seventeen miles east of the city of San Antonio and Kelly a lesser distance to the west. The terrain was flat and open, mostly grainfields; the weather normally fine, blue skies predominating. An ideal location for a flier's kindergarten. The Army Air Corps had some 1,200 active pilots for 900 first line aircraft in December 1935 and the requirement for new pilots was limited. The United States was still in economic recession with military expenditure severely curtailed. Air Corps flying training courses were reduced to three intakes per year and chiefly programmed for creating a reserve. Cadet Zemke was one of seventy young men joining the first Primary course early in 1936. On arrival he was viewed with some suspicion by his mentors until he enlightened them that a missing eyebrow and stitched cut was not due to a brawl but the result of his last boxing match. In the days that followed Hub's attitude to the service venture changed; a new enthusiasm was born as he came to realise he was enjoying the experience.

★   ★   ★

When I arrived at the flying school I fully expected to find the other students on the course would be keen guys already well versed in aeronautical matters. I expected to be quickly washed out and sent back to Montana. But in due course I found my class mates didn't know any more than I did about flying and that I stood as much chance as anyone of getting through. My career as a flying cadet began with marching and obedience drills, various ground classes on the theory of flight, navigation and the like. Once I entered into flying I quickly began to enjoy it. The primary flying was conducted in

Consolidated PT-3 biplanes, light two-seaters with open, tandem cockpits and a 225 hp Wright radial engine up front. A hardy little craft — it had to be to withstand the rough handling it took from trainee pilots. My instructor was a Lieutenant Eastman who seldom said much and never yelled at me; so much an introvert that I wonder how he ever became a pilot. On average we flew twice a day with flights of 15 to 20 minutes duration. Communication between instructor (in the front cockpit) and pupil was conducted by shouting through a Gosport tube, a flexible pipe with a funnel at each end. Once you learned to control the aircraft the instructor would get you to practise engine failure situations by suddenly cutting the throttle. This hazing was to see how you responded in an emergency; if you panicked or just couldn't handle it then you were very quickly going to be washed out.

Not far from Randolph Field there was a high tension power line on tall pylons and it was a favourite trick of instructors to fake an emergency when flying in the vicinity. On one occasion I was high over this line when Eastman suddenly chopped the throttle. I put the nose down and took the PT-3 around in a gentle diving curve and selected the best landing place I could see, a large field the other side of the power line. That was one time Eastman did get excited — when he realised that I planned to go down under the power lines. He quickly took the controls and in no uncertain terms told me to go pick another place.

Your first solo flight is the high mark of attainment in every pilot's life. To be up there for the first time without an instructor is a sensation like nothing else; you're hilarious about it afterwards and I was no exception. I soloed after about 7½ hours piloting, which was about average. Flight training then progressed to more exacting manoeuvres. One of the exercises involved a bunch of students with their instructors flying to one of the auxiliary landing fields in the district to practise short landings. The instructors would put up a string hurdle across the strip between two posts over which students had to shoot forced landings. Our task was to fly over the strip, cut the throttle, circle round and drop down over the hurdle, plonk her three-point on the ground and roll the minimum distance. The instructors bet beers on whose pupil would achieve the shortest landing without hitting the string hurdle. This was something I could usually do pretty well and I won Eastman several glasses of beer in the Officer's Club on these occasions.

By now my uncertainty about learning to fly had departed. I was really enjoying it as well as the service life. More than anything I was determined to get through the course and make a career in the Air Corps. On the evidence of past courses I reckoned there was about a fifty-fifty chance of graduating if I kept out of trouble. But trouble didn't have to be of my making. One day I was detailed to practise aerobatics north of San Antonio. I only had about six hours solo time on the PT-3 but everything had so far gone smoothly and I was a pretty confident neophyte pilot. After practising a few loops I was pulling up on a chandelle (a twisting climb) when suddenly: boom, bang, and the engine cut out. I didn't know what was going on but the immediate reaction was disbelief that it was happening to me. Then almost automatically into the emergency routine that Eastman had preached: nose down and pick up flying speed, check wind direction, find a place to land. Luckily there was a big cement plant not far away and smoke billowing from the stacks indicated which way the wind was blowing.

When the engine failed I was probably at around 2,000 feet, but pulling around in a curve the plane was losing height rapidly. The choice of landing places was limited; nothing large really suitable — the best a small field planted with grain. I side slipped to and fro, barely getting over the fence, to put the plane down hard and skid through the wheat to a stop. All the way down I had acted pretty coolly, but after jumping out of the cockpit I just stood and shook like a leaf. Then I began to worry if all had been my fault, something I'd done or hadn't done. The airplane didn't appear to have been damaged in the landing although the tail skid had torn up a wide strip of wheat. We had had classes on engines but I was no mechanic and couldn't see anything at fault externally when I looked at the radial. This only increased my apprehension. What if they found nothing wrong? Perhaps the engine was okay. Had I panicked? If so it would mean packing my bags next day.

On the other side of the wheat field was a farmhouse so I took my parachute off and walked over to get help. Two women met me, one middle aged and the other I assumed to be her daughter. It was a surprise to suddenly hear them speak to each other in German, in fact the older woman could speak no English. I asked if I could use the telephone to call base and tell them where I was. About an hour later the crash wagon and several cars arrived. To get to the airplane, the investigating party proceeded to drive all over the wheat field, causing much more damage than I had. Perhaps the farmer made more in compensation from the government than he would have got from the crop.

The engineering officer wanted to know what went wrong. All I could tell him was the engine suddenly made a lot of noise and lost all power. With some trepidation I watched him crank up the engine and was dismayed when it started and ran smoothly. He then signalled the mechanic in the cockpit to open the throttle and when he complied — bang, crash! What a noise. But sweet music to my ears confirming mechanical failure and not pilot error. The engineer's diagnosis was a broken piston rod. This was the first forced landing by anyone in our class course. For a day or two I became the regular hero around the place for saving the aircraft. It meant more to me than I'd saved my own life!

In June I moved on to basic training. We now flew the Douglas BT-2, a more robust biplane powered by a 450 hp Pratt & Whitney radial and fitted with high frequency two-way radio enabling us to talk to the tower at Randolph. Emphasis was now on cross-country navigation and instrument flying 'under the hood'. I passed through this stage without any major difficulties. The final advanced stage of the course and the move to Kelly Field came in September. Here there were four different sections to choose from: bomber, pursuit, attack and observation. As none of us anticipated a war, most wanted to go into bombers for flying time on multi-engine aircraft so that they could get an airline job. I thought about this but wanted no part of it. My ambition was to participate in pursuit flying with fast, manoeuvrable aircraft; the slow lumbering Keystone bomber biplanes had no appeal. Attack (light bombers) and observation were also too restrictive for my taste.

In the Pursuit section at Kelly we flew the Boeing P-12, a type with which some regular pursuit squadrons were equipped. A neat single-seat biplane with an air cooled engine and a top speed around 185 mph, it was the finest flying machine I ever handled, without a doubt. They ran like a sewing machine. You could do most anything with them; great for aerobatics. We were taught pursuit tactics of a kind and formation flying. The pursuit section had 27 P-12s and we usually operated as a six man flight, the leader being an instructor. There were no radios for plane-to-plane communication in the P-12s so a system of hand signals was used to convey directions.

One day we were up doing aerobatics when our instructor,

Lieutenant 'Curly' Stalter, a curly headed ambitious type — but a heck of a fine instructor — suddenly gave the going down to land sign. So we all went into a string behind and followed him down. Darned if he didn't pick a small field and what made matters worse was that it had just rained and the turf was going to be slippery. I went over the fence right behind him, skidded and slipped and barely got out of the way of the man coming in behind me. All six of us did get down safely but I remember thinking that he didn't have the best of judgement in taking us into such a small field in the prevailing conditions. I looked across at Stalter who had just gotten out of his plane. He was madder than hell. What I and the others had thought was all part of a rigorous training exercise was an emergency! Stalter's carburettor float had stuck and his engine conked out. The signal just meant that he had got to put down, not for us to follow. The field was so small there was no way we could fly out in the wet conditions so each airplane had to be taken to bits and trucked back to Kelly.

Flying with the pursuit section at Kelly was a marvellous time. With the heat of flying school rigidity off, you were recognised as a pilot cadet and pretty certain to graduate. The classes were more interesting, flights were of longer duration and we did cross-countries. The pursuit section was despatched on a great round robin of the universities in the south — Louisiana, Alabama, Georgia — to create interest in the Air Corps and promote recruitment. It was an idyllic existence for a pilot. By then you had got to know the other cadets and developed friendships. Passes into San Antonio were plentiful and the local people were most hospitable. The town had plenty of girls and about the only difficulty was stretching that $75 to last the entire month.

I graduated from flying school on 17 February 1937 with the option of either one or two years' active duty as a reserve officer. Because the funds were not yet available to the Air Corps, I did not actually receive my commission as a Second Lieutenant Reserve until 21 June that year.

Having been given cadet squadron commander status at Kelly, I was accepted for assignment to a regular pursuit unit. During the last few weeks at San Antonio some of us had been approached by a man working out of the Mexican Consulate to volunteer for fighter pilot duties on the Republican side of the Spanish Civil War. The astounding salary of $500 a month was offered. It was easy to fancy oneself as a great fighter ace. I must admit to thinking seriously about going, but common sense prevailed. With only a year's training, I didn't know enough about air combat, besides which none of us had any air gunnery experience — in fact we had never fired a shot. Most of our class reasoned the same way. I don't think any of them volunteered although, later, I knew Reserve officers who went to Spain.

After graduation we were allowed thirty days' leave. Most people went home but for me it meant a trip right across the States to Montana when winter was at its worst, and then back east to Virginia. I had recently spent $450 dollars of my savings on a little Ford convertible and there wasn't time to drive all that way. "Monk" Myres, who shared my quarters at Kelly, had been assigned to bombardment at Langley and as he too was not going home, together we drove my little Ford the 3000 miles to our new assignment station. The Air Corps paid three cents a mile travelling allowance and we actually made money on the trip.

At that time the Air Corps maintained only three fighter groups in the continental United States, the 1st at Selfridge Field, Michigan in the north, the 8th at Langley, Virginia in the east and the 20th at Barksdale Field, California on the Pacific side. My posting was to the 8th Pursuit Group at Langley Field near Norfolk, the most prestigious of Air Corps bases. Apart from the 8th Pursuit, equipped with Curtiss P-6Es, there was a bombardment group, the 2nd, which had the first Flying Fortresses, the Boeing YB-17s. Langley also housed General Headquarters Air Force which was the nearest the Air Corps had got to an independent role for its activities as against the traditional commitment of direct support of the land forces under an Army commander. My Group CO was Lieutenant Colonel Adlai Gilkeson who in July 1938 was replaced by Lieutenant Colonel William Kepner. These men, near double the age of most squadron pilots, appeared to be expected to participate more in administration than flying. Kepner, a World War 1 marine, had received a bayonet wound in the cheek and in the 1920s achieved fame for setting balloon height records. A slightly built, unimposing man, he was a very level-headed commander, a good listener and equally so at getting his points across. The Group had three squadrons, the 33rd under Major Glenn Barcus, the 35th bossed by Major Francis 'Butch' Griswold and Major Ned Schramm's 36th to which I was assigned.

In contrast to the organised life at Randolph and Kelly Fields, where you knew exactly what you were going to do each day from a pre-arranged schedule, active duty at Langley was a lethargic existence. They didn't check your rooms, you didn't have to report to dining halls at set times. When we reported for duty at 07:30 each morning we frequently had no assigned tasks. The ranking Operations and Staff officers were generally long in service years, married and pretty conservative. There appeared to be no training programme of any consequence. Little time was spent on tactics; on reflection I don't think our senior officers knew much about such things.

We did go on manoeuvres to support the Army down in the Carolinas, occasionally fly over Washington in formation to wave the flag at some special function and take part in the annual War Games. Normally we were free after 12:30 and had all afternoon to ourselves. So we junior officers took to driving into Richmond or Williamsberg or to play golf at Yorktown. It was a gentleman's life; you were a member of a country club, not a fighting unit.

Older than the P-12 flown at Kelly but up-dated, our P-6Es were very similar in both performance and handling. In 1937 we also received some Consolidated PB-2 two-place monoplanes that were quite an advance on the P-6E from an engineering standpoint but no way as manoeuvrable or pleasant to fly. The following year we received our first single-seat monoplane fighter, the Curtiss P-36 with a radial engine and retractable undercarriage.

One of the advantages of the relaxed atmosphere at Langley was that even young Reserve 2nd Lieutenants like myself had considerable freedom in the use of aircraft. The usual form was to fly a mission given by the squadron operations officer in the morning — probably of no more than an hour or 45 minutes duration. You were then free to undertake further flying, most of us indulging in mock combat or working up team aerobatics. We were also allowed to take aircraft on personal cross-country flights every weekend which enabled a group of fellows to take-off for an airport at some resort we fancied and really go to town. Officially such flights were for navigational experience and we did benefit in this respect. However, it also provided fast and free transportation to places we could not afford to reach on our pay. We had to be back to report for duty at 8 o'clock Monday morning. On the return flight the more red-eyed guys would be breathing on the oxygen tube to clear away the effects of too much drinking the night before.

To make our $75 stretch as far as possible we learned to get invited to functions where refreshment was free for the taking. For this reason the daughters of the senior officers at Langley were never short of dates as we knew the fathers who kept a well stocked bar. I lived in Dodd Hall, a batchelor dormatory, right next door to a house occupied by a Lieutenant Colonel Spaatz and family. I dated his eldest daughter a couple of times and was taken to the house. Colonel Spaatz was a quiet, serious man, while his wife was just the opposite. General Frank Andrews, the senior commander at Langley, also had a daughter. She eventually married one of the junior officers in our league, 'Rabbit' Williams, who later became General Andrews' personal pilot.

During my first weeks at Langley I noticed that practically every Sunday there were competitive events on the skeet shooting range close to the Officer's Club. Skeet, using 12-bore shotguns to knock down catapulted clay targets helped develop a flier's deflection shooting. With my hunting background I wanted to participate but learned that most of the ammunition allocated for skeet shooting had been acquired for the 2nd Bomb Group whose senior officers were regular participants on the range. Prominent was a Captain Curtis LeMay, an excellent shot. Being envious and wanting to get in on the act I asked our armament Sergeant about this situation and learned that the only bar to participation on the officers' skeet was ammunition. I also discovered that pilots were authorised to draw 600 rounds per year but the requisition had to be made on 1 July annually. As the 8th Pursuit Group had not been making a large requisition, the 2nd Bomb Group had taken all of the available ammunition and stockpiled it in their bunkers.

It so happened that I was made Armament Officer of my squadron. With this responsibility I was in a position to lobby the pursuit squadron commanders to draw the full allocation of skeet ammunition for our Group. Came 1 July, I was there with the necessary documentation. This had the effect of cutting the 2nd Bomb Group's club activity in half, and they now had to suffer a bunch of small fry fighter Second Lieutenants shooting at the club. Nothing was said but as I had signed the requisitions, the 2nd Group officers undoubtedly knew who the young upstart was who had spoiled their fun.

The bomber men of the 2nd were looked upon as the Air Corps elite in the late 1930s — they even had a special dress uniform. Their YB-17s had a higher top speed than our P-6s and PB-2s and there was a school of thought that held that the Fortresses were fast enough to evade interception. The Air Corps striving to achieve an independent role, saw the long range B-17 bomber as a prime instrument in this quest. The 2nd undertook goodwill flights to South American countries — we envied them that.

With the Curtiss P-36 we had a fighter that could just about catch the B-17s but it was lacking performance compared to what we heard about the latest European fighters. In the summer of 1939 our squadron, the 36th, was selected to service test the Curtiss YP-37, the first American fighter to have the new Allison liquid-cooled engine rated at 1,000 hp. It was heavy with sluggish acceleration but for the first time we had an aircraft with a top speed in excess of 300 mph. The YP-37 was based on the P-36 airframe, with the cockpit placed further back to improve streamlining and enhance performance. As a result, the long nose and wing obscured the pilot's vision forward and down, making it a treacherous beast to land. We also had problems with the new supercharged engine which gave the Allison people a lot of work. The following year we received some of the first Curtiss P-40s, which were basically standard P-36 airframes with the liquid cooled Allison engine. Being lighter, it was a much better aircraft but lacking the supercharger it had no altitude performance. The surprising thing to me was that the first P-40s only had two machine guns, the same armament as was fitted to all the previous fighters I had flown, when at this time British and German fighters had as many as eight machine-guns or armament that included cannon.

When war in Europe erupted in September 1939 my thinking was that in due time the US would be involved and that I'd better be prepared, educationally and psychologically, for combat. Some pilots talked eagerly about getting into combat but I rationalised there would be losses and I could be one of them. I was not looking to be a hero. That said, with the probability that one day you would be fighting for your life, the wise thing was to become as proficient as you could as a pursuit fighter pilot. Having decided to make the Air Corps a permanent career — I received a regular commission in August 1939 — it was always my endeavour to excel. At this time I was always active in flying, getting between twenty and thirty hours a month; I studied new techniques and tried to keep up with engineering developments. Whenever an opportunity arose, I flew different airplane types. By taking cross-countrys to other fields, I was able to fly the Seversky P-35 and later the Bell P-39, also the British version of the P-38.

With war in Europe, the tempo of life at Langley began to change. There was more emphasis on training and we had less time for leisure. Probably because of the war in Europe with news of the exploits of fighter pilots, the public image of the fighter pilot began to change. We came to be looked upon as dare-devils following a dangerous livelihood. You capitalised on this to a certain extent, especially with the girls. As I've said, I didn't really have any steady dates at all during my first years in the Air Corps. There was a schoolteacher I met in San Antonio while a cadet and I did take a cross-country from Langley to Atlanta to see her one Christmas, but it was a casual relationship. In fact, if I'm honest, I was pretty naive where girls were concerned.

In the winter of 1939 our squadron was ordered to Sarasota in Florida on a training assignment. The local Chamber of Commerce organised a dance one evening and there I met a girl of Italian extraction named Maria. I always considered myself a pretty level headed guy but I really lost control here. In five days we were married! She was nineteen and her parents, who lived in Tampa, didn't even know about it. I came to my senses pretty quickly and realised we were two incompatible people; a fit of passion wasn't going to sustain a marriage. Never a serious churchgoer, back at Langley I was naive enough to approach a Catholic priest to ask if I could get the marriage annulled — we had been married by a Justice of the Peace. The priest couselled me that any such action would be morally and religiously wrong; that I had got to try and make it work. So I rented an apartment off the base and arranged to bring Maria up from Tampa. Over the years we had good and bad patches but sadly the marriage never really worked out.

Late in 1938 command of the 36th Pursuit Squadron was taken over by Captain 'Freddy' Smith, a West Pointer and son-in-law of Admiral King. On whose recommendation I do not know, but Smith made me his adjutant. Never excelling at paperwork, I was not happy about having to sit at a desk. This was in addition to my duties as a Flight Commander and I could see no reason why a pilot should be wasted on such a job. However, I found that most of the work was done for me by Master Sergeant Flarity. This man, the administrative cornerstone of the squadron, was a gruff-spoken, cigar-smoking, big pot-bellied fellow; an appearance that belied his capacity for work.

While I often thought the Air Corps lagged behind other air forces in both technical and tactical matters, at this time the general standard of the senior NCOs was exceptional, particularly in engineering. Our Line Chief was Master Sergeant Ulyses S. Nero. I truly believe that this fellow had a greater knowledge of the airplanes we flew than some of the design engineers. There did not seem to be an engineering problem he couldn't overcome. We always had top line maintenance on our airplanes thanks to the high standard of training mechanics through the training they received from people like Nero. Airplane maintenance and engineering became progressively more complicated and exacting with each new type the squadron received. The old P-6E was comparatively simple and didn't take much work. In contrast the P-40 with its liquid-cooled engine and various systems was very demanding in time, particularly as it was raising a lot of mechanical difficulties. It also had problems for pilots, notably on landing, where you could easily end up in a ground loop. Its stall characteristics were such that when you came in for a three-pointer and the speed dropped past 65 mph, the air burbled over the wingroot, causing directional control to be lost and the airplane spin round. Often under such circumstances an undercarriage leg collapsed and the plane would go down on its nose. We overcame this problem by learning to land faster, taking a longer roll, keeping the tail up as long as we could while the speed fell off.

In the summer of 1940, together with two other pilots from the 8th, Gilbert Meyers and Joe Mason, I was sent to Wright Field, Dayton, Ohio, the Air Corps experimental base, to conduct an accelerated service test on modified engines. This was because the Allison engine was suffering from bearing failures. The usual form was to take off at full power, cut back and climb to altitudes varying between 5,000 and 10,000 feet, then run at normal power settings for ten minutes, then maximum for a specified time and repeating the procedure. We all had some narrow squeaks, partial loss of power but no complete failures. The trouble was solved by replacing the original main bronze bearings with a silver composition type. Later that year I was again told to report to Wright Field, this time alone. On arrival I was directed to a Lt Colonel Ira Eaker who told me to fly a P-40 up to Dearborn, Michigan and land on the Ford test track at River Rouge, about six miles south west of Detroit. There I was to conduct demonstration flights as requested by Ford engineers and give them any technical information they requested about the aircraft. As

instructed I flew up to Dearborn and landed. To my surprise the reception party not only included Fords General Manager, but Henry Ford himself!

Ford said that accommodation for my week's stay was arranged on his farm at Dearborn. During a couple of lunches with him, I was asked to sample his soya bean wafers — apparently he had been one of the first to introduce soya beans to the United States. He displayed a great interest in farming and insisted I see round his farm. The Company had turned out a few special cars for the Indianapolis races, although they never did too well in these events. Henry Ford asked me if I would like to drive one on the plant test track. Here was an opportunity I was not going to decline. Driving this race car I exceeded 100 mph on the ground for the first time; an exhilerating experience which made me fully appreciate that the sensation of speed is relative to what is near to you. Most of the time I was either demonstrating the P-40 for his engineers or explaining its capabilities and limitations. While not an engineer, I had a fair understanding of the technical details of the aircraft. Henry Ford had told Roosevelt that he could apply his car mass production techniques successfully to aircraft and the purpose of my visit was to allow Ford design engineers to evaluate the feasibility of mass producing the P-40. Apparently it was not a viable proposition with the P-40 although Ford later did successfully apply mass production to the B-24 Liberator bomber.

By the time I returned to Langley I was feeling like a celebrity after such royal treatment. I don't think it went to my head but if it did I was soon to undergo a sobering experience. In November 1940, after eight years' residence in company with the 2nd Bomb Group, it was decided to move the fighter operation from Langley to the New York area. As a result the 8th Pursuit moved to Mitchel Field, Long Island. Having recently been appointed an assistant to the Group Materiel Officer, I was given the onerous task of overseeing arrangements for the movement of equipment and stores by rail. I had been exposed to many things in the service but nothing quite like this. I was put in charge of working up the logistics for the train movement which entailed several visits to the rail yards to obtain measurements of freight wagons followed by arranging for the boxing and crating of everything from extra engines down to office chairs. After finally satisfying myself that all was safely secured on the freight train I

joined the other fliers and flew up to Mitchel while our equipment went up the line. The Group could not function until it arrived.

After three days we figured it was lost and I was running around in circles trying to get the railroad people to trace it. Finally they notified me that the freight cars were in the rail yard at Baltimore so I flew down to see what the problem was. Seems I had thought of everything except giving the nearest railroad station a destination. No-one on the railroad knew where "Mitchel Field, New York" was and all seemed too disinterested to locate. The train was duly sent on its way but after having waited around a few days without equipment my superiors were not pleased with my performance. After the chewing out I received, it was hoped relief from duties with the materiel office would follow; but this was wishful thinking. The desk and paperwork continued; mostly chasing aircraft spares and contacting Wright Field on technical problems.

During 1940 some of my fellow officers in the 8th Pursuit Group had been transferred to new units that were being formed as the Air Corps expanded. This continued apace early in 1941 and as soon as we were settled in at Mitchel part of the Group was split away to form two new organisations, the 33rd and 57th Pursuit Groups. It was one morning around this time that the Group Commander, Colonel Edward Morris, who had replaced Kepner in the previous February, called me into his office. I guessed I was in for a transfer to one of the new outfits. I certainly wasn't expecting to hear what I did: 'Hub, you and Johnny Alison are going to England as Air Corps observers of the air war.'

3

JOURNEY TO VIEW A WAR

The principal reason for Lieutenant Alison's and Zemke's despatch to the United Kingdom was to assist the Royal Air Force in operating the Curtiss Tomahawk, that service's name for the P-40. The British had purchased 1,180 of these aircraft, some originally ordered by France. When first procured they were intended for use as fighters to meet the anticipated German assault on the British Isles but, by the time of the first deliveries, the upsurge in the production of better indigenous interceptor types such as the Spitfire brought a change in plans.

The Curtiss Tomahawk was a well-engineered and sturdy aircraft. Its performance, however, was inferior in many respects to front line RAF and Luftwaffe fighters. Lacking engine supercharging, it could only give of its best below 15,000 feet. The armament of four machine-guns was also considered inadequate for a first-line fighter while the installation of armour plate, bullet-proof tanks and other war equipment severely impaired its handling. Although tests by British pilots in the United States had revealed these deficiencies long before the first shipments arrived in England, at the time the RAF was desperate for any worthwhile fighter types. With a healthy production of Spitfires, the RAF decided to use the Tomahawk to re-equip its Army Co-operation squadrons which, as the name implies, operated in direct support of ground forces. These squadrons had been equipped with Westland Lysanders during the Battle of France, a slow spotter-type aircraft which proved vulnerable to both light anti-aircraft weapons and Luftwaffe interceptors. The new support concept was to use fighter type aircraft with good low-level performance and the speed to evade the enemy's weaponry for photography. At the request of the British, several American specialists were sent to the UK to advise on their aircraft types purchased or supplied under Lend-Lease. They included US Army Air Corps personnel, whose activities were kept secret as the United States was still ostensibly a neutral nation. The Army Air Corps advisers were known as 'observers' for a secondary purpose of their visit was to acquaint themselves with RAF techniques and to learn as much as they could from the British about Luftwaffe equipment and operations. Many senior Air Corps officers were sent specifically to gather such intelligence at this time.

Hub's period of temporary duty was to last three months after which he was to return to his unit. With Johnny Alison he went to Washington for a briefing by Lt Colonel 'Pete' Quesada (who later commanded the IX Tactical Air Command in the post-D-Day operations on the Continent). They were to work from the US Embassy in London, officially seconded to the Air Attaché's office, from whence they would receive instruction and to whom reports had to be submitted. Any technical information they required from Wright Field would be obtained through the Embassy. Alison and Zemke were warned that while they should take opportunities to fly British aircraft in the UK they must not participate in any operational flights. Four Air Corps Sergeants with technical knowledge of the P-40 (Bonker, Seghrist, Tingle and Young) were to accompany them to England and act under their command. Diplomatic passports and travel tickets were provided for an ocean voyage to Lisbon and from there by British Overseas Airways Corporation flight to England. US Army financial procedures were apparently sacrosanct for there was no advance payment of salaries and to obtain British pounds it became necessary to change dollars out of their own pockets before proceeding to the New York port of embarkation. In the urgency to make the sailing date, Hub had little option other than to put personal furniture and possessions in storage near Mitchel Field and send his wife — understandably apprehensive of what would become of her husband in a war zone — back to her parents in Tampa.

For Hub it was an adventure in which he was eager to participate, though genuinely surprised at being selected for this assignment. While self-confident in most personal endeavours, Hub had always been uncertain of his standing with others, particularly those in command. Perhaps this was due to the nature of his background; the locomotive fireman's son who had prospered in a military society composed largely of men with middle class backgrounds. If he did suffer a slight uneasiness in this respect, it was misplaced so far as his service went; senior officers viewed him as a young man of much talent. Hub was a better than average pilot, always eager to increase his understanding of the machines he flew and the way they could be employed operationally. It was no luck-of-the-draw chance that he had been chosen to participate in the accelerated engine testing with the P-40 or that he was the pilot sent to show the aircraft to Henry Ford. Quite simply, Lieutenant Zemke was good at his job and his squadron and group commander recognised this. Hub was a likeable person, of pleasant disposition with a personal integrity imbued by the nature of his rearing. An upbringing that also fashioned his resourcefulness and self-reliance. Hub Zemke was his own man. Hereditary factors gave him the quick temper and stubborness of Benno — although the temper was rarely uncontrolled. Perhaps the stubborness was often really tenacity. If Hub was convinced he was in the right then he would maintain that conviction, sometimes when it would have been politic to desist. Hub would be the first to admit that there were times when he had a lapse of common sense; but then what man has not. Nevertheless, in Hub's makeup can be seen the necessary attributes of an intelligent warrior; a man as yet in no way seeking that role in life.

When Hub embarked on the American Export Lines SS *Excalibur* for his first ocean crossing he fully expected to be back at Mitchel Field by mid-summer. It transpired that his absence was to be far longer than the advised three months, involving him in journeys to places he had never dreamed of visiting.

★   ★   ★

The ocean crossing was uneventful. Our ship, painted white, was ablaze with lights at night illuminating the large Stars and Stripes painted on each side. The voyage took about a week and after docking at Lisbon we were taken to the Hotel Estoril, a fine place just outside the port. Our stay was brief, two nights. The following day the Embassy had us taken to the small airport where we were checked on a British DC-3 flight to England. We knew the British and Germans were busy poking bullets at each other a few hundred miles away so it was strange to find that at Lisbon airport Lufthansa and BOAC had facing counters. They even used the same scales to weigh passengers' luggage. We took off at night making a wide detour out over the Atlantic before heading north. Our first indication of entering a war zone was when the windows were blacked out and we were cautioned not to raise them. The DC-3 landed at Whitchurch near Bristol early next morning and, after changing from civilian clothes to our Army uniforms, we boarded a train to London.

My initial impression of England was a damp and generally drab scene. It wasn't the England I had visualised through literature. The automobiles were small and so were the rail cars. There were a lot of people in uniforms. On reaching London we were picked up by an Embassy car and on our journey through the streets to the Dorchester Hotel we saw plenty of evidence of the blitz; buildings reduced to rubble by bombing. That night we were made well aware that we were in a combat area. In contrast to the lights of New York and Lisbon, London was blacker than black after dark. During the evening the sirens began to wail. Innocents that we were, Johnny and I went up to the roof of the hotel to see what we could of any action. Searchlights were sweeping back and forth and as the German bombers arrived — a distinctive unsynchronised engine note. The anti-aircraft batteries in Hyde Park, opposite the hotel, began to fire. We were excitedly taking in our first view of a war when there was a sudden 'clunk' on the roof beside us: then another. It didn't take many seconds to realise that shell fragments were falling round about and here we were chancing our bare heads. A hasty retreat was made back into the hotel.

Next day I received orders to report to RAF Station Old Sarum, located near the spired city of Salisbury about fifty miles south-west of London. A Tomahawk Flight had been formed at this base to teach senior pilots from Army Co-operation Command squadrons how to handle the aircraft. I was met at the station by an RAF staff car and taken out to the airfield, about three miles north of the city in a river valley. It was a small grass field with brick-built barracks and hangars. Here I was first introduced to the peculiarities of British service life. I was given my own room in the officers' quarters and assigned a 'batman', a kind of personal servant.

In the RAF all officers from the rank of Flight Lieutenant up had the services of a personal batman: there was nothing like this in the US Air Corps. First thing in the morning my batman awoke me and offered a cup of tea, picked up my shoes and polished them, pressed my pants and laid out my clothes. Any personal chores I required he was there to do them. I was puzzled how a nation involved in total war could afford such a luxury with manpower. I discovered later that most batmen were either not physically fit for other duties or were reckoned too old. The other thing I couldn't equate with this nation at war was the "tea break". Whether you were in an office or out on the line with the mechanics, everybody downed tools at 10 o'clock while an enlisted man ran around with a teapot. Same thing at four in the afternoon — the officers took tea and hot crumpets. You came to accept this as some sort of sacred ritual for which even the war could wait. But then the apparent casual attitude of the British to the war was also most notable. When my services were not required at Old Sarum there was time to visit combat RAF fighter stations on the south coast and learn a little about the way operations were conducted. I met pilots just back from missions and was struck by the unexcited way they recounted their experiences. You learned that among the British Services it was "a bad show" to "get in a flap". Despite the serious situation the national attitude was one of a general calm confidence, sometimes irritating to us gung-ho go-getting Americans.

Perhaps the most notable impression of wartime England, after the plenty of the United States, was the rationing. It seemed almost everything was rationed for civilians, who needed coupons for acquisitions. The military were also subject to rationing, particularly in the matter of food. It took some getting used to British wartime food. The German and Russian rations proved to be better. Firstly there was little of it and secondly most of what there was did not please the American palate. While kippers and fried potatoes may have been nourishing, it was a gastronomical imposition for me. The principal meat on your plate was a sausage. The British joked that it was ninety per cent sawdust and ten per cent rabbit and it usually tasted that way. At Sunday lunch in the Officer's Mess we had a joint of beef on which the chefs exhibited great skill in ensuring everyone had a fair portion. The slices were so thin I declare you could read a newspaper through them. We fortunate Americans could retreat to the commisary in the London Embassy whenever the chance arose and there stock up on chocolate bars and other goodies absent from British shops.

The station commander at Old Sarum was a Group Captain, a man in his forties. He and his staff were always hospitable, in particular one of the pilots in the station headquarters, Flight Lieutenant Dave Annand, and his fiancée, an attractive young WAAF, who invited me to their engagement party at the White Hart in Salisbury.

Soon after we arrived at Old Sarum Johnny Alison and two of the Sergeants were sent to the squadrons which had or were converting to the Tomahawk to advise on repair, maintenance and operational matters. During the course of these rounds Johnny had to bale out of a Tomahawk at 9,000 feet near Saffron Walden, landing safely.

In mid-May I was sent to advise the Canadian 403 Squadron at Honiley and Baginton who were having problems with the Toma-hawks. The squadron was scheduled to move on the evening of the 28th and the station commander gave a party during which speeches were made and pilots of a Polish Hurricane squadron presented a silver bowl to the mess. This was my first real experience of an RAF party at an operational station. The reserved conduct I had observed among pilots at work disappeared once the toast to the Queen was dispensed with. It wound up in complete bedlam. The Canadians pitched me into a pond. They tore the place down. After I finally got back to my quarters I was awoken at around 4 am by something moving in the room and switching on the light found a sheep! The perpetrators of this prank were of the opinion the animal would make me feel at home.

My visits to RAF fighter bases, particularly the operational fighter squadrons, provided a wealth of information on equipment, technique and tactics that the RAF was using. I gained an appreciation of the capabilities of radar and its part in the British defence system. The fighter control sectors and the Y-Service which monitored Luftwaffe radio traffic were particularly fascinating. But as a pilot I was probably most impressed by the flying control system, which kept track of all flights, and Darky the emergency aid for use if you became lost — and it was easy to become lost in the extensive cloud more often than not encountered on any flight over the British Isles. We had nothing like this in the States and having been conditioned into believing we were best, it came as something of a surprise to see how far we Americans were behind.

On one occasion I went to North Weald, a combat fighter station with Hurricanes. The recently operational Eagle Squadron was there, its pilots being US nationals who had volunteered to fly with the RAF. I saw them return from a sweep where they had been in combat and lost one or two people. The pilots were jumpy and in a state of shock at their misfortune. In contrast another experienced squadron on the field with mostly Norwegian pilots commanded by a blond headed Dane was cool, calm and collected. The difference between the conduct of the neophytes and hardened warriors was a salutary lesson in the value of experience.

During my visits to RAF bases I was able to get permission to fly a Spitfire Mk II, Hurricane, Blenheim and Miles Master. All were far more utility in design than most US aircraft, although the single-seat fighters were in consequence much lighter and had a better performance than the P-40. Johnny and I had taken turns in flying a Spitfire against a Tomahawk and both found that the Spit had the upper edge in manoeuvrability, acceleration and climb. We could understand why the RAF had consigned the P-40 to a ground support role.

One day in late July I was summoned to the station commander's office at Old Sarum. When I entered there was a man in civilian clothes with him. The Group Captain greeted me and said that the man was a plain clothes police officer who had come to escort me to the US Embassy in London where I was to report to the Air Attaché. He thanked me for my work at Old Sarum and wished me luck. The purpose of all this was a mystery, all the policeman could tell was that he had to accompany me everywhere and prevent me from speaking to anyone! We drove to the London Embassy that evening where John Alison, also escorted, was waiting in the lobby. Eventually we were ushered in to see the Ambassador himself, John Wyant. To our astonishment we also found ourselves in the presence of the President's roving ambassador at large, Harry Hopkins, Averell Harriman, who headed Lease-Lend aid, and Brigadier General Joe

McNarney, a top US Army materiel officer. To our further astonishment we learned that we were being sent to the USSR. As an immediate gesture of help to the Russians, reeling under the German invasion launched the previous month, the British were sending a convoy of war supplies, which was to include Hurricanes and Tomahawks.

Unbeknown to me at the time, the British had, as a result of tests in the States, decided to equip their Army Co-operation squadrons with the Mustang, a fighter designed and built for them by the North American Company. Although this aircraft had the same Allison low/ medium altitude rated engine as the Tomahawk, it had far better endurance and a performance reckoned as good or better than the current British and German fighter types up to around 15,000 feet. In consequence, the British were relegating the Tomahawk to North Africa where enemy opposition was less developed, and releasing others to the Russians. In July 1941 the British offered 200 to the Soviets, 140 being re-shipped from the UK and sixty via the Middle East. To help the Russians Johnny Alison and I were to oversee re-assembly, test fly them and instruct Soviet pilots on this type. Officially we were on assignment to the American Embassy in Moscow as assistant air attaches although our directions would come from the RAF in that country. Johnny was to accompany Hopkins and Harriman's party who were flying to Moscow right away: I was to follow by sea.

Having been told to go out and buy personal equipment for both of us, as it was unlikely to be available in Russia, the following day I made requisition through the Air Ministry for two sets of winter sheepskin flying suits and boots, oxygen masks and goggles, flying helmets and parachute bags in which to carry them. Two parachutes were also acquired from the same source. Flanked by my two Scotland Yard men I then visited Selfridges, Harrods and other stores to purchase items I could not get from the RAF. Four pairs of long handle underwear, a couple of heavy shirts, heavy gloves and several pairs of woollen stockings. I also wanted a summer flying suit and was offered a choice of a black or white pre-war civilian garment and decided the former would be the more practical colour.

We sailed on the afternoon of 12 August and as we headed up the Irish sea a convoy of seven merchant ships with an escort assembled. The *Llanstephan Castle*, an 11,000-ton Union Castle Line steamer, carried in addition to a large complement of passengers several crates of aircraft lashed to the top deck. There were several senior RAF men on board, including Wing Commander Ramsbottom-Isherwood who was to command a wing of Hurricane fighters that were to operate from Russia affording protection for northern ports. There were representatives of the British government, and those of the Polish in exile, also a number of journalists including fellow American Wallace Carroll, London correspondent for United Press. Among the British were a few intellectual socialists, notably Mrs Charlotte Haldane, wife of a professor, who never seemed to stop extolling the Russian communist system. It sounded all a little too good to be true.

The convoy proper assembled at Scapa Flow and proceeded towards Iceland where we arrived on 20 August. Then to Greenland before turning towards Spitsbergen to keep out of range of German reconnaissance aircraft from Norway. The pace was frustratingly slow, about eight knots at a guess. At first the weather was mostly fine and we could see our escorts — which included the aircraft carrier *Victorious* — on either flank. As the convoy sailed further north and east visibility closed in and for days we were shrouded in fog: sometimes so dense other vessels were lost from view and each merchant ship had to trail a sea plough so the next in line would know its position. We spent the trip walking and talking, taking part in twice daily Russian lessons, courtesy of the Poles. In anticipation of the language difficulty I had picked up some English/Russian phrase books in Harrods and had started to learn the alphabet. The Poles were able to help with pronunciation and during the sea trip I picked up around 800 words in Russian which was reckoned to be sufficient to get you by.

Eventually the convoy swung south through the Barents Sea and on the last day of August, after almost three weeks on board ship, we dropped anchor off the Russian coast near Arkhangelsk. The following day the *Llanstephan Castle* moved up river to Bakaristsa Quay, about five miles from Arkhangelsk, past saw mills, timber wharfs and great stacks of lumber. The first people seen on shore were lumberjacks and when we got near these proved to be mostly women. We were soon to learn that in the USSR there was no sex discrimination in heavy manual labour. Our first encounter with the Russians was a boarding party of officials and officers who came to greet us. The commander of the destroyer that docked next to us reciprocated by inviting these people to a reception and also requested my company, presumably as a goodwill gesture as I was the only

American officer in the convoy. At first a very stiff formal affair with interpreters translating toasts and speeches; later the gathering became more relaxed as the drink took effect. Next day we sampled Russian hospitality when invited to a party ashore. The spread on the table was sumptuous and drink was plentiful. People became very merry, not least our hosts, who concluded the entertainment by firing revolvers above their heads which, because of their instability, quickly had a sobering effect upon most of the British officials.

The following morning I was still sobering up in my cabin when informed that I was to be taken to an airfield where the P-40s were to be assembled. A small staff car, similar to the old Ford Model A, collected me from the docks. In the company of an English-speaking Red Army Lieutenant we set off along rough roads through Arkhangelsk. My first impression of the town was an overall drabness; then I realised this was due to the absence of painted buildings; with few exceptions they were all of timber construction and rough finish. Outside the town the vista was tundra and clumps of spruce; a really deserted countryside. The further we drove the more potholed the road became. About six and a half miles from Arkhangelsk we arrived at three railroad cars parked on a rail spur and deckecd with spruce branches as camouflage. This I understood was to be my quarters. One of the end coaches had sleeping compartments which were assigned to me and four RAF NCOs who were to work on the Tomahawks. The centre coach served as a communal mess and recreational area, while the far coach held the kitchen, stores and, we assumed, the Russian quarters, although we were not allowed to investigate. There were always two guards outside the coaches, night and day; we never did decide if they were to keep us from straying or their fellow countrymen away.

At the rail cars I was introduced to the housekeeper. She was about thirty to thirty-five years old, blonde and perhaps of Finnish extraction, having relatively fine features and slim build whereas the average Russian woman tended to be sturdy and well rounded. Her name was Aleksandria and she spoke excellent English. Perhaps with a little make-up, a decent hair style — hers was cut short like a man's — and more feminine clothes she would have been a pretty good looking girl.

After stowing my personal belongings, the Russian Lieutenant drove me the mile or so to the airfield site. Called Yagodnik, the place was still under construction. The runway and taxy roads were like nothing I had seen before. The spongy peat of the tundra had been dug out from two to three feet deep down to the permafrost and then spruce piles driven in about two feet apart to form a foundation. Across these were six-inch square timbers, laid side by side and end to end, forming a 300 foot-wide runway extending for a mile across the site. Timber was about the one thing of which there was no shortage and the Russians, having it in plenty at Arkhangelsk, certainly knew how to use it. Only a very few bulldozers and other machines were to be seen at Yagodnik where most work was carried out by hand. There were hundreds of labourers. In following days I noticed there were also many armed guards around the area and I deduced that the workers were prisoners. They appeared to be a mixture of captured Poles, Soviet political prisoners and criminals. I never did learn what their crimes had been for the average Russian wasn't concerned as to why they were prisoners; it was accepted that they had been involved in some offence and that was that.

I was taken to see the Russian commander, Colonel Boris Smirnov, a pleasant, stockily built man of around 35 years. He had flown in Spain and against the Japanese in Mongolia in 1939 and was a Hero of the Soviet Union. He could speak a little German and Spanish although not sufficient for me to converse with him in those languages so at first we had to use the interpreter.

On return to the rail cars a meal had been prepared which I partook with the RAF men. Our hosts' obviously had no idea about the eating and drinking habits of foreigners for at this and every meal the table was liberally stocked with vodka and wines. Food was simple but good — and far more than the British ration. Tired from my first day's activities on Russian soil, I soon dropped off to sleep; only to be uncomfortably awakened. The bites in my groin were all too familiar; I immediately recalled those days in McDowell's shack out in the Montana wilds: bed bugs! This was not for me and next day, acting on my complaint, they had the coach fumigated.

Every morning the RAF men and I were collected by the English speaking Lieutenant with the small staff car and driven over a log-surfaced road to the air base. At night the same man returned us to the rail cars. It did not take me long to figure out that he was the camp political officer. Most of the Russian officers seemed slightly wary of him, even Colonel Smirnov. I got the impression that he had been specially selected to keep an eye on us and report to higher command. I came to like and admire the Russian people but their suspicion of foreigners was most apparent. Rarely were they completely at ease in our company; it was as if we were some contagious disease they were scared of catching.

I soon became aware of how closed their minds were against anything but the official Government line. As Aleksandria had a good command of English and lived in the rail coaches she was the recipient of most of our questions. You became aware that her answers were always guarded or evasive if the questioning had any political implications. After a few weeks we began to receive *Time* and *Life* magazines in the mail from England. They were quite innocuous and although left in the dining car for anyone to pick up and look at I noticed that none of the Russians ever did. Intrigued, I asked Aleksandria why she didn't look at them. Her embarrassed reply was that they were propaganda! I couldn't help feeling that the real answer was that she was afraid to be seen looking at them. Probably she did have a peep when no one was about. Even Smirnov, who I got to like and know quite well, avoided certain topics. However, on one occasion when he came to see me on matters relating to the P-40 we walked along the rail track as we talked. The conversation got round to other topics. I asked about his trip abroad to Spain. From what was said he obviously had doubts about the communist system but was too loyal to his country to make any statement that might be taken as criticism. I learned he had a wife who was a doctor of medicine and two children, none of whom he had seen for two years. He said his worldly possessions could all be contained in two bags. Despite his high rank and record I could detect that he too had a certain apprehension of the political officer. The Russians were fine people but rarely could you escape this atmosphere of suspicion.

A few days after my arrival I happened to be going through my bags and discovered my passport was missing. The door to my compartment could not be locked. Only Aleksandria and a cleaning woman normally had access. I questioned Aleksandria and complained to Colonel Smirnov. There was supposed to have been an investigation but the passport was never returned. I had to go through the long process of obtaining another via the US Embassy in Moscow. Obviously the passport was stolen and I have always been intrigued by the possible reasons. Was it used to smuggle someone out of the country? Or, more likely, for espionage purposes to help infiltrate an agent into the USA. Who knows?

The guards on our railcars didn't help towards an easy atmosphere.

Even after a couple of weeks I would be challenged every time I approached the railcars. This was a little disconcerting as the procedure was for the guard to wait until you were in striking distance and then thrust out his rifle with bayonet attached as he shouted "Stay!" You immediately responded with "I am an American" in Russian and they would lower the weapon and tell you to pass. This may have been proficiency but as the tip of the bayonet was usually only a couple of feet from your stomach, and the guard's finger was crooked around the trigger, I found the ritual both uncomfortable and irritating. So in an effort to improve the situation I asked the NKVD Lieutenant why it was taking these guards so long to recognise me and to forego the challenge. His abrupt reply was that they never would and that if I tried to ignore the challenge and push by I would end up with a bullet through me. By that time I had come to realise that life in wartime Russia was very cheap and that if I had got myself shot there might have been little concern on the Soviet side. The losses among their own people were terrible so why should they have concern for a foreigner.

The only time any Britisher or American was allowed to visit the Soviet army camp adjacent to the airfield was the weekly use of the steam bathhouse. A necessity with the visitation of bed bugs. The bathhouse was a large log cabin with a disrobing room and the steaming compartment itself consisted of a central fireplace and tank of boiling water around which were tiers of wooden benches on which the bathers sat. There were no windows and the only light was from the fire. On an early visit I was sitting there cheerfully perspiring when the door was opened to allow other people to enter. As light shafted in from the disrobing room I was startled to see I was sitting beside some well endowed naked females. My embarrassment was not shared as such mixed steaming was quite normal in the Soviet Union. In fact, I was to learn that at this time relations between men and women were far more open than in western lands. Divorce was comparatively easy; if a couple wanted to separate it was a matter of a small payment and signing a formal document. Women were truly emancipated in the Soviet Union and I marvelled at their industry. Often a section crew would come by working on the railroad with women predominating in this back-aching job. These well-built girls would shift rails and tamp ties all day long.

The cleaning woman who worked in our railcars was of some curiosity to me. She was a broad-based, stocky peasant woman, always cheerful, and smiling. Every day in washing the floor she and accomplished this by bending over from the waist. Never once did she kneel. Quite extraordinary to watch. The other thing about this woman was her teeth. They appeared to be stainless steel capped dentures. Every time she smiled you got a sight of these great gleaming pegs. When Johnny Alison arrived he likened her mouth to the the bumper of the current Ford car. She did not speak a word of English but had a great sense of humour. Her work was hard as all floors and windows were washed without soap. Her brooms were simply brush sticks bound to a crude handle. She never fretted.

The task of erecting the P-40 Tomahawks was difficult primarily because of the lack of handling equipment and suitable facilities. The crates containing the aircraft were brought from Arkhangelsk docks by rail and off-loaded at the airfield rail spur. In England we had cranes available to move the components. At Yagodnik there was only one light crane of about two ton capacity. The fuselage and engine came in a box 29 feet long by 7 feet 3 inches high and weighed three tons. The wing box was some 36 feet by 10 feet and weighed nearly four tons. The problem was the single crane. Undaunted the Russians developed a method which employed brute strength by making use of something they had in plenty; manpower. The first step was to remove the wing from its box, then extend the main undercarriage legs and lock them, levering the wing over until it was positioned with wheels on the ground. The fuselage, once removed from its box, was hoisted one end onto a stand while the crane was suspended the other end. Around twenty men would then lift the wing and manoeuvre it towards and under the fuselage, holding it in position while the fuselage was dropped and levered into the correct position with poles. Sometimes the men under the wing supported it with their backs for a half hour before the fixing bolts could be secured. Wooden pole hoists were constructed to lift the propellers into place. By this brute force it was eventually possible to erect five P-40s a day.

The RAF men, each being a specialist in some trade, oversaw the assembly, checked the synchronisation of guns, the functioning of the radio equipment and operation of hydraulics. The senior sergeant was responsible for the initial engine starting which was a difficult job because the cosmoline — the protective grease substance — had not been washed off as it would have been in the States or Britain. It tended to foul the ignition, necessitlating removing and cleaning spark plugs several times. This trouble led to a lot of over priming with its risk of an engine fire, but luckily it never happened.

The Russian mechanics learned fast and sometimes, in their eagerness, often did jobs out of sequence. They had a habit of loading ammunition into the guns before the final assembly and I warned them that this was a dangerous practice. My warning was not heeded and one morning I heard a burst of gunfire as an engine was being started. Investigation revealed a neat .50-calibre hole clean through a propeller blade. Although the guns were synchronised to fire between the blades this was not effective until 1,500 engine revs per minute had been reached. Below this speed there was a good chance a bullet would hit a blade. There were no spare propellers available and with the holed blade the propeller would be unbalanced and dangerous to fly. This was duly explained and I expected the P-40 concerned to become a 'Hangar Queen'. The Russians had other ideas: the damaged propeller was removed and returned a few days later with the hole repaired and the prop balanced. They made such a good job I couldn't tell which plane it was during my test flying. This provided an interesting aspect of their engineering abilities.

Once the aircraft had been assembled and had a satisfactory run-up on the ground it was my job to carry out a test flight. The bumpy wooden runway was quite satisfactory although following rain it gained a coat of muddy squelch, became slippery and required cautious braking. On one of the early test flights I was orbiting the field when the engine began to cut out. A quick scan of the instruments indicated fuel pressure drop and probably fuel pump failure. I immediately grabbed the wobble pump lever — the hand priming pump used for starting — and worked it back and forth furiously until the engine caught. While continuing to pump I headed the P-40 round for the runway, using my stick hand to quickly drop the flap and undercarriage levers. It was a busy few minutes until the P-40 was safely back on the runway. Inspection revealed the auxiliary drive shaft from the fuel pump to engine cam shaft had sheared. We later discovered that the failure was precipitated by the electrical generator jerking due to overloading of the electrical services.

In Britian the RAF had changed the Tomahawk's original twelve volt electrical system to 24 volt to support more electrically operated services such as cameras, VHF radios and IFF. We got word to the British of our problem via Moscow and they responded with a modification that was later put into production in Russian factories.

Before this could be effected we had a couple of crashes due to fuel pump failure. These happened after take-off and the Russian pilots involved were able to crash-land straight ahead into the tundra. Both escaped but banged their heads on the gun sight. This was a reflector model added by the British which unfortunately projected so far out from the decking that, even with the seat belt and shoulder harness really tight, a pilot was still liable to hit his face in a crash.

The Russians were generally good pilots. Those I checked out in the P-40 had little trouble mastering the aircraft. There were no landing accidents that I recall and I never did see a Russian pilot ground loop a P-40, a trap many British and American pilots fell into. While the P-40 had a performance that the British and Americans thought inferior to potential German adversaries, the Russians were eager to get their hands on any worthy combat aircraft. The P-40 had equipment yet to be fitted on their own types — such as VHF radios and reflector gun sights. Morale among Russian pilots was high despite — as we learned — having lost around half of their front-line fighters during the first two months of the German invasion.

My ability to communicate in their native tongue improved as the days went by. For very technical matters the NKVD Lieutenant was usually on hand to act as interpreter. In the evenings Soviet technicians would come to the rail cars and I would translate the technical manuals on the P-40 from English to Russian. These sessions often went on till past midnight as these people would cheerfully put in fourteen hours or more a day.

Johnny Alison arrived at Yagodnik towards the end of September. It was good to see him again and to have one's own countryman around for companionship. He had been to Moscow on duties for the US Embassy and now came to help with the P-40 programme. Shortly after he arrived Colonel Smirnov asked us why Americans didn't like parties. We told him he was mistaken; we enjoyed such social occasions. His response was to announce that he would lay on a party in our honour to be held in the railroad dining car. The occasion was memorable to say the least. Our hosts, who previously appeared to only have access to the bare necessities for housekeeping, laid out the tables with fine crystal ware and cutlery, plus an excellent selection of wines and food which I was frankly amazed to see in a country locked in a bloody war. If the Russians worked hard, they also certainly knew how to enjoy themselves. There was a can of Caspian Sea caviar and crab meat from the Kamchatka peninsula, delicacies I had not seen before.

Our hosts, who were also our guests, arrived in strength; it seemed that practically every officer on the base was there. We began by drinking toasts to one another then followed with the meal and more toasts. It was no good insisting you didn't drink; you had to drink if you did not want to show offence. As the Russian form of toasts consisted of emptying the contents of a vodka glass down in one swig it was obvious to me that it would be impossible to remain sober. The problem was even more acute for Johnny who did not drink alcohol. I had long ago learned how to make myself vomit and rid the stomach of alcohol before it took effect although until now I had never had cause to resort to this distasteful act — sticking a finger down one's throat. After staggering back inside it began again; black bread, butter, caviare and another toast. The next move was to stack the tables to the side, start the little wind-up gramophone and dance. Men danced link-arm with men. It got wilder and wilder with more toasts and after each emptied cups or glasses were smashed against the walls. At one point Johnny proposed a toast to the Russian mechanics whereupon Lieutenant Kokkinaki, a large man, clasped Johnny in his arms, lifted him up — Johnny was about five feet four inches tall — and planted a kiss full on his lips. A common compliment àmong Russian men but certainly unexpected and embarrassing for Johnny. Kokkinaki was a great extrovert and really knew how to enjoy himself. He was also a fine test pilot and in post-war years became famous for establishing flying records.

In spite of a further trip outside it was not possible to avoid the effects of all the vodka that flowed. Gradually most people keeled over or left in a stupified state. Feeling decidedly ill I eventually managed to escape to my compartment. I was lying on my bed when the door opened and in came Aleksandria. Her intentions were soon obvious. Luckily I was too damn sick for anything and after a while she left. We had been warned not to become involved with Soviet women before leaving London but in any case I had no such desire for Aleksandria having never, even jokingly, made a pass.

Wine and vodka was always available on our meal tables and was rarely touched except by the senior RAF sergeant. One evening an incident occurred that was undoubtedly aggravated by this man's frequent imbibing. We were seated in the dining car for our evening meal with the RAF sergeant opposite me. I could tell he was already the worse for drink. Suddenly, he pulled the Webley pistol he carried from the holster and poked it right in my face pronouncing: "I'm getting tired of you. You're taking advantage of my girl." Looking down the barrel of a revolver with a drink deranged man fingering the trigger is not the most comfortable of situations, I tried to placate him asking "What are you talking about? Aleksandria isn't anybody's girl." He persisted in his claim and we argued back and forth until eventually he withdrew the revolver to one side. Johnny, who was sitting beside him, immediately jumped on his arm and I sprang across the table and wrested the gun away from the man. The other RAF boys held him down while Aleksandria, who had witnessed the rumpus, sent for the guards.

Later Colonel Smirnov arrived with some of his people, a preliminary investigation was held and the girl was taken away as she was supposedly the cause of the problem. Johnny and I explained that Aleksandria was not to blame; that easy access to alcohol was a major factor and that henceforth we requested it be withdrawn from all meal tables. We also communicated with the RAF command that these people should be directly under our administrative control and subject to disciplines we chose to impose. We didn't ask for the RAF sergeant to be withdrawn as he knew his job and we hoped that without the drink he would behave. This request was conceded to and a Group Captain arrived a few days later from Moscow to give us a written directive to this effect. He also relieved the RAF men of knives and pistols — neither Johnny nor I had any personal weapons.

Undoubtedly we all suffered from "cabin fever" for there was little to occupy us in the evenings except cards and a few English books and magazines. The RAF boys wanted to play chess so I carved a set of chessmen from wood as my relaxation. In conversations with Colonel Smirnov I indicated my desire to see Moscow. He said that he would shortly be flying south in a transport plane and that Johnny and I could go along for a brief visit. On the appointed day we piled into a Russian version of the Douglas DC-3 that had landed at our airfield. After take-off we set course flying just above the tree tops. This was an incredible trip the like of which I have never experienced. For 600 miles we flew at no more than 100 feet above the trees. While the aircraft bucked in turbulence, we sat on folded blankets watching some Soviet pilots from our base nonchalantly playing cards.

After landing at an airport near Moscow, Smirnov gave us directions to return in three days and arranged to have us conveyed to the US Embassy. Here we enjoyed the pleasure of conversing with fellow countrymen and made use of the commissary for candy bars and other national delights we had been missing. We spent our time seeing the sights such as Red Square and the Kremlin; but the highlight of the visit was the Bolshoi Ballet for which the Embassy staff had managed tickets for us. We were wearing civilian clothes and my dress for the ballet consisted of service trousers, a brown turtle neck sweater bought at Harrods, my leather flying jacket, and all topped off with a Russian caracul cap decked with my US Army insignia! Looking around as we sat in our seats about three or four rows back from the orchestra pit, I guess we were as well dressed as anybody. The ballet, Tchaikovski's Swan Lake, was I think the most memorable stage performance I have ever seen. The prima ballerina, Olga Libashinskaya was reputed to be the wife of Beria, head of the NKVD. She was so graceful; her performance was spell-binding. I was duly impressed and needless to say so were the people around us. Encore followed encore and people kept coming forward with bouquets of flowers. I wondered wherever such flowers came from in this cold bleak land where we were experiencing the first frosts.

During an interval the audience went back to the foyer to promenade and sip a little refreshment. So Johnny and I went too. We were standing in the crowd when I spotted Smirnov conversing with some people. I said, "Let's go over and say hello." So we pushed through the crowd and said "Hi". There was no response as he moved away. He certainly must have heard and seen us but he showed no sign of recognition and ignored our approach. We knew instinctively something was wrong and didn't follow. A day or so later when we reported to the airport for return to Yagodnik there was Smirnov all smiles. After we were airborne he whispered in my ear in German that if I ever saw him in Moscow or any other place when not engaged in military matters I was to pretend I didn't know him. He offered no explanation. The only conclusion I can draw is that at the time for a senior Soviet officer to acknowledge an acquaintance with foreigners in public could be damaging to his career.

The pleasant weather of summer was now replaced with fall conditions, with shortening days, cold nights and frequent overcasts. Our Tomahawk flight testing continued apace. After test flying the aircraft were flown to a regular Red Air Force base nearer Arkhangelsk where Soviet pilots would take over and ferry the aircraft to southern battlefront units. We returned from the Arkhangelsk base in a little Soviet two-seat biplane, the U-2, rather primitive but very rugged. The Russian pilots did on occasion let me fly the U-2 back to Yagodnik. There were some Russian I-15-3 Chaika and I-16 Rata fighters at Arkhangelsk, the former a biplane not unlike the old P-12 and the Rata a chunky radial monoplane akin to the Seversky P-35. My endeavours to get permission to fly these were always politely turned down.

Occasionally we would see other Russian types while flying around Yagodnik — although air activity was generally sparse. One October day, when the overcast ceiling was down to 3,000 feet and visibility about five to six miles, I was on the delivery run to Arkhangelsk when I saw a twin-engined aircraft approaching me head-on. I pulled out to the right intending to get a good view as we passed. That cold feeling of alarmed surprise is difficult to describe in words; as I glanced left I saw black crosses not red stars. Without any mental deliberation I racked the P-40 round, fully advanced the throttle lever, charged the guns and started in pursuit. Gradually I began to overhaul the German but as I approached within firing range he pulled up into the clouds, obviously aware of my presence. The aircraft was a Dornier 215, probably on a reconnaissance of Arkhangelsk. Only then did I reflect that here was I, a serving officer of the USAAF, intent on destroying an aircraft of a nation my country was not at war with! Had I been successful it might have precipitated an international incident. However, the endeavour stood me in good stead with the Russians when I landed for they had seen the reconnaissance plane and were delighted that a neutral had been so intent on its destruction.

By November most of the Tomahawks the British shipped into Arkhangelsk had been dealt with. Further shipments were coming through Persia as the northern route would soon be frozen up. The cold weather was already having an effect on our operations for the P-40s had no winterization equipment. With the first frosts we were forced to drain the engine oil while warm, and heat it in a can before replacement next morning. Here the Russians were ahead of us in that their aircraft had heating devices and other facilities for cold weather operation. As winter came it sometimes took five or six hours to get one P-40 running. It was obvious that the programme would have to be moved to a softer climate. The RAF men had already been moved and there was now little left for us to do.

Before we left we were given permission to go into Arkhangelsk. As in my previous impression, the place was almost wholly of timber construction, a very drab town in contrast to Moscow. The roads were potholed and a smell of stale sewage permeated the air everywhere you went. Most of the transportation was horse-drawn although on rounding a corner I was amazed to see a fellow in a floppy hat leading a camel pulling a cart! On most corners there was a loudspeaker blasting out music occasionally punctuated by what we took to be either news bulletins or patriotic speeches. There wasn't much we could buy as souvenirs; there were no big department stores. Outside grocery and butchers shops people stood in line for food. Our interpreter acted as guide.

In December we received orders to report to Valogda, an airfield about fifty miles north of Moscow, and after a brief stay we were called to the US Embassy in the Soviet capital. The German advance had brought them close to Moscow and all foreign embassies had been instructed to move east to Kuybyshev on the Volga, north of Stalingrad. Our embassy had been allocated a couple of railcars and Johnny and I assisted in removing their records and taking them by truck to the station to load. That night heavy artillery fire could be heard in the distance and there was some panic among civilians trying to leave by train. We could never have got through those crowds but for the Russian guards on our truck. It was a frightening situation. We finally boarded the train and set off south. Next day we stopped at Tula for a while. The town had been subject to the scorched earth policy. Everything had been burned; a blackened vista and the air heavy with the smell of burning. Even the telephone poles had been chopped down and fired.

At Kuybyshev there was little for us to do but to roam around and pick up useful intelligence. However, on the morning of 7 December we were awakened early to be told that the Japanese had attacked Pearl Harbor. The United States was at war and here were two fighter pilots far away from the action. Both of us immediately put in requests for transfer.

From our Air Attaché we learned that newer types of US aircraft were expected and we would be required to help the Russians master them. Our protest was that we had no experience of other types; we were fighter pilots not technical experts. Eventually, much to my delight and Johnny's chagrin, orders came for me to report to a new Fighter Group, the 56th, at Charlotte, South Carolina. Apparently the preference was due to my being a married man, Johnny then being single. The next problem was how to get out of the Soviet Union. Winter had closed the northern ports to British shipping. The only way out appeared to be a 4,000-mile train ride to Vladivostok with the hope that I could make contact with some US agency there. Fortune was to smile on me for a contact in the British Embassy told me an RAF Dakota was due in to Kuybyshev airfield with supplies for them. I could get a ride down to Tehran when the aircraft left. With sleeping bag, parachute and a little food I was on my way. We landed at Baku near the Caspian Sea and next day continued on to Tehran where I reported to the US Embassy. Our people put me up in a French-owned hotel in the hills with fine cuisine and a delightful room, a considerable contrast to the austerity of my recent accommodation.

For two weeks there was nothing to do but walk around Tehran. I bought a couple of bochara rugs with money provided me by the Embassy. Having turned in my parachute and flying helmet I used the parachute bag to transport the rugs. Just when I was beginning to wonder if I would have to sit out the whole war in Tehran I was told that a twin-engine British transport was just about to leave for Cairo. They rushed me to the airport and I was again on my way. We landed at Habbaniya near Baghdad to refuel and then flew across Jordan, Palestine, and landed near Cairo. Once again I turned myself in to the Embassy who put me up in Shepheard's Hotel. The war situation in the Middle East was bad at this time and there was difficulty in finding me a way home. The only immediate prospect was a British ship and a long sea voyage. I became rather frustrated by the obstacles and in consequence a little depressed. One evening in company with some of my fellow Americans in the bar at the Shepheard's, I was sounding off about the toughness of the Russians and doggedness of the British and announcing that Americans were too soft and would never be able to take the punishment I had seen. A crusty old Marine Major from World War 1 heard me out and then quietly put me in my place. "Son," he said, "you haven't seen war yet and you haven't seen Americans fight. When they get discipline and training they're as good as any other fighting men in the world." I was humbled.

To add to my plight in Cairo the Air Attaché had now decided he could use me and wanted to get my orders amended. He needed a representative in the Western Desert. This I resisted, I did not want a ground job. My persistent pestering for transport home eventually paid off when at 5 o'clock one morning I was awakened from my slumbers by a phone call from the Assistant Air Attaché. If I could get to the airport right away, an Egyptian pilot would give me a ride to Khartoum where a Pan American Clipper was expected to land on the Nile next day. Once again it was panic to get to the airport. Such was my haste in departure that I did not have time to collect the parachute bag with my two rugs from the Embassy, or underclothes that the Shepheard Hotel was cleaning and pressing.

The Egyptian pilot, having trained in the UK, spoke English well. His small twin-engine plane did not have much endurance and we had to land at a couple of airstrips where I helped him fill the tanks from five gallon cans. At Khartoum the Clipper did not arrive as advised and as the days passed I again began to wonder if I was in a dead end. Then there she was; this beautiful Boeing flying boat sitting on the Nile. The crew told me they had left the States carrying five tons of .50-calibre ammunition for the beleaguered forces in Java and were now on their way back to the States. All the luxury passenger accommodation had been ripped out to give room for this load. We left the Sudan and flew across Kenya, landing that night on the Congo at Leopoldville. Refuelled, next day we headed over the Atlantic for Natal, Brazil. From Natal it was Puerto Rico and finally Miami, USA. We landed at night. The whole place was aglow with lights; a complete contrast to blacked out Moscow and London.

It was March and I had been gone almost a year. In that time the US had come into the war and the Army Air Corps had become the Army Air Forces. I went to the nearest airfield and managed to get a ride on a transport going by Charlotte, North Carolina. I reported to the station headquarters and told them I had been assigned to the 56th Fighter Group. 'It's not here,' they said 'they've moved to Teaneck, New Jersey, but we do have something for you.' They produced the parachute bag with the two Persian rugs. How it ever beat me to Charlotte I'll never know. The underwear at Shepheard's did not follow, probably because the hotel burnt down so my shorts probably went up in smoke.

Armed with travel vouchers I finally made Teaneck by train. I asked the station master where the local airport was and he said there wasn't one. Seemed as if my every move to make my assignment was to be frustrated. However, further enquiries resolved the matter. The National Guard armoury building in the town had been taken over by air force personnel and this turned out to house the headquarters of the 56th Fighter Group. I reported to the senior man there, the Group

Adjutant. 'Ah, Lieutenant Zemke.' he said. 'They wired ahead you were coming. We're assigning you to the job of Group G-4, Assistant Materiel Officer.' Well, hell, I couldn't believe my ears. Here the Air Corps had sent me to Britain and Russia and halfway round the world. I'd been one of the few US observers with the RAF. I was probably the first US serviceman to live alongside Russian fliers. I had gained a vast amount of intelligence on how our Allies operated and their equipment, to say nothing of Luftwaffe techniques and equipment. And what was the Army Air Force doing with me? Why consigning me to a desk again to move paper and secure toilet rolls and spark plugs!

4
EARLY DAYS WITH THE 56TH

The 56th Group was one of the new fighter organisations formed during the Air Corps' effort to expand when US involvement in hostilities looked only a matter of time. Activated down in Georgia in January 1941, it had little more than a token existence with a handful of personnel for many weeks. Even after the move to Charlotte, South Carolina, in May that year, it could only muster a dozen aircraft, and those mostly trainers. Soon after the United States was brought into the war the Group was sent north to the New York area to take on an air defence role. The three flying squadrons that made up the 56th were outposted to coastal airdromes around the city from which they were supposed to challenge any air raids with some half dozen Bell P-39s apiece. Not that enemy air attack was likely; the Germans had no aircraft carriers and the Japanese were unlikely to appear in the Atlantic. What is more, with no blackout and no night defences at all, New York was wide open once darkness fell. While the 56th Group went through all the motions, scrambling a couple of fighters every time some unidentified plane was reported, in reality the outfit was still in a training and formative state. Commanding was Colonel David Graves, a tall dark man who was also boss of the New York Air Defense Wing who really had his hands full.

I learned all this during my first couple of days of getting settled in and finding rooms so I could bring my wife from Montana. The thought of working in the Directorate of Materiel troubled me greatly and at the first opportunity I went across the Hudson River to Manhatten to see Graves, who spent most of his time in the Group

Operations Office which was situated on the 11th floor of the American Telephone and Telegram Building. The Colonel listened to my objections to the job in view of the experience I had gained overseas. He seemed sympathetic, said he would do what he could, but for the time being I was to stick with my current assignment. As a special duty, he asked if I would visit each of the three squadrons, introduce myself, look them over and then write him a confidential report with my views on what I had seen and learned. First I went to Bridgeport Municipal Airport on the coast of Connecticut where the Group's 61st Fighter Squadron was stationed. The airfield was also being used by the Chance-Vought people for test flying their new F4U Corsair naval fighter. Barracks were still being built so the 61st personnel lived downtown in what accommodation was available. Some officers slept in the loft of a church. The mess hall was a tent and the engineering facilities were equally primitive. The squadron had a few P-40s, the version of the P-39 the RAF didn't want, a couple of genuine P-39s and an AT-6. People were doing their best but heaven help New York if this was one of the outfits on which it relied for defence. The 62nd Squadron at Bendix airport, New Jersey and the 63rd at Farmingdale, Long Island were in little better shape.

On the other side of the field at Farmingdale was the Republic Aviation's plant and here I got my first look at their new fighter, the P-47 Thunderbolt. Some early production examples were sitting on the ramp. It looked enormous beside a P-39; more like a bomber than a fighter although it was said to be the fastest interceptor in the world. I had heard manufacturers' claims before so was more than a little sceptical. The rumour was that the 56th would be the first outfit to receive this fighter.

A few days later I received orders to report to Graves who informed me I was to be Operations Officer. Most of my time was then spent at Combat Operations where a plotting table map of the New York area had been set up and on which aircraft movements were displayed as counters. The plotters were girls and the whole set-up was based on the RAF's system of raid reporting and control. Promotion to Captain followed and with the accommodation found for my wife and myself on the 13th floor of the Hotel New Yorker, life was pleasant.

Early in June the 56th received its first few P-47Bs so mechanics could become acquainted with the servicing requirements. One aircraft was allocated for flying and to give a greater margin of safety in landing and take-off this was based at Mitchel Field which had longer runways than Bridgeport. The first P-47Bs we obtained were divided among the three squadrons so that all pilots could gain experience handling the monster. As an "off the drawing board" design, teething troubles were expected and they were not long in occurring. One of the first problems was a fault with the air ducting between engine and turbo — the turbo being situated in the fuselage aft of the wing — highlighted when the P-47 Dave Graves was flying burst into flames and he had to bale out.

Probably as a result of my frequently voiced desire to get back to flying, I received a rather unusual temporary assignment. The US government had arranged to train a number of Chinese pilots for Chiang Kai-shek and 120 of these that graduated from flying school had to be checked out to fly pursuits. With three Lieutenants I was sent to Bradley Field at Windsor Locks in Connecticut where we were to put these pilots through their paces with AT-6 two-seat advanced trainers and then let them solo on Curtiss P-36s. This was a training school with a difference because they spoke no English and understood little, so everything we told them had to go through interpreters. This wasn't too bad in the classroom but it led to more than a few difficulties when they were airborne. As they couldn't engage in radio communication with the airfield tower they were really on their own. In bad weather it was particularly worrying. On one occasion when two failed to show up we feared the worst but they had managed to land elsewhere.

They were stalwart little fellows, generally very consciencious and well disciplined, but now and then they got the wrong idea. Before letting them loose with a P-36 we took them up in an AT-6 to show how to make an airfield approach in the P-36 and demonstrate how the aircraft would behave. Before the flight they were briefed through interpreters as to exactly what was going to happen and how they were to perform touch-and-go landings. The second man I took up had his own ideas. He was in the forward cockpit and I was in the rear. We had just gotten off the ground and tucked the wheels up when I suddenly saw the ground coming up on one side; the guy was doing a slow roll! Grabbing the stick I righted the aircraft, came round to land and taxied over to where the interpreter was standing. Containing my feelings, I asked what the pilot thought he was doing. There was an exchange of Chinese between the two men and then the interpreter informed me: 'He says he is now a fighter pilot and all fighter pilots do a slow roll when they take off.' I was astounded but retorted: 'Tell him he may reckon he's a fighter pilot but he just scared the hell out of me. If he pulls that trick again at 60 feet and next to no flying speed he's gonna be a dead fighter pilot!' Despite such incidents, by mid-June we got them all through the programme without an accident.

At the end of June 1942 there was an organisational change in the 56th Group, the Headquarters Squadron was disbanded and a new Group Headquarters unit formed from a cadre brought from Selfridge Field by Colonel John Crosthwaite who became the new CO. Dave Graves remained head of the New York Air Defense Wing and some of the personnel from the Headquarters Squadron stayed with him. The remainder, myself included, were given other assignments within 1st Fighter Command. I was promoted Major and, at last, given my flying command. A new fighter group, the 80th, was being formed under 1st Fighter Command and late in August I was given one of the embryo squadrons, the 89th, located at Farmingdale alongside the 56th Group's 63rd Squadron. Perhaps this advance stemmed from my report on the squadrons of the 56th for Graves, but any personal euphoria was brief for I quickly discovered this new unit was hardly worthy of the description squadron, being a handful of pilots with worn P-40s backed by 250 largely untrained enlisted men. Few people seemed to know what their job was and fewer still how to carry it out.

The 89th was symptomatic of the Army Air Force's desperation in forming new combat units without having sufficient trained personnel or equipment. Many of the enlisted men had been given a uniform and basic military training and that was all. We had to find them a slot in the organisation and train them to do useful work. And while the few trained mechanics and specialists were busy teaching there was little hope of functioning like a fighter squadron. Most of my time was taken up with just seeing these men were fed and kept under military order. After about two weeks with my first command I received a call to go to Brigadier General John Cannon's office at 1st Fighter Command HQ, Mitchel Field. Cannon, who later headed tactical air forces in North Africa and Italy, came straight to the point. Colonel John Crosthwaite had been given the 56th Group because Dave Graves had more work than he could handle with two commands. The new man, in his forties, was not a flying commander and Cannon considered him an interim CO until a younger fellow could be found. "I've talked to the three squadron commanders about

this and your name has been put forward. We've given you some experience with your own outfit and it has now been decided that you'll take over the 56th. Report to Bridgeport tomorrow."

Headquarters of the 56th Group had been moved to Bridgeport Municipal Airport in early June 1942, where its 61st Fighter Squadron was already in residence. Soon after I arrived the 63rd Squadron was moved in from Farmingdale to give more room at that base to the expanding 80th Fighter Group to which I had briefly been assigned as a squadron commander. Bridgeport became rather crowded and it was not an ideal field for operating the P-47, the runway length being restricted by drainage dykes on two sides of the field. The third squadron, the 62nd, had been moved to Bradley Field, sixty miles to the north.

Command of a group, the Air Force's principal operational unit, was a prized appointment that most seasoned officers sought. To be honest, I was proud to have achieved this status and intended to do my utmost to make my group the best — as I'm sure did every other man given a similar assignment. There were a great many difficulties to overcome and in my determination to succeed my command became the paramount concern in my life at that time. When not actually dealing with the day-to-day problems, I spent much time thinking how I should conduct myself. There may be born leaders but for me good leadership was a skill to be acquired. It was necessary to distinguish one's qualities and weaknesses, to trade on the former and hide the latter, to endeavour to be firm yet flexible, to be receptive but decisive, to earn the respect and trust of my men. A demanding role and you can only try to carry the majority with you. Human nature being what it is, however good your performance there will always be detractors.

My first few days as a group commander were spent assessing the organisation as well as trying to find accommodation to which to move my wife from New York. The three squadron commanders were men I had known for years. In charge of the 61st was Loreen McCollom, a blonde, lean man with angular features; level headed, agile and reliable. We first met in 1935 at Vancouver Barracks when taking physicals for flying cadet selection. Mac had been two classes behind me through flying school and had followed to Langley, joining the 35th Pursuit Squadron. Dave Schilling, who had the 62nd, also came to Langley while I was there, being assigned to the 33rd Pursuit Squadron. A geology graduate of Dartmouth College, Dave was

handsome, dark haired and debonair. An easy manner and flamboyant style made him popular with everyone, particularly the ladies.
His father had a large ranch in Arizona and was divorced from his
mother, a concert pianist. The family had a bit of money and after an
education at a top eastern college, Dave had entered the Air Corps for
a lark. He was, however, a natural pilot, so good that he had spent a
while test flying production P-40s from the Curtiss plant. When he
tired of that he got assigned to the 56th. The 63rd's commander was
Philip Tukey who had been in the same flying class as Schilling and
had gone to the 8th Pursuit at Langley after getting his wings in May
1940. His dad was a dentist in Maine and Tuke completed a pre-
medical course before deciding to enlist in the Air Corps. A likeable
individual, he was probably the sharpest of the three, picking things
up quickly and running a tight unit.

To find yourself elevated from a Lieutenant to a Lieutenant
Colonel in a matter of six months — as I was — and having to assume
the authority of command and act the stern disciplinarian with long-
time friends was a difficult transition to make. Particularly so for those
of us who had been pilots in the small peacetime Air Corps which was
like a gentleman's club where you got to know just about every other
officer. Later the situation eased when most of your contemporaries
also had speedy promotion and were given commands in the rapidly
expanding Army Air Forces. I soon realised that to establish myself as
the group commander, I had to gradually distance myself from my
squadron commanders to escape the buddy-buddy situation. The day
soon came when I had to look McCollom in the eye and say "Mac, we
do it this way" — although Mac was probably more appreciative of
the changed situation than the other two. Schilling was the most
difficult to deal with because of his irrepressible nature.

One of the biggest problems facing us was that we never had our
complete authorised complement of people on hand. Individuals were
always being sent on specialist training courses, or transferred out to
other units, while replacements scheduled for us were often diverted
elsewhere. The situation became so chaotic that 1st Air Force allowed
us to recruit specialist people from the locality, providing we were
sensible about it. Dave, as was his effervescent way, went to the Pratt
& Whitney engine plant at East Hartford not far from his base, picked
out a likely engineer or two and offered them the immediate rank of
Technical Sergeant if they would join his squadron engineering
section. Here was a manufacturer desperately trying to meet the ever

Missoula, March 1915 —
one year old. The Tyrolean
hat was made by Anna.

Benno Zemke (wearing the German ceremonial forestry sword) and his friends on a
deer hunting trip in the Swan River country. It took three days by horse and buggy to
reach this remote area. Each individual was allowed to kill no more than five deer but
could shoot as many bear, cougar, coyotes or wolves as he liked.

The CMTC camp enthusiast, June 1930, Fort Missoula. In the background is the boxing ring where the Idaho v. Wyoming-Montana Middleweight Boxing Championship was won at this time — but not without a few black eyes!

By virtue of young Hubert's reputation in American football, a scholarship was forthcoming for his University tuition. Representing the Univserity squad as a line guard in numerous games against the best of the Pacific coast teams, he was renowned for his tenacity in tackling much heavier opponents.

Kelly Field looking from the west along the Flight Line towards San Antonio city. Here I spent my happiest flying time, darting around the sky in P-12 biplanes. These WWI buildings were demolished and rebuilt at a later date.

A PT-3A primary trainer at Randolph Field. Landing gear had only rubber shock cords to take the rough handling of student pilots. Top speed 85 mph.

A P-12 of the 43rd School Squadron, Kelly Field. A joy to fly.

Running up on 8th Pursuit Group P-6E at Langley.

The PB-2A was the first high-altitude fighter in the Air Corps inventory. It had poor manoeuvrability and the rear gunner froze at 25,000 feet. This PB-2A carries the 36th Pursuit Squadron insignia.

The 36th Pursuit Squadron's CO's YP-37 at Langley. The position of the cockpit severely limited the pilot's forward vision. A precarious beast to land.

A Curtiss P-40 of Headquarters 8th Pursuit Group in olive drab finish.

Извлечение из „Положения о дипломатических и консульских представительствах иностранных государств на территории СССР" от 14/I—27 г.

„Ст. 2, п. а) Дипломатические представители пользуются личной неприкосновенностью, в силу которой они не могут быть подвергнуты аресту или задержанию в административном или судебном порядке.

Ст. 4. Помещения, занимаемые дипломатическими представительствами, а равно помещения, в которых проживают лица, упомянутые в ст. 2, и их семьи, являются неприкосновенными. Доступ в них может иметь место не иначе как с согласия дипломатического представителя.

Ст. 5. Принадлежность к числу лиц, упомянутых в ст. 2, удостоверяется соответствующими, выдаваемыми Народным Комиссариатом Иностранных Дел, документами".

(Выдана на основании ст. 5 Положения о дипломатических и консульских представительствах от 14 января 1927 г., С. З. 1927).

Дипломатическая карточка

№ 1826

Настоящим удостоверяется, что пред'явитель сего Лейтинант Зелике Губерт, Помощник Военного Атташе при Посольстве США

пользуется всеми правами и преимуществами, присвоенными в СССР дипломатическим представителям дружественных государств.

Действительна по 11 ноября 1942 г.

Народный Комиссар Иностранных Дел СССР

Заведующий Протокольным Отделом НКИД

1953 Москва 11 ноября 1941 г.

The identification card issued to me by the Soviets.

There were times when I felt more like a schoolmaster than a fighter pilot — Britons, Russians and now Chinese for tuition on the technicalities of flying American fighters. In the classroom I wrote details on the blackboard and the interpreter added the Chinese characters. Slow, but we got there.

Graduation at Bradley Field. Captain Zemke pins wings on six of the twenty Chinese pilots in front of a Curtiss P-36.

While at Mitchel Field, my superiors asked me to co-operate with the Air Force publicity people who required photographs for a special project. This is one of the shots posed in the cockpit of a P-40 at their direction. As a result, my face was beaming out of recruiting posters later in 1942.

On a chill winter's day visit to the Republic plant, their publicity people set up a picture with Joe Parker (left) and Lowery Brabham, the test pilots who had done most of the experimental work with the P-47. Brabham first took the prototype into the air and Parker had the dubious distinction of being the first man to bale out of a Thunderbolt.

In my Group Commander's aircraft leading a section of 61st Fighter Squadron high over the Atlantic seaboard.

The black flying suit (the same Harrods' model taken to Russia), high neck sweater and tousled hair were hardly becoming of a group commander. While talking to Colonel Bob Landry (who later headed the 56th while I was in the States) during the UK introduction of the P-47 to the press, a photographer took this shot. Happily it didn't reach General Hunter's desk.

This and similar photos of Lieutenant Robert M. Stultz appeared in several US and British newspapers following the P-47 press debut in England. Both 'plane and pilot eventually fell to the Luftwaffe — on 30 July and 17 August that same year.

Press photographers 'shooting' our P-47s at Kings Cliffe, 10 March 1943.

The Duke and Duchess of Gloucester meet a visiting B-17 crew during the tour of Kings Cliffe, 29 March 1943. The cold blustery wind gave the ladies trouble with their hats.

increasing demands for aero engines and along comes a young Air Force Captain and proselytizes some of their top mechanics right from the factory. Well, the President of Pratt & Whitney didn't stop at our little outfit; he went right to the top, to the Army Air Force HQ in Washington. The first thing I knew about this was a phone call from an irate General. I managed to get Dave off the hook; it would not be the only occasion. You couldn't help liking the guy but I soon learned that Dave tended to go his own way despite saying yes to me. The result was that I gradually became wary of him, wondering what screwball idea he'd be pursuing next. In fairness, all three squadron commanders would hoodwink me right and left in some matters, but Mac and Tuke were more cautious.

I took the first opportunity I could to fly the Thunderbolt. There was plenty of room in the cockpit and controls were pretty much standard apart from those for the turbo-supercharger. The turbo was an integral part of the design and supposedly gave the aircraft a top speed of over 400 mph at high altitude. This was difficult to believe, for even if the big Pratt & Whitney R-2800 radial engine up front could develop 2,000 horsepower, the drag of the blunt nose and large airframe went against the current trends set by the neat, small, superbly streamlined interceptors developed by the British and Germans.

The first flight was certainly an experience. On take-off I wondered if we were going to leave the runway, the roll being so much longer than that of other fighters. It finally lifted clear and the wheels were tucked up and I began a steady climb away from the airfield. Its rate of climb was decidedly poor. At around 15,000 feet I levelled out and tried a few manoeuvres. Lateral control was pretty good and the plane recovered from stalls pretty well. A few runs were made and I soon found there wasn't any acceleration worth the name. Coming in at Mitchel the final approach was long and fast but once down the plane stuck to the ground like a leech; the wide track landing gear was a good feature. Overall the P-47 was a big disappointment, only to be expected from a fighter grossing seven tons in comparison with the four of a P-39 or P-40.

The current mission of the 56th Group may have been the air defence of New York, but it was pretty well accepted in 1st Air Force Headquarters that as soon as our organisation was fully manned and proficient in mastering the P-47, we would be sent overseas. Assembling a team of trained men was task enough but we had the added burden of what amounted to being the service test unit for a new fighter which gave us plenty of trouble. The Army Air Force provided forms for everything and for noting technical troubles we filled out nearly 200 Unsatisfactory Reports on the P-47 while in the States. Most were minor; a few were serious. The majority of people flying the P-47 were Second Lieutenants right out of advanced flying school; jovial, cocky and pretty much a hotshot crowd, but definitely not the pilots who should be given the tricky job of finding the design faults and mechanical weaknesses in a fighter built straight off the drawing board. Not if you don't want a lot of buckled airplanes and dead aviators. Test pilots are generally too wary to push an airplane to its limits or, if they do, then by careful stages. Second Lieutenants have no such constraints. The euphoria engendered by being given a powerful fighter plane blinded them to caution.

Around the time I took command of the 56th there was an embargo on high speeds with the P-47 due to several instances of the fabric cover ripping off tail surfaces. Until Republic could come up with all-metal elevators and rudders this put a check on our would-be hell raisers. The radio mast on the B models we had, was originally made of wood but when the speed restrictions were lifted there were a large number of failures. I talked to Alex Kartveli, the P-47's designer, about this and he had a metal mast designed. We tried this on an aircraft in Tukey's squadron and Lieutenant Bobby Knowle, an outstanding pilot, took it up to test in a dive. I was in my office on the base when Tuke stuck his head round the door and asked if I wanted to come outside and watch what happened to the mast. I joined Tuke and a few others as Knowle topped off his climb at about 10,000 feet, pulled a half roll and entered a steep dive. He really put on the power; only he just kept coming, straight down and into the soft ground about 400 yards from where we were standing. There was nothing left but a few small smoking pieces around the water filled crater. It was not the kind of spectacle to promote confidence in the P-47.

Soon after this another incident occurred which probably explained what happened. Harold Comstock and Roger Dyar of the 63rd Squadron were briefed to practise horizontal speed runs at three different altitude levels, the first at 35,000 feet. They completed this then rolled into a near vertical dive and came down hell for leather for the next level. When they tried to pull out they couldn't; the stick was immovable, locked solid. They tried cutting the throttle but this made matters worse. The ground was coming up pretty fast but as they got into the denser air so the speed fell off and they were finally able to recover. They had no idea what had happened and were understandably very concerned. I called Kartveli and he flew over from Farmingdale right away. He listened to the two pilots, asked questions and then announced that they had encountered compressibility. He explained about the Mach factor, the ratio of an aircraft's speed to the velocity of sound, which varies with altitude but is around 725 mph at sea level. The faster an aircraft went so the more the air built up in front, to a point where it forced against the wing and tail control surfaces and held them as if in a vice. The P-47 was such a heavy aircraft it could attain speeds in a dive that were hitherto unknown. Comstock and Dyar had probably exceeded 500 mph. Kartveli went on to talk about Mach numbers. This was the first I had ever heard on the subject.

There were a few wrinkles in the skin on Comstock's and Dyar's planes and if this incident proved anything it was that the P-47 was pretty robust and didn't fly to pieces easily. In fact, one of the good points about the Thunderbolt that became manifestly obvious during this time was its ruggedness. Because the 56th was unofficial troubleshooter on this fighter we suffered a high accident rate with several fatalities. A lot more pilots would probably have been killed but for this rugged construction. One pilot misjudging his approach at Bridgeport hit a timber framed house, demolishing part of the roof, yet still made it safely onto the field. Another had an engine cut on take-off and cartwheeled into Long Island Sound but he came out little hurt.

Some of the accidents were totally unnecessary and due solely to stupidity, the outcome of the cocky I'm-a-hell-of-a-feller, it-can't-happen-to-me attitude. There was the pilot who had a grandmother living near Boston. He had hardly been checked out in the P-47 when he goes tootling up there and starts buzzing the place. He makes a couple of low passes and comes in even lower on the next; washes out grandmother's house, the P-47 and himself. On another occasion one of the self-promoting hotshot pilots was up leading three neophytes over the north side of Bridgeport in some rat-racing. The tail-end Charlie racked around too close to follow, blacked-out and spun down. He wrote off himself, an $83,000 airplane and $250,000 worth of house property. These kind of accidents didn't go down well with General Cannon at 1st Fighter Command and I was the one who had to meet his concern. Despite Command's worry about the accident rate, it was tolerated because of the special circumstances.

Much of my time was spent making telephone calls or personally visiting the Republic factory on matters relating to the P-47. While the correct procedure was to wait for response from Wright Field to the Unsatisfactory Reports we made, it was a necessity to get action right away, before someone else got killed or another airplane was wrecked. Fortunately we were provided two civilian technical representatives, Andrew Kutler of Republic and Ray Romania from Pratt & Whitney, who were attached to Group HQ and proved invaluable in sorting out the many technical problems. Wright Field did not really approve of my direct engineering transactions with the manufacturers. However, General Cannon understanding my need for frequent liaison with Kartveli and his test pilots Brabham and Parker, placated Wright Field.

We received a few pilots who were frightened of the P-47 and had to go. Otherwise morale was good because the pilots were all eager young fellows who thought the Thunderbolt was a terrific fighter simply because they had flown nothing else. I knew the P-47 was better than the P-40 and had good performance if you could get it to high altitude. The rate of climb was the main concern for, if we were to serve in the interceptor role the enemy would be gone before we could get upstairs. I realised it was my job to help my pilots get the most out of this aircraft until one day something better would come along — hopefully before they were killed!

With energies being directed towards checking out pilots in the P-47, there had been little opportunity to teach them to fight with it. We finally managed to fix up AT-6s to tow target sleeves and received permission to engage in air-to-air gunnery over a specified area of Long Island Sound. To save on ammunition only one gun was used. This was a rare event as mostly gunnery was done with gun cameras.

The RAF had a number of veteran fighter pilots in the States visiting bases to lecture on procedures and tactics in the European war zone. One who came to us was Alan Deere, a Battle of Britain ace, who brought along a little machine with which it was possible to work out the calibration for deflection on your gunnery film. This proved to many of the hotshot Second Lieutenants who thought they could knock anything out of the sky that they were way off in their aim.

On Thanksgiving Day, the 56th was officially alerted for overseas duty although it was far from being what I considered a trained combat-ready outfit. What combat tactics we could practise were based on British experience. The most aircraft we had put up at one time was a squadron of twelve made up of three four-plane flights in string formation — each aircraft stepped down one behind the other. We had only managed a few cross-country flights to give the fledgling fighter pilots the experience they lacked. Bad weather take-offs had never been tried. My squadron commanders didn't share my concern or views on a number of organisational and training matters because they had not been to a combat zone and could not appreciate the problems. The camaraderie that had been established in the Group was all very well, but if we were going to be an effective fighting unit we had to have a high standard of training and air discipline. I remembered the contrast between the two Spitfire squadrons observed in North Weald in the summer of 1941.

This whole period had been one of great pressure for me. I was both coach and player: the administrative load was so great I could not get the flying time I would have liked. The amount of paperwork was just staggering; it was a seven day a week job despite efforts to shed some of the load on the Group Headquarters staff. From the outset I did not get along with the Ground Executive Officer; we disagreed on many matters. Because he wouldn't work my way I should have replaced him early on but I dithered, hoping the situation would improve. It did not and I finally fired him, by which time other officers were aware of my indecision. The delay was a mistake for I was exhibiting a weakness as a commander and losing respect which would take time to win back.

As if there wasn't enough work, 1st Air Force required that I occasionally participate in publicity events in the local community to support recruiting. All this meant that I could spend little time at home. As my wife was pregnant and mostly on her own in the little house we rented, once we had the overseas alert I decided to arrange for her to go to her parents in Tampa. I had come to the conclusion that wives didn't fit into the war situation, not because my own marriage was not the happiest, but for the sound reason that the emotional ties could bring added stress. There had been too many occasions when, with the chaplain, I had to confront an eighteen or nineteen-year-old bride of a few weeks with news of the death of her husband in a crash. I let it be known that my view was don't get married now we are going to war. It didn't make any difference; even more Second Lieutenants went out and got wed after we were alerted for overseas.

Now to add to my problems all our P-47Bs were taken away; it was said they were going to be made ready for shipping but in fact they were given to another group in training. Then I had to find something to occupy the thousand men under my command, hopefully for just a few days before we received movement orders; only it turned out to be over a month. Some men were sent on leave, others packed equipment and for the majority it had to be military drills. We started marching them around Bridgeport to absorb their energies. Within a week I'm told everyone's shoes were coming apart in the winter slush. Here I am with a hundred or so men with worn out shoes. So much for the quality of Army footwear.

The next idea was to get the men to dig trenches and gun emplacements as base defences and stage a few ground exercises. Then the base authorities complained that the trenches were a hazard to vehicles and the men had to fill them all in again — not without much bitching and moaning. We set up medical inspections, gas warfare training, showed instruction films and tried everything you can think of to keep them occupied. That didn't prevent a spate of Court Martials as most evenings there would be some trouble in town; some guy would get the worse for drink and start a fight or tear down a saloon in a last fling before going overseas. On top of this I had to keep going up to Bradley Field to straighten things out as Dave Schilling always seemed to be at odds with the base commander, a conservative old Colonel. One day I received a call from this man protesting that Dave's squadron had stolen two of the base lathes. I found out that Dave, who liked these tools and was always having gadgets made up, had decided they could be useful to his squadron overseas and had promptly confiscated them. This equipment was over and beyond his Table of Organisation (the official listing of his unit's equipment) and, as usual, I had to straighten out the situation. I had always had a quick temper and incidents like this didn't improve it. I lambasted Dave but was beginning to realise that he was just as likely to do the same hair-brained thing again.

Another irritation at this time was the result of my endeavours to secure our full authorised complement of personnel. A replacement centre had been established at Westover Field, Massachusetts under Gil Myers and Neel Kearby, both friends from the old days at Langley and Mitchel. In the 56th there had been a few people who were always trouble or trained in duties for which we had a surplus of men — cooks, clerks and so on. I had these people transferred to Westover as unsuitable and requested men skilled in the trades I needed. Few were forthcoming and then, just before we got orders to move, we finally got them, only to discover they were the same men we had so recently got rid of!

Just before Christmas 1942 our movement orders came through and on 27 December all personnel were marched to the railroad station and taken to Camp Kilmer near New Brunswick, New Jersey. This was the Port of Embarkation camp, a holding centre for troops so that as soon as the ship we were to board was in dock we could be moved out without a hitch. As I had suspected, we were bound for the United Kingdom. The men were restricted to Camp Kilmer so no one could go to town and to keep everyone busy a non-stop series of drills, showdown, personal kit inspections, physicals and lectures and more drills and inspections was laid on. With the cold and the mud there wasn't a man who was unhappy to leave when, after eight days, we were taken by train the 25 miles to the North River Docks, New York. There in the early hours of the morning we saw our troopship was the giant *Queen Elizabeth*, the famous British liner. The men went up the gangway a squadron at a time. I was standing with the checker as each man passed by with his bag of personal kit. When the 62nd came along there was Dave Schilling at its head, a big grin on his face, no kit, but two large jugs of whisky under each arm. This was typical Dave; I guess he'd worked a deal with someone to carry his kit bags.

The 56th Fighter Group was given quarters towards the bow. The ship was so vast it was difficult to tell how many men were on board but I learned later there were 12,000. We hardly had time to get settled in before news broke that there was a field hospital on board with a company of nurses. Senior officers quickly decided that this area should be out of bounds and that a guard would be mounted to allow these nurses some peace during the voyage. There was no lack of officers volunteering for the duty.

We sailed late on 6 January. The Captain brought us together and gave instructions on the lifeboat and emergency drills that were to be set up for the men next morning. We were also required to furnish men to run a night and day submarine watch alert. This occupied some of the officers' time although even with the heavy duffle coats provided it was a cold and boring job. The *Queen* ran by herself on a zig-zag course; no convoy. Compared with my previous ocean trips she really moved; perhaps twenty knots. This was her protection, making it difficult for a U-boat to draw a bead on her. The trip was uneventful if you disregard the regular rumours of U-boat sightings.

Five days after leaving New York the *Queen* brought us safely into the Clyde estuary in Scotland. Anchor was dropped off Gourock, near Glasgow, but we had to wait until the following afternoon for our turn to disembark. From the ship the winter vista was one of greyness; grey water, grey land and grey sky. I was probably the only man in the group who had been in the UK before and knew something of the contrast between this land of austerity and the plenty of America. Initially the discomforts that came with the new environment would be accepted through the excitement of arriving in a strange country and the prospect of combat. The first fighter group trained to operate the big P-47 Thunderbolt was entering a theatre of war. We were eager to get a foot on the stage.

5
KING'S CLIFFE KINDERGARTEN

The decision of the Allies to beat Germany first resulted in plans to establish a huge American air force in the United Kingdom to partner the Royal Air Force in an assault on the Nazi empire. In the spring of 1942 the US 8th Air Force was designated as the headquarters in England, under which the first tentative combat operations began in July. Subsequently most of its early units were transferred or diverted to form another air force to support the North African landings late that year. The 8th Air Force then became the chief instrument of the USAAF's strategic bombing campaign, executed with large formations of heavy bombers flying at high altitude in daylight; in contrast to RAF Bomber Command which operated chiefly under cover of darkness. The four groups of B-17 Fortresses and a few B-24 Liberators that made up this American force during the winter of 1942-43, suffered a fairly high rate of attrition but it was the belief of many commanders that heavily armed Forts and Libs could successfully fight off enemy interceptors without depending on Allied fighter escort. Few would continue to adhere to this belief by the spring of 1943. Nevertheless, in January when the 56th Fighter Group arrived, fighter support was not a pressing requirement.

All but one of the 8th Air Force's fighter groups had been transferred to North Africa in the autumn of 1942. The remaining group, the 4th, had been formed from the RAF's 'Eagle' squadrons manned by American volunteers. Based at Debden in Essex, the 4th took part in cross-Channel ventures with British Spitfire squadrons. In December 1942 the 8th Air Force received the 78th Fighter Group fresh from the USA with twin-engined P-38 Lightnings, but while working up at Goxhill, Lincolnshire, its aircraft and pilots below flight leaders were taken away to make good losses in North Africa. Near the turn of the year the first Republic P-47 Thunderbolts arrived in British ports. A decision was made by 8th Air Force to re-equip both the 4th and 78th Groups with Thunderbolts and eventually to employ these in support of its own operations.

This then was the situation when the 56th Fighter Group arrived on a raw January day to bolster the order of battle. Despite having to deal with the teething troubles of a new fighter aircraft during the formative months in New England, the Group was reasonably well trained, particularly its pilots and mechanics. This was in some part due to the disciplines introduced by its commander, a man about whom opinions varied. While he could show humour or receptiveness to the views of others, on other occasions a rigidly dogmatic stance prevailed. One thing was clear, he was intent on running the group his way and those who hindered or resented this direction would not long be tolerated. Such was not the way to court popularity; but then Hub Zemke was determined to command as he believed a commander should; other considerations were secondary. Thus by some of his men he was viewed as far too military and a bit of a firebrand when rubbed up the wrong way. The Zemke temper was given cause to erupt on several occasions during the days following arrival at Gourock.

★   ★   ★

We were briefed to leave the *Queen Elizabeth* by a particular gangway and board waiting lighters a squadron at a time. I was on the first and found that there was a rail station just by the end of the quay. In the station building the men were fed a meal consisting of a slice of toast on which was slopped a spoonfull of baked beans; a British delicacy not much to the liking of Americans. This was to be washed down with ersatz coffee, also exceedingly strange to our palates. While suffering without complaint in the knowledge that Britain was a nation of rationing and shortages, it was a rude introduction to the eating habits of the men's Allies.

I became concerned because for some reason McCollom and his squadron had failed to appear in the station. Marshalling the troops was a British and an American officer who gave me directions for getting my group into one of the trains. The information that one of my squadrons had still not shown up from the *Queen* failed to impress them. The American officer said there could be no delay and the ensuing argument became a little heated to say the least. Eventually he ignored my protests and signalled the train off. So Tukey's and Schilling's squadrons were on their way, while I raged on the platform over such a mixed up situation. McCollom and his men finally showed up to experience my wrath. They had apparently taken the wrong gangplank off the ship and got into a lighter headed for another quay some distance away. At first the marshals said they would try and arrange lorry transport for us, but they finally managed to make up a train with a small steam loco and about three passenger cars and off we chugged into the blackout.

I had learned that our destination was King's Cliffe in the East Midlands; not an airfield I knew from my first trip to the UK. After all-night travel we were deposited at a small station where trucks were waiting to convey us to the base which I soon recognised as one of the new wartime airfields with temporary buildings. I was driven to the watch tower and one of the first things to catch my eye was a large piece of aircraft wreckage leaning against the wall. I was confronted with the sorry tale of an aircraft crash the day before which had killed the occupants. Two officers from VIIIth Fighter Command, our controlling headquarters in the chain of command, had flown up in a Miles Master to usher in our group. Later in the day they had taken off and performed some fancy manoeuvres and buzzing which finally resulted in splattering the aircraft and themselves all over the field.

King's Cliffe airdrome was a bleak place overlooking a small river valley to the south and the village of the same name to the immediate west. The flying field had three short hard surface runways and an encircling paved perimeter track. A solitary enclosed hangar stood not far from the technical site buildings and I found this was already occupied by the 33rd Service Group which was evidently to be our permanent support outfit. Accommodation for personnel, however, was limited although there were civilian workers around the place erecting new huts which, like those existing, were what the British called utility buildings, mostly of Nissen type clad with curved corrugated iron sheets. The presence of the construction men meant that there was plenty of mud everywhere.

From US representatives and the RAF liaison men on the base I learned that until the new accommodation was completed, one squadron of the group would have to be housed at nearby RAF Wittering. King's Cliffe had originally been a satellite for Wittering, an airstrip set up for use if the home station suffered enemy air attack. The satellite fields did not have the facilities of the home field. Tukey's 63rd was sent to Wittering where they were happy to discover it was a pre-war RAF base with steam heated barracks and much more pleasant living conditions than at King's Cliffe. As Wittering was an operational night fighter station the RAF had to shift some of their own men in order to squeeze in Tukey's outfit.

My first morning at King's Cliffe did not get off to a good start. At breakfast I found the RAF cooks dealing out beans on toast and this, twice in 24 hours, was more than I or my men could take. My rage was not intended as discourtesy to our hosts, but more an assurance to my pilots that action would be taken. We had American cooks in the kitchens from then on and if the food was not what it was in the States at least the dishes were more to the American palate.

King's Cliffe might have been a pretty place in summer but as an introduction to an English winter it did not impress Americans who had it in their nature to bitch about any discomfort, however slight. Many of the airmen's barracks had no close toilet facilities and to go for the John meant a long trip over squelchy duckboards. Many of the existing buildings had not been occupied for some weeks and were cold and clammy. The small iron stoves in each hut became the centre of continuous activity in an effort to get some heat from them. Schilling's comment that you could stoke for three days and still pick one up with your bare hands without fear of blistering, wasn't far off the mark. The trouble was probably the poor grade coal supplied for use in the stoves. Some guys declared they generated more heat stoking than ever they got from the stoves. It took time for the Americans to become acclimatised to the persistent damp chill of the English winter and within days of our arrival everyone seemed to be coming down with colds; coughing, sneezing and blowing noses. McCollom was hospitalised for several weeks with pneumonia. It was March before he was really fit again.

As there was no suitable building on the airfield, I set up my headquarters office in the lower part of the flying control tower, a substantial brick and concrete structure. My first concern was to get the organisation accommodated and functioning while establishing the various command and supply channels. A telephone call from the commanding general of VIIIth Fighter Command, Brigadier General Hunter, provided a basic outline and an invitation to visit him at his headquarters, which was code named 'Ajax'. Being anxious to discover what our role in the 8th Air Force was to be and when our P-47s would arrive, the trip was an early priority.

There was the matter of transportation as the only vehicles available were a few Jeeps and trucks. My request for a staff car was met by the RAF who temporarily loaned one of theirs until, after a week or so, providing a huge civilian limousine on a more permanent basis. This brute must have been commandeered from the British nobility — no ordinary civilian could have afforded to run such a gas-hungry auto. The engine under the hood of this big black Wolseley was enormous. There were separate compartments for the driver and passengers. The passenger compartment had a rear bench seat for three and two fold-down jump seats on the front bulkhead. There was a sliding window if you wanted to talk to the driver as well as a speaking tube. Not a very practical car for my purposes and although it had a fast turn of speed, around the base I preferred to use a Jeep. Because of its carrying capacity the Wolseley was often employed to wander the surrounding countryside picking up girls for parties. For this reason it soon became known as the 'Sex Machine'.

'Ajax' was situated near the town of Watford, about sixty miles down the main London to the north highway, and proved to be a two hour run. The headquarters occupied a large, centrally heated, English mansion called Bushey Hall, standing in parkland, a pretty nice place, far removed from the mud, cold and poor conditions in the field. Near London and, at the time, with little operational function, it was a good number for anyone stationed there.

I did not have long with General Hunter, who asked my problems and then turned me over to his aides for introductions to the various members of his staff. What I did learn was that the 4th Group had priority with the P-47 as its pilots had combat experience, but we would be getting our aircraft any day now. There were promises from the appropriate members of the staff to deal with my requests for action at King's Cliffe.

With each passing day it became more frustrating for the pilots to have no aircraft to fly. We were able to send some on RAF ground courses and set up our own ground training, but this was no real substitute for aircraft. We needed to practise formations and manoeuvres. Someone had the idea of simulating formations using the British bicycles which each pilot had been issued as personal transport. The spectacle of a dozen men pedalling hard round the perimeter track in echelons of four must have confirmed to the British that we Yanks were crazy. As it turned out this trick proved a useful exercise. We had to set up courses in geography as the average pilot had little idea of the terrain over which he would fly and fight. They had to form a mental picture of the important towns and landmarks in their presumed radius of action. In this we were assisted by a couple of able RAF officers, one of whom had lived on the continent and was of considerable help in the geographical studies. It was also necessary to instruct pilots in the British flying control system and the various radio aids to navigation and location. Despite all this, morale was low waiting from morning tea to afternoon tea in the hope a P-47 would show — it didn't take us long to pick up the English habit of tea breaks.

There was no purpose in confining the men to base and within a few days of our arrival all the neighbourhood pubs were swamped with new business. The locals couldn't keep up with the GIs and their pay checks. Hard liquor was rarely available — 'Kept under the counter', the English said — and what they called beer was an ale unlike the German type beers brewed in the States. Furthermore, wartime had caused the use of inferior malts and the alcohol content was much reduced. That didn't stop Americans drinking it like they had a ravenous thirst; which they needed to get any effect. The pub was soon recognised as the centre of entertainment in all the little towns and villages and here you might learn the mysteries of a game of darts. We were also liberal with issuing passes for London where everybody wanted to go, and returned with tales to entice others.

During these first few weeks at King's Cliffe it was brought to my notice that the Special Services officer was trying to get up a boxing team from the 56th to take part in a tournament to be staged in London. As the mood of our men was pretty low, I felt some sort of filip was needed. So I told them I'd enter for a bout and to put me down as Corporal Billy Mills, the name I had used in the professional ring back home. Boxing was strictly an enlisted man's sport and not for officers — most certainly not group commanders. However, I figured the news that the "Old Man" was going into the ring would soon spark interest around the base. Lieutenant Tom Bowie, a professional coach in civilian life, looked after the group's sporting recreation and he found me an enlisted man as a second. On the appointed date the three of us rode to London in the 'Sex Machine'. The programme of contests was staged in the Albert Hall, a famous London building more usually connected with orchestral concerts. Billy Mills, who hadn't been in a ring for eight years, was a little out of trim and practice. His opponent was pretty tough and knew what he was doing. After three two-minute rounds Billy Mills took the decision on points. This and my subterfuge caused much pleasure at Kings Cliffe. Unfortunately word that Zemke had been boxing under an assumed name found its way to General Hunter's ear and I received a curt reminder that officers didn't get involved in staged fights. Billy Mills would have liked to fight again, instead he had to hang up his gloves.

The Group had been at King's Cliffe two weeks before the first

P-47s arrived on 24 January. Thereafter they began to come in quite fast although I learned that the 78th Group at a base called Goxhill around eighty miles north of us was also being equipped with the Thunderbolt after having had its P-38s taken away. My pilots became a pretty excited bunch and I could see some discipline must be brought into the situation. These aircraft had only recently been assembled at a depot and I didn't want anyone wrecking a plane or killing themselves in the haste to get off the ground. Theatre modifications had to be made too. All this was going to take several days. So I called the pilots together and said that no one was to take up one of these aircraft until they had been thoroughly inspected and I gave the word. Anyone breaking the rule would be fined £5, which was around a fifth of a 2nd Lieutenant's monthly basic pay and a big enough sum at that time to make it prohibitive. I should have known it was like issuing a challenge. So what happens? Some bright guys in the 61st Squadron are out with the mechanics and the instant the first P-47 is checked out they pass the hat around the squadron and draw lots as to who should be the lucky guy. I'm sitting in my office when the door opens and in comes Eby and a few others grinning from ear to ear. A hat full of coins is dumped on my desk and I'm told that is my £5 and they are going to fly right away! Eby made the first flight that afternoon. In a few days everybody was flying like mad and things really began to pick up.

My biggest organisational headache during the first months of my command in England was with the 33rd Service Group which provided the 56th with base engineering and maintenance service. The 33rd had been formed mostly from National Guard units in the New York area and very few of its personnel had any practical experience in supporting a flying unit. Many of the men were long in years and were not about to change what I considered rather leisurely habits to suit my requirements. In particular I didn't seem to get the co-operation I wanted from their commander. If we were ever going to get our act together it was obvious that the service group CO would have to take his orders from the combat group commander.

In the States the 33rd Service Group had not been under any strenuous mission and they ran an eight to four schedule. They still tended to do this now we were in a combat zone and my squadron commanders and I wanted 24 hour service. Over the weeks my relationship with its CO, Colonel Lawrence Brower, deteriorated through my objection to what I saw as his intention to serve the combat group only on his terms.

To speed our equipment some of the P-47s arrived at King's Cliffe in wooden crates to be assembled by the service group. This was no real problem as our mechanics had worked on the P-47 in the States changing wings and engines. They soon showed the 33rd how it was done. The big fuselage boxes were around 36 feet long and eight feet high, big enough for a man to stand up inside. They were beautifully made, having an inner skin of ply sheet on wood studding, tar paper lining to ensure for moisture proofing and an outer skin of tongue and groove boarding finished in camouflage green. Made by Dade Brothers of Long Island, they must have cost the Government quite a sum. It was quickly seen that the empty boxes would make excellent huts, particularly if a door was fashioned at one end and windows were cut in the sides. They were the answer to the ground crew's problem at the exposed hardstandings round the airfield where there was no shelter other than tents. It was all right by me that they were put to this use, until it was brought to my attention by Larry Brower, that all the boxes had to be returned to a depot as salvage. We discussed the matter and I suggested he support me in requesting of VIIIth Fighter Command that we retain sufficient of these boxes to give our crew chiefs weather protection. However, it appeared Brower preferred to stick with the original requirement and the boxes were moved off the field. This brought things to a head. Despite my frequent complaints and requests to the staff officers at 'Ajax' and their reassurance that matters would be attended to, the plain truth was that as far as I could see little was being done. I appreciated there were supply problems but many of my requirements were only dependent on a decision being taken and orders given. I brooded long on this ongoing situation; there had to be changes if the 56th was going to be able to operate efficiently in a combat role. Apart from my own local problems with the service group commander there had to be better response from 'Ajax' staff officers. The higher headquarters staff were there to assist the field commander: in my opinion, at that time many of those at VIIIth Fighter Command saw it the other way round.

Again I made a phone appointment to see Hunter and had my driver take me down to Bushey in the 'Sex Machine'. My inner rage probably had the better of my caution for when ushered in to see the General and asked my problem, I came right out with: 'For a start

Sir, I think you have the lousiest staff I've ever seen.' His anger probably equalled my own. He immediately sent for his staff and I was asked to read out my complaints which were then discussed with the officers concerned. I realised I was in a precarious position and that I was most likely making enemies of men with whom I would have to continue to work — if not relieved of my command. Perhaps a man concerned with personal advancement would have been more guarded in his statements but it was in my nature not to pull my punches, so I proceeded to lambast those who I considered at fault. Naturally every staff officer defended his own position and tried to make out I was being unreasonable. I also brought to Hunter's attention my dissatisfaction with the commander of the service group and that I did not think we could continue together. In my view it was essential that the service group commander should fully comply with the wishes and dictates of the combat group commander and that both combat and service units should be able to function as an integral team. Hunter responded that it was up to me to put my complaints in writing and if Brower did not comply then I had the right to ask for his replacement.

On the return journey to King's Cliffe I had time to reflect on my own position. Hunter had not fired me but would my outburst achieve its aim. I felt the General suspected there was a certain amount of slackness in his staff and that Zemke's outburst may have sharpened them up a little. In the months ahead I would gain a better understanding of 'Monk' Hunter, who was a cohort of Arnold and Tooey Spaatz and other old timers. A batchelor with a liking for the ladies, he was always smartly dressed and well groomed. The big black moustache gave him a rather stern look. Of medium build, he always carried himself erect. He had a fine World War 1 record as a fighter pilot and he didn't forget this. He liked to mingle in the upper strata of society although he was not a high liver. While not a dynamic individual, he expressed himself well and I always found he was willing to listen. I came to realise that while he was right to delegate to his staff, he rarely followed up to see they had satisfactorily dealt with the matter entrusted. This tended to make his staff officers commanders in their own right which was wrong. He lacked the spark of real leadership. It also became obvious that Hunter didn't understand the active air and ground control of that day and age. I don't think he was ever able to grasp this and therefore tended to leave it to the RAF, who were in any case providing the operational control of USAAF units flying combat at that time.

As it happened, my confrontation with Hunter and his staff did bring about improvements in lines of supply and administrative action to remedy some of my complaints. This showed they were valid and not just the bitching of an upstart group commander as they might well have been seen. I did as Hunter had suggested and gave Brower a written directive stating my dissatisfaction and what was required of him, hoping he would conform.

We still did not have a full complement of pilots and were unlikely to receive more while P-47 trained replacements were going to build up the 78th Group. One day I received a phone call from 'Ajax' asking me if we wanted a Captain Gabreski who had operational experience on RAF Spitfires. Both the 4th and 78th Groups had declined to take him because they had enough people with rank and did not have a slot for him. For the same reason I hesitated, but finally said 'yes'. Likewise none of my squadron commanders were keen to have him. McCollom, however, eventually took this lean, energetic young captain as a flight commander. We were soon to find we had gained a real fighter.

Early in March the USAAF decided to release news of the Thunderbolt's arrival in England and we were surprised to receive notification that on the 10th a party of journalists would arrive at King's Cliffe to view the aircraft. The party turned out to be 47 strong and included photographers and movie cameramen. We did not know at the time that on the same date the 4th Group at Debden was to fly the first P-47 mission. When, in the following days, it was announced in the press that P-47s were in Britain, the photographs in the newspapers were those taken at our base. The sweep carried out by the 4th Group was little more than a publicity exercise because radio communication between pilots was almost impossible due to intense noise in the sets. This was a problem we had encountered in the States but which was magnified by the powerful crystals that were necessary in England. The P-47s we were receiving were the C-2 and C-5 models which had several improvements over the Bs flown in the States; notably a slightly repositioned centre of gravity giving better flight stability. There were still problems with spark plug fouling and distributor ignition leaks which were old hat to us. We heard they were also giving the 4th and 78th Groups plenty of trouble.

Because the P-47 had a radial engine and the only other combat fighter in the European Theatre of Operations (ETO) with a radial was the German Focke-Wulf 190, the authorities decided there might be some difficulty in distinguishing between the two and issued an instruction for special markings for the P-47. We had to paint white recognition bands around the nose and tail surfaces, add extra large white stars under both wings and outline the fuselage national insignia with yellow. It didn't say much for the average standard of aircraft recognition as apart from the blunt nose the FW 190 was nothing like the P-47. Around this time we were also ordered to paint special squadron letters on the 'planes that identified each squadron. The 61st's marking was HV, the 62nd's LM and the 63rd's UN. Additionally, each plane in a squadron was distinguished by a different letter and it became the practice of squadron and flight leaders to choose the initial of their surname for their assigned ship. My P-47B in the States had been crewed by Sergeant Sylvester Walker of the 61st Squadron. As I didn't wish to be seen to favour one squadron more than another, my P-47 at King's Cliffe was in the 62nd Squadron with Sergeant Theron Dillon as its crew chief. It was marked LM-Z.

Once the pilots had regained the feel of flying the Thunderbolt we put them to practising formations and gunnery. In the States we had used the string formation almost exclusively. In England we found the RAF were using the finger four formation and we decided to adopt this for general purposes. It was composed of two elements of two aircraft, a leader and his wingman, and staggered just like the fingertips of a hand. Each finger four was called a flight and three flights made up a twelve-plane squadron. The trailing flights were stepped down behind the squadron leader's flight so that pilots could easily keep him in view and follow his changes of course. So there should be no confusion in radio messages, the flights of a squadron were known as white, red and blue and the individual aircraft within a flight as Leader, Two, Three and Four. In this way you knew instantly the position of the pilot making the call. The three squadrons of the group were issued radio call signs — a two syllable word which prefaced any radio call. For example, if the leader heard someone call — say — 'Shaker Blue Three', he knew instantly it was the second element leader in the last flight of the 61st squadron.

Little gunnery had been done while we were at Bridgeport and one of my early requests to VIIIth Fighter Command was to lay on tow-target aircraft and range facilities. We learned tow-target flights had been set up using Lysanders, a British high-wing monoplane originally assigned for observation work, and these were located at Llanbedr on the coast of Wales and at Matlask near the Wash in Norfolk county. As the facilities were limited each squadron was sent for a period of two weeks. I joined Tukey's outfit at Matlask where a flight of our P-47s would take turns in trying to hole the sleeve towed by a Lysander up and down a range over the sea. Matlask had no spare accommodation so we were billeted in a nearby pub which had a large flour grinding wheel implanted in the floor. Our pilots called it the Wheel House, which seemed appropriate as I was in attendance and their 'big wheel'. From then on the group commander was frequently the 'wheel' and his abode the 'wheelhouse'.

The weather was fairly good while we were at Matlask, whereas the 61st Squadron that went to Llanbedr could rarely get off the ground because of persistent cloud and rain. When they did, one hotshot guy continued firing at a sleeve when the Lysander went into a turn and hit the aircraft which had to be ditched in the sea. Happily the crew were saved. The rule of the day in the States was that fighters would not fly cross country if the weather was less than 1,500 feet ceiling and three miles horizontal visibility. Well, you were not going to fly many days in the UK with those restrictions — and the Luftwaffe certainly wasn't going to call off its operations to oblige us when such conditions prevailed. We had to master bad weather flying and people were sent up from King's Cliffe in conditions which would have grounded us in the States. As a result all pilots kept getting lost and discovered first-hand the advantages of the British Darky system set up specifically to aid lost aircraft. On such occasions everyone eventually got back to King's Cliffe safely.

Lawrence Brower had discovered that the King's brother had a country estate a few miles from our base and somehow it was arranged that the Duke and Duchess of Gloucester would pay us a visit. The day turned out to be blustery and having hastily learned the protocol for welcoming British royalty we entertained them in our Officers' Club and arranged a P-47 fly-by. The Duchess proved to be a most gracious lady with a keen mind. The Duke didn't say much and it was difficult to judge his attitude. At least the visit helped morale and gave the men something to write home about.

At the beginning of April word came from 'Ajax' that we were about to be put on operational status and would shortly receive orders to move to an new base, Horsham St Faith, just outside the city of

Norwich. The move was received with mixed feelings because we had by then just about knocked King's Cliffe into shape. I decided to fly over with the squadron commanders and take a look. We found a grass field but to our great delight the place was a pre-war RAF station with permanent brick-built barracks, excellent mess halls and good technical facilities. On 5 April all serviceable aircraft of the 56th took off from King's Cliffe, assembled first into three squadron formations and then set off east with me in the lead. It was the first time we had put a whole group formation into the air. After landing at Horsham St. Faith I was standing with a small group of pilots watching the other P-47s come in when the acting RAF station commander came up and introduced himself. In turn, I introduced him to the particular pilots I'd been talking to: Schilling, Goldstein, Shiltz and Altschuler. The RAF officer smiled and said, 'Sounds as if I'm handing over to the Luftwaffe!'

6

HORSHAM ST FAITH
AND OPERATIONS

One of the notable characteristics of the United States serviceman of the
Second World War was his unflinching allegiance, even if he or his family
originated in a country that was now the enemy. Many of the young men who
arrived in Britain with the USAAF were first generation Americans born of
parents who were part of the massive emigration from eastern and central
Europe in the late nineteenth and early twentieth century. In addition to those
of Russian, Polish, Balkan and Scandinavian extraction, were many who had
relatives in Germany, Austria and Italy, thus facing the prospect of having
cousins as opposing enemies. For Hub and other pilots in his group of similar
background, an awareness of this situation was countered by unquestioned
loyalty to the cause of Uncle Sam; they could not have been truer Americans if
their forebears had sailed on the *Mayflower*. Indeed, the US serviceman's
confidence in the superiority of his nation was flouted to an extent that often
irritated allies. Nevertheless, the general spirit of these young warriors from the
New World was remarkably cohesive considering their diverse roots.

Fighter pilots were eager to go to war. Their task appeared one of personal
combat where the best man became the victor, albeit that this was an over-
simplification of the real situation. For the pilots of the 56th, as Hub was well
aware, while proficient in handling the P-47 their appreciation of air combat
through lectures and training could in no way make up for lack of actual
experience. The same was true of the 78th Group which had also been placed
on operational status at the beginning of April 1943 and, like the 56th, moved
to a new station, in their case Duxford near Cambridge. The 78th had been
filled out with Thunderbolt-trained replacement pilots from the States while its
flight and squadron leaders who remained after the P-38s were sent to Africa
had to retrain locally on the P-47. Most pilots of the 4th Group at Debden, a
few miles south east of Duxford, had seen a little combat, though some had
extensive experience. They had to convert from Spitfires to P-47s which was
not achieved without several accidents, in contrast to an almost trouble free

pre-combat training work-up period in England for the experienced 56th in their P-47s.

The 4th, having been formed from the RAF's Eagle Squadrons the previous autumn, understandably considered itself the senior party of the three groups. Colonel Edward Anderson had been installed as CO to endeavour to bring the 4th into line with USAAF procedures. In his fortieth year, he was somewhat old for such a command and his task proved difficult as his pilots were reluctant to forsake the ways of their RAF mentors. The British influence would remain for many months. Their most notable adherence to RAF practice was retaining a flying executive, a duty vested in Major Chesley Peterson, a highly experienced leader who had also shot down eight enemy aircraft. Most 4th Group pilots were unhappy about converting from the nimble Spitfire to the heavy Thunderbolt which they felt would be no match for the Luftwaffe's FW 190 and Me 109. The 78th leadership was not enamoured with the P-47 either, as having originally flown the agile Lockheed P-38 they considered their new equipment a retrograde step. As the pioneering unit with the type, the 56th did have confidence in the P-47; but then most of the pilots had flown no other modern fighter.

After all American fighter groups in the UK except the 4th had been moved to the North African invasion force in the autumn of 1942, General Spaatz directed that future fighter group assignments to 8th Air Force should be used to support daylight bomber operations. The P-38 Lightning, with its good range was the preferred type for such duties, but the demand from other theatres of war and limited production prevented further allocations to the United Kingdom for some considerable time. Range, however, was not of immediate concern when the equipment of fighter units destined for the UK was planned, it being anticipated that these would be employed in similar type operations to those undertaken by RAF fighters where high-altitude perfor-mance appeared to be an important factor. At the end of 1942 the only high performance fighter readily available from current American production was the P-47 Thunderbolt, of which some 200 were shipped to the UK in December 1942 and January 1943.

At Bovingdon airfield, not far from Bushey Hall, VIII Fighter Command had an experimental unit under an able test pilot, Major Cass Hough. Acquiring a P-47C, he ran a number of flight tests to determine performance, and in the process had a brush with compressibility, the vice-like action of air as the speed of sound is approached, while in a power dive. Comparison tests were run by other pilots against captured Luftwaffe fighters operated by the RAF from which various conclusions were drawn.

At altitudes up to 15,000 feet, both the Me 109G and FW 190A had all-round better performance than the P-47C, most notably in rate of climb. Above 15,000 feet the P-47's performance progressively improved so that from between 25,000 and 30,000 feet it surpassed those of the enemy fighters except for rate of climb and acceleration. This was to be expected of an aircraft double the weight of an Me 109 and half as much again as the FW 190. Under full power in level flight the Thunderbolt was faster than both enemy types above 15,000 feet, the advantage rising to as much as 20-30 mph at 30,000 feet. Although both Messerschmitt and Focke-Wulf could initially accelerate well in a dive, the P-47C soon overhauled them and easily out-dived both from high altitudes. It was also found that the P-47C could turn with both the Me 109 and FW 190 provided its speed kept above 200 mph.

As a result of these trials Thunderbolt pilots were advised to avoid combats at low altitudes and slow speeds; and never try climbing away from an enemy unless having gained good momentum in a dive. This latter advice can be understood when considering that an Me 109G averaged eleven minutes to climb from near ground level to 30,000 feet, and an FW 190 fourteen minutes, while a P-47 required twenty minutes. No wonder 4th Group pilots, in particular, bemoaned the Thunderbolt's sluggish climb when the Spitfire Vs they had foresaken could equal that of the Messerschmitt.

In practice the comparable performance of different types was dependent upon a number of other factors, notably the mechanical condition of an aircraft — there could be substantial differences in performance between aircraft of the same type — its loading and prevailing meteorological conditions, all of which might tip the scales. Even more critical to success in combat was the advantage in surprise and, of course, the skill of the pilot born of experience.

While 8th Air Force aimed to employ the P-47 force in support of its daylight bomber operations, the Thunderbolt pilots were first to gain operational experience under the controlling watch of RAF Fighter Command. A portion of the sizeable force of Spitfires, built up initially for defence of the British Isles, had been employed in offensive cross-Channel operations since the spring of 1941. These mostly took the form of 'Rodeos', the code word for several squadrons carrying out a high speed sweep over the enemy occupied territory to entice enemy fighters to combat.

As the Luftwaffe usually saw no reason to meet such challenges and suffer unnecessary attrition, a ruse known as a Circus was flown. This consisted of a small number of bombers with very strong fighter support, the bombers acting as bait to bring up the enemy fighters. A fighter escort for a true bomber operation was known as a 'Ramrod'. In these types of offensive operations by RAF Fighter Command, pilots frequently had to fight defensively as they were usually the ones attacked. Until the spring of 1943 the majority of squadrons flew the Spitfire V which, while it could better the FW 190s and Me 109s in a turning climbing fight, gave its best performance at around 20,000 feet whereas the German fighters, particularly the Me 109, had superior performance at high altitude. In consequence the Luftwaffe usually chose to attack with the advantage of altitude. Moreover, both enemy types could outdive the Spitfire. Thus the almost standard Luftwaffe tactic employed against Spitfires was to dive out of the sun, open fire, and then dive away to lower altitude before climbing to reform. The appearance of the Spitfire IX with its excellent high altitude performance, in the summer of 1942, altered the balance of what had been an unfavourable situation for the RAF, but the enemy types still had the advantage of being able to outpace Spitfires in dives.

Following Hitler's move to attack Russia in the summer of 1941, the Luftwaffe fighter force in the west consisted of approximately three full fighter regiments — Jagdgeschwader: JG1 based in north-west Germany, JG26 in the Pas de Calais and the Low Countries, and JG2 defending the Atlantic coast ports of France. JG2 and 26 had nine Staffeln each, a Staffel being a squadron with a strength of about twelve aircraft, organised into three Gruppen each. In total, about 200 fighters. At intervals Gruppen or Staffeln from JG2 and JG26 would be sent to other fronts and their place taken by units from other Jagdgeschwaden so that a strength of approximately 200 was maintained. This was the scene when the 56th Fighter Group became operational in the European Theatre of Operations. Hub expected the Group to be scheduled for its first mission at any time.

★   ★   ★

'Three days after the move to Horsham St Faith I received an order from 'Ajax' to take a four-plane flight to the 4th Group base at Debden to participate in a Rodeo set up by the RAF. I picked Dave Schilling and two flight commanders in the 62nd Squadron, Captains John McClure and Eugene O'Neill. Colonel Arman Peterson and three of his pilots from the 78th Group were also involved. The combat-experienced Chesley Peterson led the combined force of two dozen P-47s that took off from Debden late in the afternoon of 8 April, climbed to 30,000 feet and swept over Dunkirk at full power. But for the radio interference and knowledge that we had penetrated some dozen miles over enemy held territory, it could have been just another ninety minute practice mission over England.

'We stayed on at Debden to gain further operational experience. A few days of unsettled weather kept us on the ground until the morning of 13 April when we again formed part of the 4th Group formation in a sweep over the Pas de Calais. The 56th Group flight was placed in the highest flying squadron of the three. Over enemy territory we had a bit of excitement when there were radio calls from a lower squadron indicating the presence of enemy aircraft. The leader of our high squadron immediately and without warning made such an abrupt turn that I could barely hold formation with him and never did see what was going on below. That same evening another sweep was laid on and this time McCollom and Tukey brought a flight each from Horsham St Faith to rendezvous with my flight at Debden before we all set off to fly as the third squadron in the 4th Group formation. Climbing out over southern England towards the coastal town of Hastings, I found my oxygen supply was not working properly. After manipulating the regulator switch to no avail for some time, I had no course but to waggle my wings to signal I was aborting — turning back due to equipment failure — and feeling pretty chagrined headed for Debden. Schilling took over the lead of the 56th's squadron and followed Chesley Peterson's boys into France over Le Touquet and out ten minutes later near Dunkirk where a few bursts of flak were seen hovering in the sky. One of Tukey's men, Captain Roger Dyar — who had been involved in the power-dive incident in the States — suffered a complete engine failure over Dunkirk. From 31,000 feet he was able to glide 25 miles across the Channel to belly-land in a meadow near Deal. Seeing his approach at prohibited low altitude for crossing the coast, a British AA battery fired a warning shot — as they often did when such breaches of procedure were observed. It gave them a nasty shock when Dyar's P-47 crash-landed as they thought they had shot him down. A burnt out ignition harness was found to be the cause of engine failure. We had a lot of similar trouble with this equipment.

'Two days later I led the first full group operation from Horsham, another sweep of the Pas de Calais. When RAF Debden sector radioed a warning of enemy aircraft to the west of us and a swarm of fighters suddenly appeared from that direction, we thought we were in for a fight — only to quickly discover it was another P-47 group. By this time the 56th squadrons were scattered and made their own way back to Horsham and a lecture on air discipline from me. The 4th Group did get into a fight on this occasion and Major Don Blakeslee was credited with the first enemy aircraft shot down with a P-47. His group leader, Chesley Peterson, had to bale out into the Channel due to engine failure. He was picked up wet but well.

'On 17 April another Rodeo aimed at diverting enemy fighters away from a B-17 mission, was unsuccessful and for the 56th uneventful. A sweep along the Dutch coast a week later was similarly devoid of any contact with the enemy. I tried out a new formation staggering the squadrons and flights so that the group formation was like a giant V when viewed in plan. No hard and fast orders had been laid down by 'Ajax' on formations to be flown and the 56th, like the other P-47 groups, experimented to find the most desirable for control and deployment against the elusive enemy. The enemy, however, was around and simply biding his time to teach those upstart Americans a lesson.

A member of the 56th Fighter Group, destined to become one of the most famous American fighter pilots of the war, was Robert S. Johnson. In the early days his relationship with his group commander was a little uneasy.

'I had broken the rules on several occasions and received sharp reprimands from him. He probably thought I was trouble. He had a mission to perform and was quite serious about it. Very stern but also very fair. He was not an easy man to get to know. He didn't socialise much at the Officers' Club and had little contact with the Lieutenants outside working hours. But somehow I got the impression there was a guy just like us imprisoned inside that disciplinarian. Despite my misdemeanors, I learned that our Colonel could and would turn a blind eye to doubtful activities if he thought they were of benefit to our combat mission.

'For example, I was confined to base for two weeks as punishment for my contribution in perforating the ceiling of a Nissen hut with 45 cal. slugs. While my buddies were free to roam off-base or wherever, I would slow time P-47s. These were aircraft that had had new engines installed or were new aircraft. The engines required a number of running hours before they could be used on operational missions. I used the time to practice combat tactics.

'On one occasion I was devising escape manoeuvres should I find myself being pursued. At high cruise speed and fairly low altitude, I rolled the airplane over into a tight split-S, pulling the nose through as tightly as possible, thereby reversing my direction and skimming just over the treetops at a very high speed. I repeated this manoeuvre several times to find the minimum altitude required by the P-47 to *stay above* the treetops instead of *into them*. I then dropped my altitude even lower and rolled the airplane into the same manoeuvre-only, as the nose of the P-47 reached about a 45 degree angle to the ground, I rolled it back to the upright position and skimmed the treetops in my original direction. The idea being that any enemy would think I was going to crash and break off his attack. I repeated this several times and then, as it was getting late in the day, I buzzed the field one more time and came around to land. In this final run I saw our Commander standing near the control tower watching me.

'I fully expected a severe chewing out for dangerous flying. After landing and going to the pilots' room there was no message for me to report to the CO's office. I later learned that he had watched me for several minutes, but I never heard from him. He didn't miss much.'

'On the 29 April the group was again alerted for a high altitude 'Rodeo' in conjunction with the 4th and 78th, each group sweeping a section of enemy coastline with the 56th briefed to go in south of Flushing, turn north and come out near The Hague. Having led every mission the group had flown to date I felt someone else should be given the opportunity. Dave Schilling was the obvious choice, having previously taken over the lead when I had oxygen problems. Soon after midday 36 Thunderbolts were marshalled at Horsham St Faith and took off to follow the usual procedure, an orbit of the base to make formation and set course for the enemy coast, climbing at around 700 feet a minute. Once the group had passed 20,000 feet Schilling found his radio was faulty. Instead of turning back and handing over to one of the squadron leaders, he chose to continue in defiance of standard operating procedure. While still over the sea and about fifteen miles from the briefed point of landfall, Blankenberge, a Staffel of FW 190s coming down out of the sun attacked the leading 62nd Squadron. Schilling was unable to direct his squadrons or call for assistance. In consequence the 61st Squadron flying top cover was at first unaware of the battle and when it was, waited for the radio call that never came. The flights became scattered and unsure as to what was happening and what to do. By the time the English coast was regained fuel was so short many pilots had to land at the first airfield they saw.

'I was in the tower and from the radio talk realised the group had seen action and that all was not well. When Schilling landed I hopped in a jeep and drove over to where he had parked near a hangar. The P-47 had been shot up and the crew chief and mechanics were already trying to patch the holes. Schilling, in an agitated state, wanted to set up another mission to go out and seek revenge. I had to remind him that this could not be done without approval from higher authority and that he should settle down as this was going to be a long war. At the debriefing it became clear that two pilots were missing and that the mission had been a fiasco. Paramount among errors was the leader's failure to abort the mission when his radio was found inoperative. Without hesitation I took Schilling aside and admonished him for ignoring a golden rule. There was also some plain speaking to squadron and flight leaders who failed to communicate or respond in the situation. Two good men had been lost and two returning aircraft damaged — although happily the missing pilots survived as PoWs. We were a green outfit but this really was an ignominious combat debut.

'A change in tactics following this mission involved the formations we flew. Hitherto individual flights had gone out in close finger-fours, each shifting into string trail behind its leader at the enemy coast. This flight battle formation, advised by the RAF in our Stateside training days, placed the rearmost aircraft in a very vulnerable position. Other pilots were usually in no position to warn him of a surprise attack from the rear and in such an event the enemy was ideally placed to pick off the remaining planes ahead in the line. To improve matters, we staggered the two-plane elements in a flight and spread flights out in very loose formation. This gave better positioning for spotting attackers coming in from the rear and more flexibility in evading.

'After one more sweep VIIIth Fighter Command adjudged its P-47 groups sufficiently experienced to be used for bomber support. On 4 May when Fortresses were sent to bomb a factory at Antwerp, the 56th was briefed to meet them as they left the target. My radio again failed, just before the group reached the Dutch coast. Incensed, I handed over to McCollom and turned for home. This was my second forced turnback for equipment failure and I was concerned that some of the men might view this as the excuse of the faint hearted. As I turned back for Horsham St Faith to vent my wrath on the radio mechanics, I thought I saw a parachute far below. Only later did this connect with what happened on this mission.

'The bombers were seen shortly after crossing the enemy coast and the group turned to cover them. Near Walcheren Island some FW 190s were reported making passes at the leading bombers as McCollom led his flight down to attack. Mac lined up behind one fighter and opened fire. As pieces flew off his victim and it spun down it was clearly seen to be a Spitfire! Back at Horsham St Faith I listened to the debriefing and the confused and contradictory nature of individual pilots' reports. It was clear that some people were not only mistaking FW 190s for Spitfires but P-47s for FW 190s. Reports of Spitfires with 'solid yellow tails" could also be discounted. Excitement, speed of closure, sun glare and restricted vision through the cockpit canopy all contributed to mistaken observations; a situation confronting all fighter pilots but in this case exascerbated by inexperience. The RAF and 'Ajax' were, understandably, far from pleased with the 56th's performance, although our errant group could rightly plead that it had not been briefed for Spitfires in that area.

'For me this was particularly galling for as group commander I was ultimately responsible and had to meet General Hunter's summons to explain. For all our endeavours there was no hiding the fact that the 56th's bad score to date; two 'friendly' aircraft shot down and two P-47s lost, was certainly not a creditable showing. It was, therefore, something of a surprise to receive a message that as from 9 May I was promoted to full Colonel. On consideration, I realised this was due to policy whereby group commanders long in the service were to be upgraded in rank to provide greater opportunity for merit promotion of junior officers.

'The group's performance was constantly in my mind. I occasionally took myself on lone walks across the airfield to think over problems. I realised that lack of air discipline was our major weakness, for despite schooling in the tried and tested RAF fighter control procedures, too many pilots were given to doing their own thing on the spur of the moment, be it through excitement, eagerness or fear. I had long ago recognised that to achieve order in the air it had to be developed and maintained on the ground. It was easy for a commander to lapse into a buddy-buddy relationship with fellow pilots, particularly in the close camaraderie of a fighter outfit. Back in the States I had deliberately distanced myself from my squadron commanders in order to achieve an awareness of command and this policy had been pursued in England. Following my reprimands of Schilling and McCollom I became aware that I was becoming isolated. After dinner at night I found myself left alone in the Horsham mess while my squadron commanders sought the social company of their subordinates. I was obviously stuck with an over-military tag. My efforts to build respect for the necessity of strong command were raising a barrier and that was no road to success. The only way out of this that I could see while retaining the hard-nosed commander stance, was to order McCollom, Schilling and Tukey to move from their present quarters with the squadrons to the same building as mine. This was not popular with the individuals concerned but it proved the correct move as it brought us into regular social contact where they had to stand up to me rather than turn away.

'The aircraft maintenance situation had to be improved; too many P-47s out of commission for too long. There were several instances of engine, oxygen and radio failure and while some of this could be attributed to inherent weakness in the equipment, I was not satisfied with the support that crew chiefs were getting from the service group. Brower had continued to run his organisation in his own manner and could not accept a situation where he had to be subservient to a bunch of fighter pilots half his age. My own staff were well aware of the friction between us and I began to detect in their attitudes that they identified a weakness in me for allowing this deteriorating relationship to continue. Finally, aware that I had procrastinated too long, I took the necessary action to remove Brower so that service and combat groups could better operate in unison. I had dismissed subordinates in the 56th but to exercise my prerogative against a refined man of equal rank and many years my senior was a task I had hoped to avoid. It was not made any easier by Brower breaking down when the decision was put to him. Brower's executive officer took over the 33rd but I soon found that he too was not measuring up to my requirements.

'While the problems and administration of the 56th were constant, in order to gain technical and tactical intelligence and discuss ideas it was necessary for me to have regular contact with the staffs of the two other P-47 groups, the fighter technical section at Bovingdon and VIII Fighter Command Hq at Watford. At Horsham St Faith we were a considerable distance from these other installations which were all within forty miles of one another north of London. While I would normally fly down, if the weather was poor the 'Sex Machine' would be brought into service for what was usually a hundred mile or more time consuming trip.'

Hub's regular driver of the big black Wolseley was Sergeant Curtis Houston. This luxury limousine had some complex systems, notably an electrically operated carburettor that on occasions proved troublesome. Returning from one of Hub's trips to Ajax the route selected was via the A12 highway out of London to Ipswich. At one point the Wolseley's engine suddenly petered out and Houston diagnosed carburettor trouble. Hub found that by tapping the mechanism with a screwdriver whatever was sticking became unstuck and the engine would run. Hub hopped in beside Houston and away they went, only to have the vehicle stop again a few miles further on. More tapping again brought the engine back to life and enabled the journey to continue. Just outside Ipswich a British soldier thumbed a lift and Hub told his driver to stop and pick the man up. The soldier, no doubt surprised to find the civilian limousine in American service hands, climbed into the back compartment. The car had not proceeded much further when the engine again spluttered and died. Hub went through the revival procedure but this time the engine ceased to run as soon as he stopped the tapping. In Hub's view there was only one solution, so he positioned himself on the long mudguard and with the laterally hinged bonnet (hood) open, instructed Houston to drive on while he kept up a periodic tapping on the carburettor. The British soldier, curious as to the problem, slid open the rear compartment connecting window and enquired of Houston. The mechanical difficulty explained, the soldier then asked: 'Who's your mate out there?' 'He's my Colonel.' replied Houston. The look of amazement on the soldier's face and his subsequent uneasy silence indicated that the significance of the situation was not lost to him. For some 25 miles up the Ipswich-Norwich road the large black Wolseley purred along with a full Colonel lying on the mudguard tapping away at the works, while his Sergeant drove and an embarrassed British private sat uneasily in the splendour of the passenger compartment!

★   ★   ★

'Having recently received several new bomb groups, the 8th Air Force was able to double its bomber effort. On 13 May I led the 56th in support of some of the new B-17 outfits bombing an airfield in France. In the terminology of our combat report the show was "uneventful". Next day the bomber effort was again increased as two more new groups joined the battle. This time the 56th was assigned to meet one force of B-17s over Antwerp and shepherd them to the coast.

If the Luftwaffe was true to recent form and after the B-17s, I figured there was a good chance we would be able to get into a fight. Flying my LM-Z — now carrying the slogan *Moy Tovarish* (My Comrade) — I led 34 P-47s to rendezvous with the bombers over St Nicholas, arriving at 13:15 hours at just under 30,000 feet. For once visibility was excellent, a beautiful spring day.

'My hunch was right: over Antwerp FW 190s were reported diving towards the bombers. I saw two around my 2 o'clock position disappear from view under the P-47's nose. Immediately calling 'Shaker White Flight Follow Me,' a 180 degree diving turn was executed to pursue the enemy but they had disappeared. Looking round to check the rear I saw that my whole squadron appeared to be with me so I called for them to climb ahead and reform. Then I noticed that four aircraft about a mile to my left continued diving and I realised they were an enemy flight. I called for a left turn and gradually got myself in a position behind the enemy which I identified as FW 190s. They were flying a string formation apparently unaware of our P-47s.

'In manoeuvring to get in a firing position I continually joggled the throttle and side-slipped my P-47 so as not to over-run. My flight must have wondered what the hell I was doing as they struggled to follow my gyrations. The enemy number three man was placed best for a target and he began to fill my dot and ring sight. When the range appeared to be around 500 yards I pressed my right index finger on the 'stick' trigger and the recoil of the eight 'point fifties' shook the Thunderbolt. The Focke-Wulf was still ahead. My fire had missed completely. I brought the P-47 down more and gave a second burst. There was a flash on top of the enemy's canopy. Again my fire had been too high and the '190 immediately rolled over into a dive. As he passed across my sight I gave him a third burst and had time to see flashes along his left wing root and fuselage before he disappeared from sight below me.

'An exhilarating feeling of accomplishment came over me with a mental, 'I got him'. It was short-lived as my earphones rang with a warning that I was about to be attacked, making me break left into a climbing turn. I saw three or four aircraft coming down head-on and as the leader got within range I pumped a three second burst. I saw no hits or return fire before he was past and gone. In case other enemy fighters were around I began to turn and then saw that my wingman, Lieutenant Justus Foster, was still with me as was one other member of the flight, in spite of all my gyrations. The number four man, Lieutenant Robert Johnson, was missing. The enemy were gone and with fuel reserves low I led the flight out over Flushing. My composure returned and while feeling elated that I had made a "kill", I realised the action had affected my normally reasoned behaviour. Had the grip of combat caused me to neglect leadership? Throughout the action I had been conscious of a great deal of radio use by other members of the group somewhere above.

Back at Horsham St Faith I found that another flight of the 61st Squadron, which I had been leading, had attacked other FW 190s and made probable and damaged claims. More particularly I was relieved to learn that all our aircraft had returned safely, Bob Johnson having come home on his own. On more sober reflection I realised I had to enter a 'probably destroyed' claim for the FW 190 attacked and await expert evaluation of the gun camera film (this was a small 16 mm movie camera in the wing actuated automatically when the guns were fired to record bullet strikes). Evaluation of combat film was carried out at VIIIth Fighter Command where I learned my claim had been reduced to a 'damaged' credit. Later, during a visit to 'Ajax', the evaluation officer told me I was lucky to even get a 'damaged'. My range estimation was way off, fire had been made at more like 1,000 yards than 500 yards. My prey, which had seemed to loom large in the sight, showed as a distant smudge on the film. Most of the 67 rounds I'd loosed off had been sprayed harmlessly around the sky. In short, my gunnery was terrible. A mental note was made to pull up real close next time — I was confident there would be a next time.

The day following my first combat, Tukey took the group out for his first time. They swept over Amsterdam, had a few skirmishes with enemy fighters and made some damaged claims. Despite another fourteen trips in May, the 56th never had an opportunity to come to grips with the enemy again. Frustratingly the 4th and 78th had several clashes and chalked up a few victories. I had a feeling that the 56th was viewed as the ne'er-do-well of the three P-47 outfits by General Hunter and his staff. It was therefore surprising to receive notification that the Assistant Secretary for War, Mr Lovert, was coming to Horsham St Faith to see over an operational fighter station. The choice of venue, however, had apparently been Lovert's as he remembered the report I had written on the Russian war front the previous year. Coincidental with his inspection, the 56th had its complement of aircraft increased from 18 to 25 per squadron, although there was the thought that this may have been expedited lest the 56th's commander should comment that the other two groups had been brought to full strength a month ago. Most of the aircraft that came in were the new P-47D models although they were little different from the P-47Cs with which we commenced operations.

The up-grading allowed us to put up sixteen-plane squadrons of four flights each for an escort to Rennes on the 29th, a task necessitating using Exeter airfield in the south-west corner of England as a forward base to obtain maximum range. A formation of Me 109s was surprised and McCollom took a flight down to bounce the rear elements and was awarded a 'probable' on the evidence of his gun camera film. The sixteen-plane squadrons allowed a tactical division into two sections of two four-plane flights. This was a far better force for bomber escort as we could split a squadron over each side of a bomber box and better spread our support. But it presented us with control problems.

On the last day of the month I took the biggest force so far to set out from Horsham St Faith — fifty P-47s — on a sweep over the Belgian coast. So as to be seen to show no favouritism, I rotated the squadron I flew with in the lead and this time had the 63rd up front. Near Courtrai, Pat Williams, flying in my flight, suddenly wheeled over and went straight down. Sensing oxygen failure I screamed at him over the radio to pull out in the hope that if he were partially unconscious I could get him to respond. I kept screaming "Williams, pull out" but to no avail. His P-47 still dropped like a stone and when last seen plunged into the clouds 20,000 feet below. He never returned.

Inclement weather restricted operations during the first few days of June during which another original pilot of the group was killed. Allison was on a cross-country when he spun out of cloud. Non-operational losses were always harder to take than those through combat; an unnecessary waste of life in my view. On the other hand, morale at Horsham St Faith was good, the pilots eager to get to grips with their adversaries. But I was ever mindful that after two full operational months during which the group had flown 26 missions our score on the enemy aircraft shot down ledger was nil, whereas both the 4th and 78th were running up towards double figures. The only consolation was that where bomber support had been required, we had fulfilled our duty on several occasions by driving the Luftwaffe away from the B-17s. Still, I couldn't escape the feeling that I was the guy up against the ropes.

7
THE BURDEN OF COMMAND

Early in June 'Ajax' instructed me to appoint a Flying Executive officer as had the 4th and 78th. This concept was based on the RAF policy of having a flying wing commander on a station who only involved himself in flying matters and was not encumbered with base administration and other leadership duties. Our 'Flying Exec' would also act as Deputy CO of the group. This was a good move, for in my determination to succeed I was trying to shoulder too much of the leadership and should have been astute enough to realise this. There was a Ground Executive, Major Stanley Swanson, who took care of the routine paperwork but it still left plenty for me. Also, so far I had set out to head twenty of our 26 missions and there was a need for someone else to gain leadership experience. The new Flying Executive's chief job would be to alternate mission leads with me. He was also to be responsible for operational training and combat intelligence and the orientation of replacement pilots to the 56th in our particular policies.

Now came the tricky business of selecting one of the three squadron commanders to fill this post. All were highly qualified and as only one could be chosen, two were bound to be disappointed. On a long walk in the evening I evaluated each officer in my own mind. Dave Schilling, natural pilot, flamboyant and popular leader would have probably been the front runner but for his lapse on his first mission lead. I was unwilling to trust Dave's impulsive nature until he had more experience behind him. Tuke was a capable commander and ran his squadron well although I thought he did not seem to show as much inherent flying ability and aggression as the others. Tuke needed more opportunities to prove himself, I figured. This left Mac. Level-headed and quiet, aggressive yet cool in combat; McCollom was the man. After dinner that evening I called all three to my office and announced my decision. Dave looked aghast, the disappointment showed on his face. Tuke kept his calm, giving no outward appearance of disappointment at being passed over. Mac smiled his whimsical smile and took the others' congratulations calmly. Inwardly I knew he was elated. I directed Swanson to cut orders for McCollom's appointment effective next day — 9 June. Then there was the matter of finding a new CO for the 61st. Mac and I talked this over and at first favoured Merle Eby but finally decided that the job should go to Gabby Gabreski because of his greater experience.

Mac took out his first mission as the Flying Executive shortly after mid-day on 11 June and that evening I led another sweep. If nothing else, we were certainly getting to know the coastline on the other side of the Channel. The following evening McCollom took the group out on another sweep over the Pas de Calais. They went in at 20,000 feet, far below our usual altitude. Mac figured that the Luftwaffe always expected us to be up around 30,000 feet and might be caught off guard at a lower level. I gave the okay, stressing no lower. Sure enough a Staffel of FW 190s was seen about 5,000 feet below our boys while over Belgium. Schilling's flight went down to attack and Dave took a long deflection shot at an enemy 'plane as they broke and dived. One Jerry flight, however, went into a climbing turn, probably hoping our boys would fall into the trap of trying to follow the diving '190s. What the Jerries hadn't seen was that another flight of P-47s was up sun. Seeing what was happening its leader, Captain Walter Cook of the 62nd, went down on the Focke-Wulfs that were trying to circle round. Coming up behind the last man Walt held his fire until around 300 yards away and then let fly. His first shots struck the fuselage and then as prop wash caused his plane to veer slightly his fire began going into the enemy's left wing. A large puff of black smoke indicated he had hit the ammo compartment and a large piece of wing came off. Cook broke off the attack and pulled away. The FW 190 was seen going straight down in an uncontrolled spin. As the enemy pilot took no evasive action it seems likely he was killed by Cook's opening burst. At last the 56th had made its first confirmed kill! At the same time I couldn't help speculating that at the current rate of attrition it would take a hundred years to decimate the Luftwaffe.

The following morning we were alerted for yet another sweep. My turn at the lead. The report made out on return from that mission was probably one of the most detailed of that type I ever wrote.

★   ★   ★

'As flying wing commander of the 56th Fighter Group on this mission, I had decided that I would lead the 61st Fighter Squadron as bouncing squadron. The 62nd Fighter Squadron was to be close escort at the same altitude and slightly to the rear. The 63rd Fighter Squadron was to be high cover for the other two squadrons with a superiority of 1,000-2,000 feet more or less to the inside of the course and slightly ahead where I could direct their direction and disposition.

'Take-off and climb of the squadrons was normal in that nothing of importance can be mentioned. The squadrons positioned themselves on the climb so that the 63rd was to the left and the 62nd was on the right. From Felixstowe to Gravelines the course was 174 degrees through a thin layer of about 6/10 Cirrus clouds. This gave me considerable anxiety as the 56th Group was to give high support to the 4th Fighter Group. The layer being at 26,000 feet. At this time, which was about 09:30 plus hours, contrails were reported ahead going into France and were believed to be the 4th Fighter Group. Shortly thereafter, the Ground Operations reported bandits in the vicinity of Ostend heading west along the coast. Since the group had not reached France and were trying to give support to the 4th Group, who were only in visual contact by their occasional condensation trails ahead, it was decided to continue on plan.

'At about 09:35 hours, while still over water, the Ground Operations reported that twenty-plus bandits were is the Lille area, heading to the north-west (in our direction), altitude unknown.

'When the coast was reached at 09:37 hours, a slight turn left was made placing the 63rd slightly ahead and well to the left, they having gained 2,000 feet of altitude over remainder of the group. Again Ground Operations gave me instructions that twenty-plus bandits were flying north-west at 20,000 feet in the vicinity of Ypres, this being due ahead of us on course.

'A split second later I looked ahead at 11 o'clock and down slightly toward a very large hole in the cirrus clouds and saw fifteen or twenty spots climbing in our direction. Some of these spots were leaving distinct vapour trails. They must have been fifteen or twenty miles away at the time. They, as well as us, never altered course but closed at a very rapid rate.

'When a distance of two or three miles between forces had been reached, I saw that they were flying in three groups of approximately six each in what would be called a company front formation. They were then below some three or four thousand feet and well to my left. The altitude of my squadron was 27,000 at that time.

'The squadrons were told that I was taking the first section of eight of the 61st Fighter Squadron in a left diving attack. It may be noted that I forgot to touch my throttle and it remained at 31 inches Hg manifold pressure and 2,550 rpm for the entire combat.

'At first I dove to attack the lower lead unit but changed my mind and continued down to attack a group who were slightly to the rear and above the lead unit. As the attacking dive commenced, the lead E/A group began turning to the right and the remainder to do likewise. This fact plus the fact that they never flew more than two or three lengths apart, leads me to believe that I was never seen but that all eyes were on the 63rd Fighter Squadron which was well to my left and directly over the hole in the overcast.

'As I approached the last of the four enemy aircraft, directly astern, I noticed that the tail end aircraft had white stripes around the horizontal stabilizer and elevators. This made me hesitate for I thought these aircraft might have been P-47s coming out of France. Perhaps this hesitation helped me, for I closed to 150 to 200 yards before firing. There was no doubt in my mind then. To destroy this aircraft was a mere matter of putting the dot on the fuselage, and pulling the trigger. A split second after firing, the fuselage burst into flames and pieces of the right wing came off. I immediately went down to the right leaving the number three plane of the four aircraft string just ahead.

'This plane for some reason must have been weaving so that I had to give it some deflection. The deflection proved to be a bit excessive and I noticed strikes out on the right wingtip. The plane being in a right bank went down placing me directly in back of the number two plane of the string, which sat in the gun sight as one would imagine for the ideal shot. Again, when the trigger was pulled this aircraft exploded with a long sheet of flame and smoke.

'Unfortunately the number one man of the flight of FW 190s must have become aware of the unhealthy situation and left the scene of battle in a dive so I didn't see him go.

'Each gun fired an average of fifty rounds in the three bursts mentioned above. Recovery was thereafter made due ahead to 26,000 feet where a slight turn to the left revealed that Dunkirk was directly down to the left. On looking over the sky again, everything was well broken up and miles away. Only two other P-47s were with me out of the sixteen first taken out. Combats were noted at great distances away so I ordered an assembly over Dunkirk. This was exceedingly difficult as the R/T was as nearly jammed with pilots reporting each other as E/A as can be imagined.

'The assembly point was moved out over the sea from Dunkirk as quite heavy anti-aircraft was put up over the area. The squadrons were then ordered home, since the E/A had gone to the deck and it was believed all organisations were disorganised. In reality the 62nd and 63rd Fighter Squadrons never entered battle. I had failed to call them down until too late.

'The group continued on to home base with the two above mentioned squadrons giving support and picking up my stragglers. I claim two FW 190s destroyed, and one FW 190 damaged.'

The Ground Controller was located at the RAF sector control building near Debden. This received information on enemy air movements from radar and radio monitoring stations, passing anything pertinent to our mission to us via 'A' Channel, one of four push-button switched channels on the P-47's VHF radio. A different frequency was used for each fighter group to avoid confusion. Every message sent was prefaced with my group call sign. As radio silence was essential to prevent alerting the German monitoring organisation of our position, the only acknowledgement to the ground controller was a quick 'Click, Click', made by pressing the microphone switch on the throttle handle. The control centre was eventually taken over and manned by VIIIth Fighter Command. While the RAF ran it, most of the controllers were often members of the Women's Auxiliary Air Force, 'WAAFs' as they were called. It was a little disconcerting to be six miles high in hostile airspace and suddenly have your earphones filled with the clear and precise tones of a cultivated English girl. On the occasion of my first successful air fight I owed a lot to the girl whose cool and taciturn control certainly played a major role in the proceedings. She could not have executed her job more efficiently. Naturally I wanted to thank her personally but such contact was not permitted by high command and so, sadly, she remained anonymous.

Back at Horsham St Faith I discovered that another FW 190 had been shot down by Lieutenant Robert Johnson. Johnson had been flying Shaker Blue Four, the number four position in Gabreski's flight, which was flying high on my left before the action. When Johnson saw the Focke-Wulfs below us he just peeled over and went down after the leader, got close up behind him and blasted him out of the sky. This was in direct contravention of the rule whereby a wingman always stayed with his element leader unless otherwise directed. It was not the first time that Johnson had been guilty of ignoring the rules and he had to be disciplined. It was difficult to give a man a chewing out for action which resulted in the destruction of an enemy 'plane. In so doing I doubt I endeared Bob to his group commander. Privately, it was good to know that I had pilots of such aggressive calibre. Also, I was aware of my own failure to call other flights down to attack and realised that in future flight leaders should be instructed to use their own discretion and go into the attack if the group leader was preoccupied in combat. Without checking individual initiative the team effort had to be fostered to such a degree that every squadron and flight leader automatically followed our battle plans for a given situation. More and more I was coming to realise that if we stood any chance of really beating the Luftwaffe it was going to be through bringing as much of the group's firepower into action on each operation, rather than just picking off one or two enemy planes when the opportunity arose. To this end we had got to increase the emphasis on training. A lot of our people already thought themselves 'gung-ho' fighter pilots but they still had an awful lot to learn.

'After this mission it was necessary to re-emphasise the importance of radio discipline. I understood that in the excitement and fear of combat there was a natural desire to call and comment. This was taboo, for the more people transmitting on the assigned frequency the more likelihood that the commander's instructions or warning calls could be blotted out. The importance of radio silence was difficult to instil in some individuals who frequently talked unnecessarily during a mission. I recognised the same voices. One persistent offender was Lieutenant Anthony Carcione in Schilling's 62nd Squadron, an outgoing, affable boy of Italian descent. He flew as well as anybody but the loneliness of a fighter cockpit seemed to stimulate his desire to converse. He just could not keep his thumb off the radio transmit button on the throttle and blow off steam. Schilling had talked to him about this without avail. Now I took him aside and said, 'Tony, that radio chatter of yours is going to get you in hot water some day. Keep it down. There are 47 other chaps in the air when you're flying with us. You just can't all talk at the same time, or even occasionally. If everyone was to talk when he felt like it then important calls will be drowned out.' His reply 'Okay chief', did not convince me he was going to control his temperament.

Life was pleasant at Horsham St Faith and group personnel enjoyed going into Norwich when off duty. Many friends were made among local people. Tukey got to know some of the RAF types at Coltishall, a British fighter base north of our field. We went to their mess and they came to ours. Apart from the social contact we picked up quite a lot of useful intelligence on RAF operating tactics and those of the enemy. The effervescent Dave Schilling had different yearnings. Between Norwich city and the North Sea coast lie many connected fresh water lakes and channels known as the Norfolk Broads. In peace-time sailing on the waters is a popular English pastime. Pleasure craft could be hired and Dave had soon rented a large houseboat. One evening I was invited to go aboard to find the boat weighted down with strong liquor, lobsters, girls and some of our eager pilots. Dave's parties were a ball but it was no place for the group commander: I pulled out after the first encounter.

When we moved into Horsham St Faith I thought we would probably be there for the rest of our time in England. Just as we were getting nicely entrenched it was a blow to learn from 'Ajax' that we were going to have to move elsewhere. Horsham was wanted for a bomber field. On 21 June we were advised we would be moving temporarily to a newly constructed bomber base at Halesworth, about 25 miles south-east of Norwich. I decided to take the Cub liaison aircraft and fly over and have a look. Dave Schilling came with me. From the air we could see it was a standard type bomber field as built by the British with three-mile-long intersecting runways within a concrete perimeter track off which were numerous aircraft hardstands. Only one of the two hangars was fully erected.

On landing we were met by Squadron Leader Archer, the RAF officer in charge, who conveyed us round the base in his little car. We discovered that many living sites were uncompleted and currently there was insufficient accommodation for the personnel of a whole fighter group. The communal site was built in the timbered grounds of a gentleman's country estate and in the centre of this park stood a small mansion called Holton Hall. Now part of the base, I decided to use this house for our group staff until better arrangements could be made. We learned from the RAF officer there was also an abandoned farmhouse and outbuildings on the airfield, so we requested he drive us out along the dirt covered perimeter track to inspect it. He said that as the buildings were within the perimeter track they were scheduled to be bulldozed. Although the house was old and dilapidated we decided it could be useful and asked that it be spared. Dave decided he would use it as the pilot's room for his squadron.

Halesworth, to say the least, was a disappointment. The thought of having to forsake the comforts of the compact and orderly permanent aerodrome outside Norwich city for this mud patch way out in the farmlands was not a pleasing one. The only good point about Halesworth was that being only five miles from the coast it might allow us longer time in enermy airspace. After contemplation and discussion, I decided to see if anything could be done to keep us at Horsham St Faith. A call was put in to Bushey Hall with a request that I be granted an appointment to discuss the projected move with General Hunter. I deliberately refrained from airing any complaints at this stage, not wishing to be forestalled by his staff. My request granted, next morning I was at Colonel 'Woggie' Towele's desk (Hunter's Chief of Staff) to keep my appointment. The General came out and ushered me intc his office.

I commenced by asking why it was necessary to move us from an excellent fighter field to make way for bombers when Halesworth was being built as a bomber base and surely they should go there. As expected, Hunter didn't know the reasons. He called in his G-4 officer who revealed that Horsham St Faith was going to be torn up and concrete runways laid, ready for bombers expected in the winter. This was part of a plan outside VIIIth Fighter Command control. There was obviously no hope of getting the order changed so I then told the General about my inspection of Halesworth and its shocking condition, the uncompleted facilities, lack of accommodation and so on. I stressed that this was another example of derelection of duty by his staff who should have seen the base was fit to receive an operational group. We were entitled to expect them to take care of these matters while we fought the war. I was careful not to direct my criticism at Hunter but I knew my remarks would sting him. I left with the promise of action, but suspected little would come of it.

During June the group was sent out on the familiar sweeps over the Low Countries until the 26th when we were given the task of supporting B-17s attacking Antwerp. Due to an error not of our making, the group was late for rendezvous and a very confused situation resulted with our intercepting other P-47 units. After a while I picked out an FW 190 below and about five miles away attacking the rear of the bomber formation. The enemy saw me coming and took evasive action. There followed a diving, climbing, circling combat in which we both loosed off rounds at each other, but mostly at too much range. Eventually my ammunition ran out and I broke away in a fast dive having been lured down to 3,000 feet. This episode gave me first-hand experience of the FW 190's low altitude recovery and climb advantage over the P-47. Throughout his manoeuvring the enemy had been able to gain substantial altitude while we circled. Fortunately for me he broke off combat when I did. From that day on I was mindful to avoid such engagements and stick to a dive and recover technique of air fighting.

Four days later we were handed another bomber support job. McCollom took 49 P-47s down to Manston in Kent to refuel from whence they set out in the late afternoon to perform their mission over France. I was in my office around half seven when Flying Control called to tell me that they had been advised the group had been in combat. I went up into the watch office and it became clear from messages coming in that some of our planes had been badly shot up. A few weeks earlier it had been suggested that it might make life more interesting for the ground men and make them feel more involved if some of the radio conversations with our tower were put out over the Tannoy — a system of loudspeakers around the hangars and servicing areas. I agreed to this on a trial basis. What was about to transpire was heard by a good proportion of the men on the field. We got a call from Lieutenant Wayne Brainard saying he was escorting in Lieutenant Ralph Johnson of the 62nd Squadron who, due to battle damage, had one main landing gear wheel down. When Johnson arrived over the field and began to circle I went to another P-47 and took off so that I could get a close look at his landing gear. Our radio exchanges were recorded by the tower.

Tower: 'You have one wheel down.'

Johnson: 'I know it — I'll try to shake it out. I'll buzz the tower once more.'

Tower: 'No, it is not down.'

Johnson: 'I'll take it up and try to get it down if my pills hold out. I do not have any hydraulic fluid. What is your position, Colonel?'

Zemke: 'I am over the field, I'll come over the tower for you.'

Johnson: 'Roger.'

Zemke: 'Let me form on you.'

Johnson: 'Roger.'

Zemke: 'Have you tried to shake it down?'

Johnson: 'Yes.'

Zemke: 'Get way up and try again. If you can't shake it down, you'll have to jump. Be careful. Go over to the lake straight ahead. Put your landing gear handle in down position, do a bank on the left wing and snap it over to the right. Let me get a little ahead.'

Johnson: 'Okay.'

Zemke: 'That hasn't done it. Do some violent weaving back and forth.'

Johnson: 'Sir, my landing gear handle is stuck.'

Zemke: 'Is it stuck down?'

Johnson: 'Yes sir.'

Zemke: 'Let's get upstairs. Follow me. Do you want to try one wheel?'

Johnson: 'I certainly do sir.'

Zemke: 'Let me take a good look at you. You don't have any flaps and you'll need plenty of field.'

Johnson: 'Whatever you say, sir.'

Zemke: 'Better bale out. How much gas have you?'

Johnson: 'About 30 gallons. (pause) That fellow didn't do a very good job of gunning on me.'

Zemke: 'I'm afraid of a landing.'

Johnson: 'You're not half as scared as I am, sir.'

Zemke: 'It's not so bad.'

Zemke to Tower: 'His plane is in bad shape. I'm going to have him bale out north-east of Norwich.'

Zemke to Johnson: 'We'll go up to ten thousand feet. Did you come back alone?'

Johnson: 'No, sir. One of the boys came back with me.'

Zemke: 'Be sure you hold your legs together when you go over, and count ten. Try shaking it once more.'

Johnson: 'Yes sir.'

Zemke: 'You don't have to sir me up here. Head her out to sea.'

Johnson: 'Yes sir. Is it okay now?'

Zemke: 'Open up the canopy.'

Johnson: 'It is open sir. It's been open for a long time.'

Zemke: 'Okay, mighty fine.'

Zemke to Tower: 'The crate is heading out to sea. I'm following him down.'

Tower: 'Do you think he will land in the sea?'

Zemke: 'No, I don't think so. Switch to "C" and call "Bullfinch".'

Tower: 'Roger.'

'Bullfinch' was the Air/Sea Rescue call. I circled as Johnson floated down and saw the wind was carrying him out to sea. He got out of his 'chute and into his dinghy and a boat picked him up later. He was back on operations three days later.

Most of the group landed back at Manston to refuel before coming home. It soon became clear we had taken a real beating. Four pilots were missing and would eventually be notified as dead. They were Weatherbee, the Group Operations Officer, Eby, Dyar and Barron, the first three being among the best and most experienced pilots in the group. In addition to Ralph Johnson, three other pilots were lucky to get home, their aircraft being badly shot up. Foster landed at Hawkinge with the back of one wing root blasted away by cannon shells. Lieutenant Eaves had several cannon shell hits on his. Lieutenant Clamp's ship had five 20 mm cannon shell and ten to twenty bullet holes all over his plane. An arm wound made Clamp our first pilot to be eligible for a Purple Heart. Perhaps the luckiest pilot was Bob Johnson who had a great hunk of tail shot away by cannon shells and his canopy damaged so that it would not open. His attacker apparently ran out of ammunition and flew alongside to look Bob over before turning back. Four pilots and five planes lost, four more planes seriously damaged — one of which was scrapped — and several with minor damage on the minus side for claims of two FW 190s destroyed, two probables and six damaged. One of the destroyed credits was by the third Johnson in the group, Gerald, a flight leader in the 61st.

There were some pretty shaken pilots around the base that night. Even so, I think this particular day did more to bring the group together for a concerted effort to succeed than any other event so far. It checked those few who thought the Luftwaffe was a push-over and this was some sort of thrilling game. We held a critique, spending some two hours going over every detail of the mission. A confused picture emerged and in some instances it was difficult to establish exactly what did happen. What could be established was that by going in at around 25,000 feet, instead of the usual 30,000, the group had been more vulnerable to bounces from above. Some of the enemy formations were detailed to attack us when we expected them all to go for the bombers — as was usually the case. As a result our people got in a number of circling fights at altitudes where the P-47's performance was beginning to fall off. Again there was lack of co-ordination between squadrons.

I resolved that re-emphasis of certain basic policies was necessary and certain changes were required for bomber escorts. In future we would jack up the altitude so that we were four to five thousand feet above the bomber formations. Altitude means potential speed in a diving attack which we did not have when flying close to the bomber flanks. We had found the P-47 more than able to match the enemy above 25,000 feet, provided high speed was maintained; slow turning climbs and climbing engagements were the kiss of death. In my view the way to fight with the P-47 was dive, hit and recover, using the momentum of the dive to regain altitude. We should apply these tactics to break up enemy assaults on the bombers. With three squadrons averaging a total of 48 aircraft we should be able to work out tactics to confront the enemy with massed firepower. By hitting him with flight after flight and not just the lead flight while the rest of the group stooged around upstairs. Co-ordination had to be smooth and automatic. There was no room in this outfit for the guy who thought he could take on the Luftwaffe all by himself and go rat-racing around the sky. Further, I was fast coming to the conclusion that the close escort we were ordered to perform by high command was not the best way to protect the bombers. What we needed to do was to range ahead of the big friends and break up the enemy concentrations before they got into a position to launch attacks. Most of their onslaughts on the bombers were head-on and once launched were very difficult to intercept and deflect.

The loss of so many good men in one blow made me rethink policy on the Group Operations Officer. This man, together with two assistants, was responsible for posting all incoming missions ordered by 'Ajax' in the briefing room and working up all training and operational orders plus many other tasks related to flying operations for the group. Hitherto the Ops Officer had been permitted to fly combat in addition to his other responsibilities. As it took time to develop an Operations Officer and to keep continuity, I ruled that henceforth he was grounded for six months as far as combat missions were concerned. At the end of that time he would be returned to his squadron by which time another grounded flier, acting Assistant Ops Officer, would be able to take over. Thus, Captain Lucian 'Pete' Dade, a pleasant, studious Kentuckian, was plucked from the 63rd Squadron as Wetherbee's successor. This was not without protest as few pilots wanted to be banned from combat flying.

As if I hadn't enough problems, the night of our bitter lesson from the Luftwaffe, eleven enlisted men got the worse for drink at a party in the nearby village of Drayton, got fighting and swearing and broke up the place. Next day they were sent back to clear up the mess. The local English must have begun to wonder whose side we were on, as earlier in the week somebody working on a P-47 set off a faulty firing mechanism and sprayed local civilian houses with several rounds. Fortunately no one was hurt.

There followed a string of 'uneventful' missions and early in July the WAAF voice in our earphones gave way to more familiar accents as the Debden Control Centre was taken over by an American fighter wing headquarters.

On 1 July we ran a Rodeo over southern Holland. Bandits were reported but the 56th didn't see any. That night I heard that Arman Peterson, CO of the 78th, had gone down, believed killed. Arman was likeable, astute and a brilliant leader. Under his guidance the 78th had so far been the most successful of the three P-47 groups in combat. In my trips over to Duxford I had appreciated Arman's grasp of the problems facing us in my trips over to Duxford. His death was a blow sorely felt and a sober reminder that group commanders themselves were not invulnerable.'

8

A NEW HOME PLATE

Warriors who address the possibility of death, invariably counter it with that inherent belief in survival through personal prowess. Fighter pilots were generally less given than other combat fliers to dwell upon such matters of extinction, because of the nature of the conflict in which they were involved: the average fighter pilot was sufficiently aggressive to be primarily absorbed with the destruction of his adversary rather than his own safety. Nevertheless, the news of Arman Peterson's loss was a jolt to Hub Zemke; but no more so than when junior officers in his own command failed to return. While always touched by such losses, he had already come to terms with the probability that many faces would disappear before this war was over. Perhaps his bounding desire to succeed, coupled with a natural resilience, helped insulate him against the qualms of responsibility a commander feels for those of his men that fall.

To many of his men Hub was something of an enigma; the usual sunny disposition and ready sense of humour could quickly be replaced by intense anger and stern command. A mood of receptive ease and tolerance might give way to dictate and obstinacy. No one seemed to be his intimate confidant, although he was a genial friend to many; indeed, no one was quite sure what label to hang on him. If they were uncertain of his personality there was no dispute that Hub was the catalyst of the 56th Fighter Group; the abbreviation of his first name was truly apt, he was the hub of the organisation. He displayed a dynamism and grip on command that was admirable. A tireless worker since the days of Bridgeport, Hub had made a point of frequent visits to the varied elements of his command and in England this was even more noticeable. Mechanics servicing a P-47 at some far airfield dispersal point or guards on sentry duty were not unused to the Colonel dropping by in the middle of the night to enquire about problems. The man never seemed to sleep.

A responsible leader, he did not hesitate to protest if he found higher command lacking in support. His outspokeness on such occasions did not help to make him popular with staff officers pricked into action. Some thought him cocky, others arrogant, but all were agreed he was an excellent group commander. Hub did not seek accolades; his quest was success for his group in meeting the challenge set them, which was to shoot down enemy aircraft. So far real success eluded him; the 56th was still to often the 'also ran' of VIIIth Fighter Command. The man who had once found success in the boxing ring knew that resolute tactics and training were the keys to success; one day the 56th was going to land that right hook. To this end he encouraged his pilots to discuss tactics and put forward ideas. Hub was receptive but having listened he would make a decision and that decision was final. His dogmatism was resented by some squadron and flight commanders who saw him as dictatorial and inflexibile. But Hub, fearful of wavering command, had to establish firm policies. Perhaps some of his decisions were wrong, he was not infallible; and while he might acknowledge this to himself there were no admissions that might weaken trust in his leadership. Strong command was of paramount importance if the essential air discipline was to be forged and the necessary tactics developed to bring combat success. But as the group entered its third month of combat flying there still seemed a long way to go.

★   ★   ★

As related, the RAF turned over the Debden sector control centre at Saffron Walden to the American fighter wing headquarters that had been established there. With this change VIIIth Fighter Command accepted responsibility for the daylight defence of our part of East Anglia against German raiders. In addition to our offensive operations our group was to take on this air defence role and, in order that pilots understood the RAF procedures involved, one of our squadrons at a time was detached to fly with RAF Spitfire outfits at Biggin Hill, Kenley and Tangmere airfields south of London. The detachment lasted twelve days so for most of July and the early part of August we could only fly two squadrons on offensive operations. As it happened we were never called upon to perform the defensive role the squadrons had trained for.

Also early in July we received orders to quit Horsham St Faith and move into Halesworth. This was accomplished on the 7th and 8th and next day we were able to send out a mission from the new base. As planned, Holton Hall, the large three-storey mansion, was utilised as an officers' billet and accommodation for some of the Headquarters staff. Already in occupation of the top floor was a colony of small bats and these were soon used by the practical jokers to unnerve the squeamish among us. The 62nd Squadron quickly set about renovating abandoned High Tree Farmhouse and adjoining buildings for their offices. Dave, true to form, quickly conjured up all the materials for the job and in a matter of days had the place shipshape. A plaque over the door announced *Schilling's Acres*. The work was done solely by the pilots and other officers.

While the contractors continued construction of accommodation and other facilities, mud was a constant nuisance. The soil, being of a heavy clay texture, was not free draining. When dry it was as hard as rock but even after a summer shower the vehicles churned the surface into a glue-like substance that clung to tyres and shoes getting everywhere. One of the first things we had to do was get a line of our men with brooms to sweep the perimeter track clear of the mess left by contractors' trucks. I was constantly protesting to the RAF liaison officer about conditions and the contractors' slow progress. He did his best but the contractors were a law unto themselves. Their men seemed to be always sitting around drinking tea. Once I remonstrated with a group, pointing out that we were trying to fight a war and they should make an extra effort to help. Then I discovered they were Irish as were most of the contractors' workforce. It wasn't their war, they were there for the money. To apply additional motivation and work effort to these placid Irish labourers was like counting more beads on a prayer Rosary.

At Halesworth it was necessary to re-vamp our mission take-off and assembly procedure because we were no longer operating from grass. On Horsham St Faiths it had been SOP for a four-plane flight to take off together across the field, with the other flights of a squadron lined-up and following in quick order. We could get a squadron into the air in under two minutes and the whole group in five. Now we had to operate from concrete runways. As the place had been built for bombers the runways were wide — 150 feet — which allowed us to fly two P-47s off side by side, each pilot watching his edge of the runway. Further, we found it was possible to marshal a whole squadron of sixteen planes on the end of the runway and for each element pair to start their run when the pair ahead were halfway down. For safety, in case someone had an engine quit, this was the minimum separation advisable. We found we could still get a squadron airborne in around two minutes and formed in a half orbit of the field. The delay came in getting the next squadron's planes positioned for a follow-on. We solved this by having the second squadron marshal on the end of one of the intersecting runways and the moment the last planes from the first squadron had lifted off, the second began its runs. By the time the second squadron was airborne the third was in position at the head of the runway used by the first. This way we could get the complete group into the air in five to six minutes.

The more time spent in take-off and forming up, the less in enemy airspace. The Thunderbolt's appetite for gas averaged around 200 gallons an hour for the high altitude, high power setting missions we were flying. Average duration was eighty minutes with some Channel sweeps taking little more than an hour, while on bomber support shows we spun out the fuel to stay up an hour and a half. Three months of operations had made plain the enemy's policy of generally ignoring our sweeps and concentrating his fighter force on the bombers. Intelligence reports revealed that the Luftwaffe had more than doubled its fighter strength in the west during this time by redeploying units from other fronts. Most of this force was held back from the area over which we and RAF fighters could operate, with the result that the B-17s had a progressively rougher ride the deeper they penetrated enemy airspace. To get to the enemy we had to increase our range on the bomber support missions.

The most obvious way was to carry more fuel and to this end Cass Hough and his team at Bovingdon had been developing auxiliary fuel tanks that we could carry and dispense with when empty. As a start they were proposing we used the ferrying tank originally designed by the P-47's makers to enable the aircraft to be ferried long distances across the United States. These tanks, made of impregnated paper laminates, were big and bulbous, and attached by four mounting points under the fuselage just to the rear of the engine cowl. The tank had a 200-gallon capacity but would not supply fuel to the engine much above 22,000 feet because of insufficient atmospheric pressure.

Flying a P-47 with a loaded tank was not a pleasant experience because the tank affected the aircraft's aerodynamics. I figured that if the Luftwaffe caught us while hugging these things, we would be in trouble. I didn't hesitate to air my views to Cass Hough and probably didn't endear myself to him through my ready criticism. Extra range, however, was a priority for our fighters, not least with General Eaker and senior 8th Air Force commanders who must have been alarmed at the growing losses the B-17s were sustaining. On the other hand, the bomber gunners regularly claimed a heavy toll of the enemy fighters that attacked them, totals that made our claims appear insignificant. At the time we did not know that these B-17 gunner claims were vastly exaggerated although I think it was suspected.

When an enemy fighter was shot down by the bombers, a dozen different gunners each made a separate claim for its destruction, such was the confused nature of an air battle. In consequence, bomber crews thought they were doing more to defeat the Luftwaffe than we were. I was made well aware of this attitude when, not long after we moved into Halesworth, I received orders to fly down to a bomber station for a command meeting where it was proposed, amongst other matters, to discuss fighter support of the bombers. 'Monk' Hunter and a few of his staff, Colonel Andersen of the 4th Group, Melvin McNickle of the 78th — who took command after Petersen was lost — and myself represented the fighter lobby but we must have been outnumbered ten to twenty to one by the bomber brass. As the discussion progressed a certain amount of indifference to our fighter effort was apparent and General Hunter didn't appear to be able to contribute much to support our case.

When Brigadier General Bob Williams, who commanded the 1st Wing B-17s, recommended that in future P-47s be directed to fly close formation with the lead bombers so they could meet any head-on attacks by enemy fighters with massed firepower, I could remain silent no longer. Gulping in disbelief I got to my feet to ask the General how he expected a seven ton Thunderbolt to fly formation at 150 miles per hour indicated at 25,000 feet? Did he realise that when a P-47 pilot pressed the trigger and eight point fifties opened up the aircraft slowed by twenty to thirty miles per hour? P-47s would be spinning out of B-17 formations like leaves in a fall wind. With the combined rate of closure in frontal attacks and difficulty in bringing fire to bear, I doubted if our fighters would be effective even if they could hold position.

When I sat down there were some moans and cryptic comments from the bomber commanders. The general view of our worth was put plainly by Colonel Curtis LeMay, commander of the 4th Bomb Wing, in his subsequent appraisal. He said, in substance, that as far as he was concerned his Wing would carry out its mission 'with or without fighter escort support'. For that matter the only fighters he had seen on missions 'all had black and white crosses on them'. From his further remarks it was obvious he had a pretty low opinion of our efforts to support the bombers. I smarted under this scathing comment. Perhaps we hadn't been very effective as yet but we were doing our best; I contained my feelings and swallowed my pride; this was a time to hold one's tongue.

After the meeting had ended, everyone was invited to the Officer's Club bar where refreshments had been laid on. In the course of having a drink at the bar with acquaintances, a Brigadier General of bomber background joined our group and immediately continued the tirade on fighter ineptitude. At first I thought this gentleman to be joking, but as he continued to press the subject I began to defend myself and the fighter league. When he made the castigating statement that he 'wouldn't pay a dime a dozen for any fighter pilots' I reached in my pocket, brought out a couple of pounds worth in loose change and threw it on the floor at his feet: 'Here General, this is all I have handy at the moment. Any time you have a couple of dozen fighter pilots handy send them my way. We can really use them.' With that I stalked out of the room to call a staff car. Back at the flight line I cranked up my P-47 and took off for Halesworth, but not before making a low-level high speed pass right over the building I'd left. One day, I hoped, that General would have to eat his words.

Despite my outspokeness in his presence, General Hunter must have approved of some of my actions for on 19 July I learned that I was the first man in the 56th to be awarded the Distinguished Flying Cross. The United States tended to decorate its servicemen generously compared with other countries — except possibly Russia. I always felt this was as much for the morale of the folk back home as for the recipient.'

During July 1943 Lieutenant Colonel John Alison passed through the UK on his way back to the USA after service in China.

'I visited Hub's group and we had a great time comparing notes on the war in the Far East and the one which Hub and his boys were just beginning to wage over the Continent. Although Hub praised the P-47, he wasn't convinced that it was superior to the '109s and the '190s. After listening to him praise the performance of the German pilots and machines, I asked him what type of missions the 56th was flying at that time. I found that Hub's group flew sweeps as far over France as they could to engage the enemy before returning to England and that, currently, they were achieving one victory for every P-47 lost. I commented that the German pilots didn't look that good with that ratio of win-loss. I then asked Hub a hypothetical question: "Suppose the 56th was defending New Jersey and a group of '109s based on Long Island flew as far into New Jersey as range would allow and then tried to get out, how many would you let get home?" He responded with a twinkle in his eye, "None". I think that probably exemplified the spirit of the 56th Fighter Group.'

★   ★   ★

Following our move to Halesworth the group made fourteen missions before it was able to get into a fight with the Luftwaffe. On a few occasions we had sighted enemy fighters and a flight had been sent down to attack, only to be seen by the enemy who then executed their standard escape manoeuvre — a split-S (our term for rolling over into a dive and curving round to reverse direction). The temptation to follow and make a kill was great but the hot-rod pilots were now more appreciative of air discipline. With each mission we became progressively more polished in formation control. On Rodeos we opened up the flights, positioning them side by side so that the whole group covered a line some five miles wide. This gave us more opportunity to spot the enemy and, if he bounced us, we did not present a concentrated target, it being easier for individual aircraft to break into his attack.

Our radio discipline had also improved with the emphasis on brevity and simplicity. The move to Halesworth had brought us new call-signs for the squadrons and the group leader's call was 'Yardstick'. Through regular classes in aircraft recognition and European geography we endeavoured to ensure a pilot's visual observations were correct. I encouraged the group to put in as much flight training as possible and it wasn't long before 'Ajax' wanted to know why our fuel consumption was so much greater than that of any other group in the Command. On missions we did our best to save fuel. We experimented with engine settings, leaning out the mixture and reducing engine revolutions for a slow climb out at 500 feet per minute to stretch endurance and range. On Rodeos once in hostile airspace we had to go round the course at 210 to 220 indicated — which meant we were clipping 300 to 325 mph. As the enemy aircraft seldom pursued us out over the water, on leaving enemy territory we would adjust the mixture and throttle settings to cut back engine revolutions still further and come home losing altitude all the way. Wingmen, who were constantly having to jockey their throttles to keep with element leaders, always had greater fuel consumptions, so often saw the red panel warning light popping on, indicating only forty gallons of precious fuel remained — a maximum twenty minutes' flying time. We didn't sweat too much in setting the crate down on home plate and there were only a few cases of pilots coming back on a sniff of fuel and a prayer. On bomber support missions when we knew the Luftwaffe would be unlikely to be around to welcome us, we reduced our altitude for penetrating hostile airspace, continuing to climb as we went on to rendezvous with the bombers.

Towards the end of July I was beginning to despair of getting to grips with the enemy again. His ground control was good and must always have advised his pilots of our coming while attempting to jam our radio communications with audio noise. The radio interference was irritating, particularly the harmonic vibrations Jerry tried. Despite the din, somehow we always managed to communicate. Then in the last week of the month a high pressure area settled over western Europe giving the bombers the near cloudless conditions needed for precision bombing. VIIIth Bomber Command struck deep into Germany on several occasions and we were asked to provide fighter cover to the limit of our endurance.

Leading a Ramrod on the 28th I kept the boys aloft for over ninety minutes. The 4th Group, making use of the 200-gallon auxiliary tanks, penetrated deeper than P-47s had been before and, catching the Jerries by surprise, knocked down nine of them. Next day the B-17s didn't operate and we ran a couple of Rodeos over the Low Countries. On the first of these one of our flights fell into the old Luftwaffe trap. Seeing some Focke-Wulfs far below, they went down to get them and on the way were jumped out of the sun by some '109s. Two of our people tried to mix it but having lost speed the P-47s were sitting ducks. Both were hit, one pilot baled out and the other managed to nurse his crate home to Halesworth. We had Eddie Rickenbacker, the top American ace of World War 1, visit us with Hunter that day and I was chagrined having to tell that we were the people who had been scalped with nothing to show for it.

The Forts were out in force on the 30th and Mac led the 56th on our longest trip so far, 210 miles to a point west of Arnhem in Holland. The group came back with three victories, two falling to the guns of Captain Leroy Schriber who had been an instructor in the States before joining the 56th recently as a replacement. Mac was mad for just as he and his flight were about to open fire on some '109s they were bouncing, someone called out that they were Spitfires. Mac immediately broke off his attack, no doubt mindful of the unfortunate incident back in May. Whoever made the call needed to improve his aircraft recognition as they were Me 109s.

We flew nineteen missions in July and at best could only claim a draw with the opposition. Real success still eluded us while the 4th and 78th Groups were really going to town. Our experience had confirmed that the Luftwaffe aircraft and pilots were good, very good. The thing I couldn't understand was their decision to avoid picking fights with us in the early days when we were inexperienced and unsure of ourselves: they could have decimated our ranks. Now, we knew the game, had confidence and — I was convinced — the ability to take them on. Our day would come. While I had originally been critical of the paper tanks we were in the process of being equipped with, what the other groups could do with them, so could we.

At the beginning of August we were handed an additional task. The first new fighter group to reach the 8th Air Force since we came in was to go operational and was moving into Metfield, another new bomber airfield hacked out of the Suffolk clay about seven miles west of Halesworth. We were asked to teach them our trade and assist in their operational debut. This outfit was the 353rd Fighter Group with three P-47 equipped squadrons led by Colonel Joe Morris. He and three of his officers joined a Rodeo I led on 4 August and on the 9th I took their group on its first mission when we swept over Holland. As neighbours, we would have much co-operation with the 353rd in the months ahead for, like us, they were separated by many miles from the main VIIIth Fighter Command area. On their arrival at Metfield we loaned them men to operate their tower and provided help and advice on several matters. Around this time we were also receiving a bunch of replacement pilots to swell the complements of our squadrons. The newcomers had to be orientated in our particular procedures which made for a very busy time.

For our next Ramrod we were scheduled to use the 200-gallon paper tanks and trial installations were made so pilots could get the feel of flying with these ungainly attachments. On 11 August I was in my office when the 63rd pilots' room called that one of their aircraft, up on a local tank trial flight flown by Captain Walker 'Bud' Mahurin, a flight leader, had just collided with a B-24 and gone down. No parachute was seen. A little later we had a call from Metfield telling us that Mahurin had managed to parachute safely and apart from shock was pretty much unharmed. Word also came through that the B-24 had managed to get back safely to its own base at Hardwick. It transpired that Mahurin had seen the B-24 — there were very few around at that time — and pulled up close to fly formation. Then when he tried to pull away the tailplane of his Thunderbolt went through a negative gravity patch under the propeller arcs and got drawn up. Less tail, the plane plummeted into the ground; Mahurin was lucky to get out alive as the accident happened at under a thousand feet. A message was left with the 63rd that when Mahurin arrived back on base he was to report to me.

When Mahurin finally walked into my office the talking that followed was pretty one-sided. I was more than a little vexed and pointed out that a Flight commander should know better than to do such a damn fool stupid thing. He had destroyed a $100,000 airplane and caused considerable damage to the B-24, all of which wouldn't make the 56th very popular at Ajax. His punishment under the 104th Article of War could be a Court Martial or, alternatively, loss of rank or pay for a period of three months. The option was really an easy one, he chose the fine. 'Bud' Mahurin was a handsome young man, high spirited and debonaire. He didn't look his 24 years. He had proved a good flight commander in combat and while I could have dealt out much tougher retribution he was the type of pilot we needed.

The following day Mahurin, the disgraced warrior, was in another P-47 when the group set out on its first Ramrod with the drop tanks. The forecast was for clear skies over Europe and the heavies set out to bomb Gelsenkirchen in the Ruhr. The 56th was to act as general support on their penetration. We were airborne about 07:30 in the morning and, as planned, switched to the drop tank and went into a climbing orbit over the base until reaching 12,000 feet. I then set a direct course for Walcheren Island where we jettisoned the cumbersome tanks at 22,000 feet. Soon after we saw the bombers and positioned above them. I was hopeful we would catch the enemy coming in at the B-17s but, although we escorted farther than ever before, circling back and forth over our charges, few enemy fighters were seen. Schilling took a flight down after some '109s but these dove away down through the bombers. When we got back to Halesworth we had been in the air two hours and ten minutes, more than a half hour over our usual endurance. Otherwise the mission had been something of a disappointment, particularly as the 4th Group had again got into a fight, claiming four victories. I could only console myself that our presence with the bombers probably kept the enemy fighters away and reduced B-17 losses.

The bulky paper bathtub tanks were used again on a couple of occasions during the next few days and while they gave us an extra half hour over enemy territory, it was at the expense of a lot of trouble for the ground crews. If fuel were left in the tanks too long it started to dissolve and weaken the sealing material. Leaks were frequent and hard to stop; attachment was difficult as the fittings did not align properly on many tanks. They also had a habit of banging against the underside of the plane when released or not coming away at all, forcing an abort.

Mac took the group to Paris with the B-17s on 16 August. Those the 56th escorted didn't have much trouble from the Luftwaffe. Mahurin and a few of our boys had inconclusive combats. One pilot had to bale out when his engine failed over France. After the group returned we learned that the 4th Group had made a record eighteen kills; news that made me even more frustrated. Later that day I had a call from General Hunter. The 353rd Group CO, Joe Morris, had gone down; their first loss. If the weather held an important show was coming up next day and Hunter wanted me to loan McCollom to the 353rd as they had no one of sufficient experience to lead them.

The forecast was good apart from early morning ground mist but this amounted to a summer fog when the day dawned. We learned that in a maximum effort the B-17s were going to targets deep in Germany. This proved to be the day of the first attack on the Schweinfurt ball-bearing plants and the Messerschmitt aircraft factory at Regensberg when the bombers flew on to land in Africa. We were briefed to go out with the Regensburg force in the morning and meet the Schweinfurt bombers coming back in the afternoon. The original plan required a turnaround of about 2½ hours, but it wasn't possible to refuel the aircraft with the few gasoline tankers we had on the base in that time. The matter was settled through a telephone call to 'Ajax'. I had arrived at Group Operations early to be given the details by Majors 'Pete' Dade of Operations and Dave Robinson, the Intelligence Officer, familiarly known as the 'Silver Fox' — a reference to what passing years had done to his hair. 'Stormy', the inevitable nickname for the Weather Officer, assured me the fog would lift. I had my doubts; we had a very low ceiling and it was not the conditions I wanted to penetrate with fifty P-47s and their bulky loads. Such was my concern that a call was put in to Colonel Bobbie Burns at Fighter Command Operations to tell him of my misgiving about trying to get off in such restricted visibility. His response was that if I felt so sincere about the risk of being able to take off in the prevailing conditions I had better speak to General Hunter. Listening to my views, Hunter reminded me that this was a maximum effort mission. He finished by saying, 'I don't know what the weather is like at your base or just how capable your unit is to partake in weather penetration,' then, after a pause, 'But I suggest you better think of going on this mission.' His meaning was plain; I thanked him and hung up. It was simply go or else.

Many of the replacement pilots had done little or no bad weather flying as in the States they conformed to the ruling that pursuit pilots didn't fly if the ceiling was less than 1,500 feet and visibility at least three miles. Even the most senior pilots in the Group had only limited bad weather experience. At briefing I ordered a new assembly procedure. After take-off each separate element pair would make a wide circle under the cloud, come back over the field and climb on a pre-determined heading, holding this until breaking through the overcast. As it turned out we popped free of the clouds at around 5,000 feet and were able to make formation with little trouble. We picked up the rear box of bombers near Antwerp and stuck with them to Eupen before having to turn back. Gerry Johnson opened up on an Me 109 before it eluded him but my expectations of meeting the Luftwaffe in force did not materialise and we returned home after another disappointing flight. As usual, the German ground control system had us marked and as soon as we turned back they vectored their fighters in to hit the bombers.

The second mission of the day was off at 15:20 hours, our brief being to meet the returning Schweinfurt bombers near the Dutch border. I wanted to penetrate as deeply as I could safely go, and as with the morning raid, deliberately chose to cross the enemy coast at around 20,000 feet on a direct line from base. The 'bathtubs' were dropped as we passed near Antwerp and while we continued a steady climb. Wingmen were reminded to swivel their heads regularly to see we weren't jumped. Visibility was excellent. The sun beamed and the fields and waterways of the Low Countries laid out below in high relief. Fifteen minutes later, when we had topped 27,000 feet, I saw black specks in the deep blue ahead, like a swarm of bees — the bombers and they were under heavy attack. Turning left Tukey took his 63rd Squadron out over the lead B-17 box while Gabby positioned above the left flank of the trailing formations and I led the 62nd to the northern flank at the rear. My headphones were filled with excited radio calls as flight commanders ordered their elements into action. We had managed to stretch our penetration some fifteen miles beyone Eupen into Germany and the Luftwaffe had either not expected to see us there or were so absorbed in attacking the B-17s that they were unaware of how far west they had come.

To my surprise, to the rear I saw a small formation of some eight

Me 110 twin-engine Zestörers apparently preparing an assault on the bombers. Even more surprising was that some appeared to be painted white — perhaps recently withdrawn from the Murmansk front in Russia? No time for speculation. 'Yardstick to Woodfire White and Red Flights. Follow me.' A wide sweeping 360-degree turn was made to get into a position to attack. But we had lost surprise; the Me 110s had seen our eight P-47s coming down and thereupon scattered. Picking out a slate-grey Messerschmitt pulling away on the right flank, I dropped down to position dead astern and slightly below, trying to keep his tailplane between my aircraft and the aim of the gunner which I knew these types carried in the rear cockpit. At around 300 yards I fired a short burst. The next instant a body came hurtling out of the Me 110 and passed under my plane. Still closing, I put two more bursts into each engine, causing long trails of smoke to stream back. My victim was now diving straight down so I broke away to recover altitude. Looking round to check my tail, the other '110s were nowhere to be seen. I pulled up to the section; two P-47s were missing. Now north of Antwerp, fuel reserves were reaching the point for return. I called for the group to break off and withdraw, Spitfires having arrived to take on the escort. We had been in action no more than seven minutes and as we made tracks for Halesworth, carefully monitoring fuel gauges as we went, I wondered how the rest of the group had fared.

Back on 'home plate' I found a very excited bunch of men; it was quickly evident that we had shot down several of the enemy. At debriefing the picture gradually emerged. All three squadrons had been engaged and the enemy obviously hadn't expected to find us so far inland. When we arrived he didn't appear to have any top cover for the Messerschmitts and Focke-Wulfs ganging up on the Forts. His chief tactic was to fly out ahead of the bomber boxes, do a 180 degree turn and attack them head-on.

The 63rd was able to divert many of these attacks and shot down eight, mostly FW 190s. When the enemy began his run on the bombers one of our flights dived to intercept and then zoom-climbed back up to re-form. These tactics, long favoured and practised, had proved successful. Lieutenant Glenn Schiltz, an element leader, downed three FW 190s while the recently disgraced Bud Mahurin knocked down two. The 61st Squadron on the south flank of the bombers had six victories, three made by the cool Gerry Johnson. The 62nd had two claims and with my own the group total was seventeen plus one probable and nine damaged. Our losses were three, a 63rd element leader shot down by an FW 190 and two 62nd pilots who when last seen were chasing an Me 110 during our initial bounce. We could only speculate that they had been jumped by '109s or '190s.

The losses didn't dampen our spirits that night; they were an accepted part of the deadly business in which we were engaged. What mattered there and then was that after three months of usually taking the worst of contacts with the Luftwaffe, the tables were now turned. And in a spectacular way; for we had contributed all but two of the total 'destroyed' claims made by P-47s that day, 17 August. Later, I learned that one of the German pilots we had shot down was among the Luftwaffe's most promising fighter leaders, Major Wilhelm Galland, commander of II/JG 26, an ace with 55 victories to his credit and considered an excellent pilot. His brother was the famous General Adolf Galland, Hitler's General of Fighters. In the confused air war we fought, the man who stayed alive was the one who continually kept his guard — a swivel head. If you saw your attacker in time you could usually evade and live to fight another day. Swivel head was the wingman's job while the element leader did the shooting. The wingman was there to spot the enemy trying to attack you and shout a warning, but a wise element leader continually looked around too. Perhaps Wilhelm Galland dropped his guard for a moment; or his wingman didn't swivel his head. Who knows.

That night I received a telephone call from General Hunter offering congratulations and asking to what did I attribute our success. Catching the Jerries with their pants part way down was my explanation; I wasn't inclined to talk tactics. There was, however, another perhaps ulterior reason for his call; he was making McCollom the new CO of the 353rd. I protested that Mac was a key member of the 56th and that our ability to perform would be harmed by his transfer. This was all to no avail, Hunter insisted the 353rd's operational advancement would be accelerated under an experienced leader and that neither the 4th or 78th Groups had anyone he rated as highly as McCollom. Reluctantly I had to agree. In the circumstances Hunter's decision could be understood. Mac had been with the 56th since the beginning, having started out as a 2nd Lieutenant. He had all the qualities of a leader and deserved his own group command but it was a blow to lose him. As it happened, while on his first mission with the 353rd that morning he had shot down an Me 109, his first confirmed victory. Although he was still assigned to the 56th his victory was credited to the 353rd.

Next morning I had orders cut for Mac's transfer to the 353rd and decided Dave Schilling — who was on leave at the time — would be my new Flying Executive Officer and deputy. There was no doubt in my mind that Dave had the necessary leadership qualities and aggressive outlook. Even if I still had reservations about his propensity towards outlandish action, I felt he had made a better showing than Tukey up to this time. Captain Horace 'Pappy' Craig was elevated to take Schilling's place as CO of the 62nd.

From the early days of my command of the 56th I had been mindful to listen, observe and take an interest in the record, intelligence, manners and general demeanour of all officers knowing that there would be attrition and spaces to fill. I could foresee a time when the replacement situation would be aggravated by pilots getting towards the total 200 combat hours required to complete a tour. As well as the necessary promotions required by transfer and loss, I also found myself writing up decoration recommendations for pilots who had performed well on the 17th. Ironically, there I sat advocating a DFC for Bud Mahurin only a week after fining him $500!

A day's rest and the B-17s were out again, this time to airfields in Holland. As their target was within our radius of action, fighter cover could be arranged all the way. We went to 27,000 feet and positioned the squadrons around the B-17s, flanking, ahead and between three and four thousand feet above as we had done on the 17th. The Germans probably thought this was another thrust at some vital installation in the Reich and sent up the Luftwaffe as soon as the first bomber crossed the coast. Our boys were calling out over the radio that enemy fighters were on hand and combats ensued. By again employing the dive, attack, zoom-climb back to altitude tactics we achieved success and back at Halesworth found the group's score to be claims of nine destroyed and three damaged. The other three groups could only claim probables. We were an elated bunch, having really proved our worth. I wondered what the bomber General who made the deprecating remarks about fighter pilots thought now, the 56th having disrupted the Luftwaffe assault on the Forts and undoubtedly reduced their losses.

Particularly pleasing was Gerry Johnson's destruction of an Me 109 which brought his total of victories to five and made him an 'ace'; our first. This accolade had no official standing, being devised by First World War pilots to distinguish the successful air warrior. Gerry, a dark-haired, chubby-cheeked Kentuckian, had a quick eye, was good at gauging deflection aim through his gun sight and an excellent shot. In recognition of Gerry's feat we looked round for some means to distinguish him from the rest of the gang. Someone recalled that General Custer's elite cavalry wore bright scarlet scarfs when they went into battle against Red Indian braves. We decided that the mark of an ace in our group should be a red silk jacket lining. Thus Gerry was relieved of his tunic which was sent to London for the addition of this scarlet trim.

Our showing on the 19th was all the more pleasing as the Luftwaffe had shot down none of the 56th. Our only loss was due to an engine failure, the pilot successfully crash-landing in shallow coastal waters and being taken prisoner. However, the group leader came near to getting an extra parting in his hair. Having dived after an FW 190 seen near the bombers and opened fire with apparently little effect, a hole suddenly appeared in my windshield. Only later, after my crew chief reported finding a spent .50-calibre bullet in the cockpit, did I appreciate my person had experienced a very near miss. The bullet most likely came from one of the B-17s we were shepherding.

The 56th's change of fortunes was in some measure due to the tactics we were developing. At joint bomber-fighter conferences bomb group commanders had continually called for close escort of their formations by our P-47s. They wanted us to emulate the RAF mode of escort where sometimes the ratio was a dozen Spitfires to every bomber. For a start we did not have the numbers to provide that sort of saturation — on current maximum efforts the 8th Air Force was putting up two or three bombers to every fighter. Experience had shown us that keeping our small force in close proximity to the heavies severely restricted our ability to intercept enemy attacks on them. What was needed was flexibility in control so that we were positioned to spot and break-up enemy assaults as they developed. While our own Fighter Command reiterated the bombers' demands for close escort, the measures the 56th was taking were increasingly in the other direction.

With the three squadrons positioned around the bomber formations as the mission dictated, we sought optimum flexibility. The flanking squadrons were separated into two sections, often at different levels, while the third squadron, or one of its sections, frequently became a freelance unit. If escorting the leading combat wing, this squadron or

The press again, 24 April 1943. This was taken while I was standing in front of Schilling's P-47 watching the fly-by. The pilot's kit over my flying overalls includes a Mae West life saver and parachute harness. The sun was bright that fine spring day.

Pilots of the 61st leave their Squadron Ready Room in a hangar side at Horsham, 24 April 1943. Leaders are (left to right) Tracy, Brooks and McCollom. Following three are Les Smith, Gabreski and Wetherbee. Bringing up the rear, Mudge, Curtis and Powers. Of the nine, two would be killed and three made prisoner in the days ahead.

Captain Walter Cook from Cincinatti, Ohio. 'Cookie' was credited with the first enemy aircraft destroyed in the 56th.

US Assistant Secretary of War for Air, Robert Lovett, visited Horsham St Faith with Major General Hunter on 22 May. Photo was taken as we were walking away from my LM:Z. Nearest camera are Dave Schilling (CO 62nd) and Major Wilbur Watson (Ground Executive).

Major Philip Tukey on the wing of the P-47C at Horsham, 28 May 1943.

Captain 'Pappy' Craig leads a formation of 62nd Squadron P-47s over Norfolk county, 28 May 1943. LM:X is piloted by Conway Saux, later killed in a collision after take-off at Halesworth. Eugene O'Neil, who became an ace, flies LM:O.

When my crew chief asked what personal name I would like on my P-47 the answer was Moy Tovarish — Russian for 'My Comrade.' He duly had this painted on in Russian characters. However, on consideration I didn't think it fitting for a group commander to indulge in such a display of individuality. The name was later painted out.

A joke shared in the Officers' Club between RAF Intelligence Liaison Officer, Flight Lieutenant 'Scotty' Barron, 'Gabby', 'Mac' and 'Tukey'. Mac had just been made Flying Executive.

Sergeant Joe Froncek, assistant crew chief of my P-47C (number 41-6330, battle letters LM:Z) points to two crosses he painted on to signify the victories of 13 June. Later, I had these painted out.

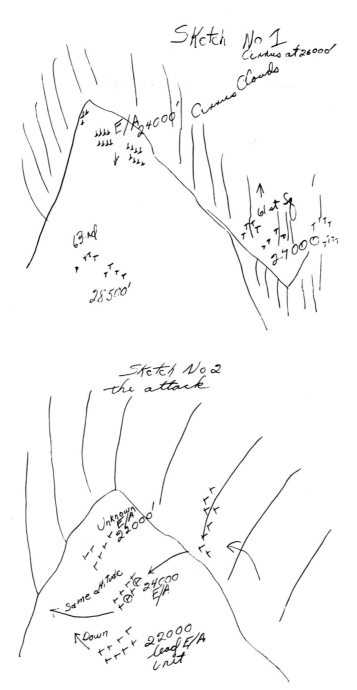

Hub's sketches of the 13 June 1943 action as attached to his combat report.

Dave Schilling with one of the many gadgets he liked to manufacture. This one was an Army Colt .45 pistol with extended ammunition clip and steadying handle to turn it into a machine pistol. It tended to spray bullets over the landscape and many a barrel was burned out.

Andrew Kutler was the Republic Aviation technical representative attached to the 56th. He consistently cut red tape and corners to help us keep abreast of the numerous changes and fixes brought out by the factory. Although a civilian, we decked him out in Army garb, figuring it was better if he appeared to be one of us.

Captain Gerald Johnson, our first ace, beside his P-47, a presentation aircraft 'bought' with bonds by the folk of Jackson County, Michigan. This able, good looking young fellow from Kentucky would, some thirty years later, command the 8th Air Force in another conflict.

The mess a .50-calibre slug made to the windshield of my LM:Z on 19 August. There should have been a sheet of armoured glass in front of the gunsight to protect the pilot, but a few weeks before I had it removed as a saving on weight to improve performance. Not a wise move and I was lucky. It was duly replaced.

The ceremony to mark the official transfer of Halesworth to the USAAF was not without a hiccup or two. The band and parade attracted a few English onlookers from the public road that ran beside the HQ site. One of the new airfields hacked out of farmland, the various sites were spread around the countryside to lessen damage if the field was bombed.

Dave Schilling's P-47 under repair on 3 September 1943, the day I collected some bullet holes in it. In the background 'Pappy' Craig's LM:R and Schilling's Acres.

one of its sections, ranged out some miles ahead. It could also act as a support squadron to the other two, answering calls for assistance. With squadrons being widely separated, each leader was given the responsibility of initiating attacks against the enemy and a greater independence of control. In this way we had been able to pick up many enemy aircraft ganging up to hit the B-17s. In written reports and conversations with my superiors I was careful not to elaborate on just how loose our close escort had become. Better to let results establish the worth of these tactics.

9
HEYDAY AT HALESWORTH

The group was now nicely settled in at Halesworth and during the better weather the contractors had made progress on completing camp facilities. We now had our second hangar and more living accommodation. Since our arrival there had been a small RAF contingent who were responsible for the base. In line with the agreement between the British Air Ministry and Washington, whereby all installations occupied by the USAAF were to become their responsibility, the RAF unit would be withdrawn, and Halesworth was to be handed over on the 20th August. A ceremonial parade was laid on when the RAF officer in charge would hand over the station for safe keeping to me. We duly had an honour guard lined up outside Group Headquarters and appropriate words and good wishes from the two parties. The RAF ensign was brought down the pole and the Stars and Stripes raised — upside down! After this was sorted out our band managed to strike up with the anthem at the wrong point in the proceedings. We may have been knocking hell out of the Luftwaffe in the air but we would not get many marks on the parade ground.

The comparative rural isolation of Halesworth appeared to give us less trouble with our English neighbours. We did have to enforce strict control on guard rifles when the local police complained that enlisted men had been using them to shoot rabbits. Bullets had been whistling around the farmsteads. With 1,500 young bucks on our patch there was always going to be some fellow who got into trouble. They were always complaining about the warm, weak English beer yet some boys couldn't seem to drink enough of it. There wasn't as much trouble over women as when we had been near the big towns; in August our VD rate was nil — or perhaps this reflected the morality of the country girls.

Following our mid-August successes I detected a more favourable attitude towards us amongst the officers at 'Ajax'. I had never considered General Hunter to have what was needed to head VIIIth Fighter Command and was not surprised to learn he had been replaced. Apparently General Eaker had been unhappy with Hunter's performance for some time. His replacement was Brigadier General William Kepner. He had been at Langley when I was a fledgling 2nd Lieutenant and I knew him to be an able commander. Moustached, angular featured, and small in stature, he had a reputation for verbosity, but behind his wordy dictates there was a razor sharp mind. I felt he would make a much more efficient organisation at Bushey Hall. I tended to take my requests straight to 'Ajax' although the Fighter Wing headquarters at Saffron Walden was an intermediary headquarters in the chain of command. The fighter wing was principally concerned with operational matters but I felt they were a paper headquarters and bypassed them whenever possible. Brigadier General Ross Hoyt was the CO, replaced by his deputy Colonel Jesse Auton a few weeks after Kepner took over 'Ajax'. Debden being right on their doorstep I always felt the wing people were overly influenced by the 4th Group.

During the last week of August there was intensive activity by the service group as they tried to fit the seventy-odd P-47s on the base with B-7 shackles under the belly of each aircraft. This was really a two-point bomb shackle but was being fitted to allow us to use the teardrop-shaped metal drop tanks that were arriving at the field. These tanks rated for a 75 gallon capacity, were found to hold just over eighty gallons. Cass Hough and his merry men at Bovingdon had devised a means of pressurising the tanks so that fuel could be drawn from them at any altitude. Ingeniously, they harnessed the exhaust of the aircraft's vacuum pump — used in the function of bank and turn, artificial horizon and other instruments — to pressurise the drop tanks automatically as we gained altitude. This meant that we could hold our drop tanks until they were completely drained or until engaging the enemy — they were too cumbersome to retain in combat. We first used these on the last day of the month when Schilling led a Ramrod over France and was airborne for a record two hours forty minutes; double our original duration. The mission was 'uneventful' as far as contact with the enemy was concerned, whereas our previous Ramrod a week before had resulted in three victories for no loss, one of these being the first for 'Gabby' Gabreski, CO of the 61st.

When I led three twelve-plane squadrons off from Halesworth on the evening of 2 September to escort B-17s over Brussels, we were again hopeful of tangling with the enemy. Climbing over the North Sea towards our landfall point at Ostend increasing amounts of cloud were encountered. By the time of rendezvous with the bombers we were flying between two layers of stratus, one at around 10,000 feet which was getting progressively thicker, while directly above, at 25,000 feet, was another band, thick but patchy. The group spread out to cover the bombers but I was not happy as we had to stay just below the cloud at around 23,000 feet. The Forts were having trouble finding their airfield target through gaps in the cloud and I saw that they were turning for another run over the same area while we continued orbiting over them. The B-17 task force leader finally decided there was no hope of a precision attack and rather than risk dumping bombs where they might kill Belgians the Fortresses started out over Ostend still lugging their loads.

As the bomber formations crossed the coast I decided to circle back one more time to cover any stragglers there might be. Visibility was poor and the sun was now low, making it difficult to look to the west. We were just curving round to the north when suddenly an alarmed 'Yardstick Break Left!' filled my headphones. Instinctively, I pulled the stick hard over. As the port wing went down and the 'Bolt' started into the turn, above the roar of the engine there was a loud ping. Similtaneously the instrument panel shattered. With the impetus of fear, accelerated movement of the stick skidded the aircraft into a dive. Then came the realisation that the engine had ceased; only the radio static and shouts of other pilots filled my ears. A glance at the gauges remaining intact showed that all power was gone. A quick check in the mirror and back through the side windows. No sign of a pursuer. I eased out of the dive and tried to prime the engine to life. Nothing.

'Yardstick to Postgate White 2, I'm hit. Will bale out.' My wingman had called the warning but I did not know if he was still around. My initial fright gave place to anger that I was about to become a prisoner of the Third Reich, fleeting thoughts replaced by the intention to evade capture, go underground, seek out the Belgian Resistance, get back to England. Must free-fall and open my 'chute at the last minute so there was less time for enemy troops to spot me before I hit the ground. I began to prepare myself for departure from the rapidly descending Thunderbolt.

Just as I was about to slide back the canopy the engine, with a cough and splutter, suddenly sprang to life. Instantly gloom was dispelled as I realised the turbo-supercharger in the rear fuselage must have taken a hit, causing the engine to die through insufficient air to the carburettor. Now, as altitude diminished, air density increased and the point had been reached where there was sufficient ram air into the carburettor to revitalise the mixture and allow ignition. Cautiously I levelled off, turned out over the coast and checked that there were no Focke-Wulfs on my tail. Confidence returned and despite several inoperative instruments I had no trouble in getting back to Halesworth. My diagnosis was correct; a 20 mm shell had hit the turbo under the rear fuselage. The P-47 had also taken a 30 mm strike, severing a trim control cable in the wing root.

My wingman, Lieutenant Edgar Whitley, had called the warning brake. No one had seen the '190s dive out of the clouds and come in on our tails in time. The other members of Postgage White flight had no doubt momentarily dropped their guard to concentrate on holding position in the turn. The other element, Lieutenants Wilfred Van Abel and Walter Hannigan, had both been shot down in this attack. We learned later that Hannigan had been killed and Van Abel made prisoner. Two more 'originals' lost. Perhaps my final sweep back over the bombers was a mistake; but a commander learned not to torture himself with such speculation. Lieutenant John Vogt in a following flight was also shot up and wounded. Johnny went down to the deck, his assailant in hot pursuit, and high-tailed it out of Belgium with the Focke-Wulf pilot peppering him until his ammunition was exhausted. Johnny managed to put down on the grass field at Eastchurch and, having no brakes, nosed up. The Luftwaffe outfit that had hit us out of the clouds in that effective slashing attack turned out to be II/JG 26, the same unit we had decimated on 17 August.

I needed to get back in the air and next day led the group on another Ramrod to support Fortresses going to hit airfields in France. We went to 32,000 feet and conducted the escort without sight of the enemy. Near Romilly, just as another group had taken over shepherding and we had started for home, Captain 'Goodie'

Goodfleisch, number 3 in my flight, called in that FW 190s were below ganging up to hit the Forts head on. We were at 28,000 feet and the Focke-Wulfs around 8,000 feet below us. 'Yardstick to Postgate White Flight. Follow Me.'

Down we went, keeping the sun between us and the '190s to maintain surprise. Closure on the enemy was quite rapid and I selected the number 3 man who was somewhat behind the rest. Just as he was framed in the gunsight, tracers were seen flashing over my right wing. 'Postgate White 2. Cease fire!' My wingman, Lieutenant William Jansen, had opened up while we were still out of range. Again concentrating on the FW 190 ahead, I closed to 400 yards and fired a long burst. No strikes were evident. Two more bursts were loosed before the underside of the '190 belched black smoke. As I skidded my P-47 to line-up on the number 2 man the smoking '190 fell away in flames. The rest of the enemy formation were now alerted for as I fired at my next intended victim he broke for the deck in a half roll, as did the leader and number 4.

Using the momentum of the dive, I pulled away to gain altitude. It might have been tempting to follow the surprised enemies down but I had enough sense to practise what I preached — strike and recover. Back on home plate the group totted up the score as four victories for the loss of one and I found 30 mm bullet holes through the prop and flaps of Dave Schilling's plane which I had been flying, my own being under repair. It had not been my wingman's tracers seen going over my wing. Unknown to both of us, another flight of four Focke-Wulfs were following some way behind those we dived to attack. As we came down these Focke-Wulfs nosed-up and opened fire. Fortunately for me, Goodie had seen them and changed his angle of dive to fire at and shoot down the one who was spraying my P-47.

For most of September the B-17s went to airfield targets in occupied countries and did not evoke the opposition that could be expected from a mission to the Reich. Intelligence suggested that the Luftwaffe had withdrawn its Staffeln to airfields further away from the coast and thus the extra range our drop tanks provided did not bring us the combats we planned for. Even so we were able to snatch a few more victories as the days passed and maintain our showing against the other P-47 groups, now joined by three newcomers. The VHF radios, the vital aid to the success of our operations, were now utilised on Ramrods to receive transmissions of 'C' channel direct from bomber leaders who could call us to their aid. On Rodeos we now had the benefit of intelligence gathered by the RAF monitoring Luftwaffe radio communications and this, together with radar plots, was used in directional transmissions from our fighter controller to give us much more information as to where the enemy were. The Germans tried continually to blot out radio transmissions by broadcasting noise on the same wavelengths. Now they introduced voice noise and on one mission somebody appeared to be repeating the threat 'you can't get home' over and over again. Our own radio discipline was much improved but there were lapses. After a Rodeo over the familiar Belgian race track one pilot left his transmitter key down for fifteen minutes all the way back across the North Sea which meant no one else could transmit on that band. All that could be heard was his heavy breathing.

I received notice that General Eaker, 8th Air Force boss, was going to visit at one o' clock on 17 September. He flew in with just a few of his personal staff and without a cortege of brass from 'Ajax' or the fighter wing. There had been quite a bit of rain and Halesworth was back to being a mud patch. I gave the General a short trip around the field and answered his questions. He was affable and interested. I guess I was flattered that the top man had chosen to come and see the 56th. He had another base to visit and before departing he congratulated us on our recent showing. He also made some very pointed remarks to me about the unkempt and varied clothing our people were wearing which made it sometimes difficult for him to distinguish between officers and men. I took the hint and thereafter stipulated that no man appeared in the Officers Club or at Group meetings without a tie or clean uniform. My decree could not extend to footware as the mud necessitated high boots and galoshes.

We began to appreciate concrete runways and think Halesworth wasn't so bad after a trip to our forward base at Thorney Island near Southampton on 23 September. This grass field was a sea of mud and what with pilots having to pre-flight their own planes some twenty minutes was lost in take-off and we arrived late for rendezvous with the bombers. On 27 September the weather was deemed good enough over north-west Germany for the bombers to hit Emden, and Schilling led the group to escort on penetration. The anticipated opposition from the Luftwaffe materialised and our boys came home with a five for one score. Next day I received notice from 'Ajax' that Phil Tukey was required at Bushey Hall to become an VIIIth Fighter Command operations officer. Having lost McCollom the previous month it began to look as if the 56th was becoming a replacement centre for command pilots. Tuke wasn't keen to go so I 'phoned Colonel Burns to argue the case, asking how 'Ajax' could expect us to maintain our current showing if they kept proselyting our best men. Burns responded that VIIIth Fighter Command needed the expertise of somebody who knew the realities of fighter leadership. My plea was dismissed.

So Tuke, who would have stepped into Schilling's place if anything had befallen me, packed his bags and moved to Bushey Hall, ostensibly on a six month detachment. The following spring he was given command of the none too successful 356th Fighter Group at Martlesham Heath and much improved its fortunes. Phil Tukey was no derring-do, hell-for-leather fighter pilot but a reasoned, steady air leader. Although he flew missions until the end of the war he never had an opportunity to shoot down an enemy. Captain Sylvester Burke, a flight leader who had already led the group on a few missions, took command of the 63rd in Tukey's place.

The cloudy days and unsettled weather of the latter half of September gave way to clear autumn days as a high pressure settled and VIIIth Bomber Command unleashed a number of missions going deep into the Reich. On 2 October we were alerted for our second Ramrod to Emden, 250 miles from Halesworth. The Me 109s and FW 190s appeared from the south in isolated groups and did their familiar trick of rolling over and diving down to escape us. On the way out I saw a lone FW 190 west of Terschilling Island which appeared to be stalking a straggling B-17. While attempting to get my flight into a better position for a bounce, the '190 circled round and headed south. 'Yardstick to Keyworth White. Follow Me.' Rolling over into a dive I came in fast behind my quarry. As the distance between us closed, he started a right turn and thinking he was about to break away, I fired a short burst, having allowed three-fourths of a ring deflection in the gunsight. Immediately strikes were registered over the entire aircraft. Surprisingly, the Focke Wulf flew on in a straight line. Another burst brought smoke and flame and a third caused the left undercarriage leg to drop. Only then did the stricken plane fall away in a vertical dive. As no evasive action had been observed I concluded the first burst had killed the pilot. Number five for me, making the second man in the 56th to earn ace status. The two other victories the group obtained that day were FW 190s downed by Dave Schilling, his first after 52 missions.

Dave had been leading the 63rd Squadron, this being one of the few occasions when, because we were temporarily short on flight and squadron leaders, I let both group and deputy CO fly on the same mission. Dave had been a late starter but he was to surprise us over the next few days. On 4 October it was his turn to lead on a Ramrod in support of bombers going to Frankfurt. With the new 108 gallon drop tanks the 56th sped 240 miles to Duren in the Ruhr before turning for home. They caught a formation of Me 110s coming up on the bombers and shot down fifteen of these twin-engined fighters which were no match for the P-47. Dave was responsible for one of the victories. Four days later he led the group on a Ramrod to Bremen and again shot down a Jerry, one of four the group claimed. On the 10th, when the Forts had a fierce battle at Munster, Schilling and the 56th came to the rescue, knocking down ten of their adversaries. Dave picked up his fifth victory this day to become an ace in just four consecutive raids.

Schilling also became one of the firm advocates for developing the team spirit that was fundamental to our success. Being an outstanding pilot and above average shot, his continual desire to fly did much in our rear area training to improve the assault-support-reserve concept of escort. Dave Schilling was undoubtedly the commanding personality in the 56th, his charismatic charm won the attention of all who came into contact with him. In the Officers Club you could be sure he would have a gathering around him. An entertaining raconteur, he was quick to establish friendships with visitors and was not above a joke at their expense. Dave discovered that Lieutenant Sam Cabot Jr, one of the ground officers in the 62nd Squadron, had an amazing capacity for mental arithmetic which Dave employed to his advantage. A visiting 'gent' from 'Ajax', or other newcomer to the Officers Club, who encountered the two at the bar, would be told by Dave that if he, the visitor, wrote down a column of four figure numbers, Cabot could total them up as fast as they were written down. The assertion was usually made in the form of a bet, accepted by the visitor, and always lost. Cabot did add the numbers as fast as they were written. The follow-on was a bet that Cabot could do the same with six figure numbers. The challenge accepted and lost, Dave pocketed the money. I've seen him take several pounds off people in this way during an evening. Presumably he split the proceeds with Cabot, but I never asked.

A characteristic of the English is their reserve, keeping themselves to themselves and not pushing their presence onto others. Dave was the complete opposite; he was often out introducing himself here and there and through that effervescent manner made many friends. How, I cannot recall, but not long after we moved into Halesworth Dave became friends with Mr and Mrs Andrew Venneck, gentlefolk of some standing in local society it was said. The Vennecks had a large estate stocked with pheasant and other game birds, but due to wartime restrictions no twelve bore ammunition. We had plenty of twelve bore ammunition provided by our government so that pilots could fire on the skeet at clays to develop aim in deflection shooting. There was, however, no stipulation that the targets had to be clays. So Venneck provided the birds, we the twelve bore shells, and all enjoyed some excellent days shooting. On my first visit it was quite apparent that the Vennecks were people of considerable wealth. Their home was a vast Georgian mansion called Heveningham Hall, standing in formal gardens and above a small lake. Only part of the house was lived in due to the wartime restrictions on heating. Schilling became very friendly with the Vennecks who were frequent visitors to our Officers Club. It was soon clear there was a mutual attraction between Dave and Mrs Venneck, a tall, attractive woman of Swedish birth. But then, Dave rarely failed to attract the ladies.

Following our run of successes it was vowed at an Officers Club party that the group would shoot down its 100th enemy aircraft by Sadie Hawkin's Day. Before we came overseas we read *The Mirror*, a popular newspaper in New England, and came to enjoy the syndicated strip cartoon *Li'l Abner*. Drawn by Al Capp, it featured a mythical hill-billy family of wild mountain folk. In England, the strip was featured by the US service newspaper *Stars and Stripes*, so we could still enjoy the comic characters which had become famous in the United States. Schilling and some of the 62nd boys decided that it would be fun to decorate their individual P-47s in honour of some of the *Li'l Abner* characters and wrote to Al Capp. He sent appropriate drawings which were copied onto the planes. Part of the folk lore in the *Li'l Abner* strip was Sadie Hawkins Day on which any gal was allowed to wed the man of her choice — if she could catch him, the men being extraordinarily disinterested in matrimony. Sadie Hawkins Day was 6 November and 100 victories seemed a reasonable goal to attain by that date.

Early in October I had received a call from General Kepner. He told me that General Eaker was getting together a small party of officers under Curt LeMay who were to return to the Zone of the

Interior (military jargon for USA) to participate in a presentation tour outlining 8th Air Force achievement, aims and method of operations. Zemke was to be one of the party! I was somewhat taken aback. First my right-hand men and now me: it seemed high command was intent on denuding the 56th of all senior officers. My protests were loud and long. After months of perseverence my group was now showing itself to be the best in the theatre; I wanted nothing more than to stay with them and continue my command. By now, however, I knew enough about Kepner to know when I was pushing my luck too far. Reluctantly I agreed and made the bold proviso that I could have my group command back when the tour was over. Kepner said yes, I could return to the 56th. I was ordered to report to 'Widewing', 8th AF Headquarters, for briefing and missed out on the fruitful missions early in October.

At 'Widewing' I was told I had to prepare a lecture to deliver in Washington. It was to describe the execution of a fighter escort mission. My draft was submitted to Brigadier General LeMay who didn't like it and told me to try again. Thinking it over, I decided that pictures could provide the information far better than just the spoken word. So I returned to ask LeMay if I could make a short film. With his affirmative I drafted a scenario and provisional script, enlisting the expertise of Major John 'Tex' McCarry from 8th Air Force public relations. McCarry had been a well known radio commentator before volunteering for military service.

A matter of some concern to me was who should command the 56th during my absence. Dave Schilling was shaping up nicely as the Flying Executive and had the necessary qualities to make a good leader; but I still had misgivings about Dave's impulsive nature. Such was my jealous guard of the 56th that I wanted to do all I could to preserve its current status and standing in VIIIth Fighter Command. Because I was not happy about leaving Dave in charge, I hit on an idea which at the time I believed was the answer to my concern. On Kepner's staff was Colonel Robert Landry who I had known back in my early days in the Air Corps. He was 34 and an able staff administrator and I figured that if he took command of the 56th he would a tight rein on activities at the base... Schilling and Gabreski could lead in the air until Landry had enough experience to become involved. Having sounded out Bob Landry and ascertained he was receptive, I put my case to General Kepner who agreed that Landry could go to the 56th until I returned from the States. Viewed in retrospect, I was unnecessarily cautious: Schilling and the rest would have been quite able to carry the show along responsibly.

After collecting a British DFC at 'Widewing' I went back to Halesworth. The group had flown to Duren again on 14 October, the date of the infamous second Schweinfurt mission when sixty B-17s went down. The Luftwaffe did its best to avoid the P-47s and we were only able to shoot down three of their number although the Metfield boys got ten. Schilling led the 56th, going as far as possible before dropping the 108 gallon tanks and keeping the group in the air for a record 2¾ hours.

On the 18th I led a Ramrod to Duren but the weather was so bad the bombers abandoned their mission. We flew through giant canyons in the towering fall storm clouds to our rendezvous point over the Maastricht area of Holland where we circled, waiting to see if the bombers appeared. Far below in one of those cloud canyons a lone Me 210 was spotted flying straight and level to the north-east. It was possible this was a decoy and that somewhere '109s or '190s lurked hidden from our view. After checking all avenues of enemy attack and telling the group to continue orbiting, I took my flight down to 15,000 feet to try and despatch this lone target. At any moment I expected our quarry to see us and flick over into the undercast and safety; but no, he continued to fly straight and level, oblivious of the danger. In the descent speed built up rapidly and had to be checked; even so, when I came up behind him the P-47 was travelling at 400 mph. Because of my rate of closure I opened fire when still a thousand yards away, firing short bursts until I over-ran the target and chandled up. He had been hit hard, without doubt, as pieces were seen to fly off. Looking back over my shoulder there was no sight of the enemy aircraft, only several P-47s. Later it was learned that Red, as well as White Flight, had attacked the Messerschmitt and that over 500 rounds had been pumped into it; certainly over-kill. At debriefing a few tail feathers were plucked; when I said one flight I meant one, not half a squadron. Six pilots were originally credited with this 'kill'. Fighter Command awards evaluation team studied the gun camera films and awarded fractions; I told them to give mine to the poor.

The bombers ran the Duren mission two days later. Again an undercast hid the ground. This time, however, the B-17s were making use of the new radar bombing devices which, hopefully, would let them attack when bombardiers could not use visual sighting methods on targets. Leading Postgate White flight, I despatched other flights to deal with enemy fighters encountered on penetration and in the target area I attacked and shot down an FW 190 in the clouds. We were using 75-gallon drop tanks and found they gave insufficient fuel for missions of this length. We were up 82 minutes, but having been involved in full throttle combat flying, many red lights were winking by the time we reached England again.

The group's score now totalled 94 and with just over two weeks to go to Sadie Hawkins Day there seemed a good chance that we could obtain the six victories needed to fulfil our boast. The Clerk of the Weather had different ideas, however, as one front after another swept across north-west Europe and kept the heavy bombers grounded — or recalled, when they did attempt to scale the clouds. This was frustrating for our eager beaver pilots but I had much to do before my impending departure for the States. The production of the film documentary required scenes of preparation and departure for a mission. To obtain these Tex McCarry and a movie team from 'Widewing' arrived at our base on 27 October. We ran a mock briefing and went through all the other procedures for the cameras. Some aerial shots of P-47s escorting bombers were required, and as we also lacked suitable film of enemy fighters making attacks it was necessary to simulate this using P-47s. I arranged with LeMay's headquarters for a local B-17 group — the 95th over at Horham — to put up a training formation and for the movie team to fly with them while I put some of our P-47s through their paces around the bombers.

My protective concern over the group was at this time increased by yet another request from 'Ajax' for personnel to be transferred. Early in the month we had lost Lieutenants John Patton and Joe Curtiss as instructors to the P-47 operational training unit, and a ground officer to the new fighter group at Bodney. Now they wanted the 62nd Squadron's Intelligence Officer for another recently arrived fighter outfit. I again argued that just because the 56th had become one of the most successful fighter outfits in England it should not become a replacement centre for the rest of VIIIth Fighter Command. In the end high command had to be obeyed but not before I had made my concern very plain. The way things were going I expected to find the best men in the 56th transferred out to other groups by the time I got back from the States. It was, however, officially no longer my concern when Bob Landry arrived to take command on the 29th and I went to London.

The next few days were chiefly taken up with the completion of the film *Ramrod To Emden*. Tex McCarry narrated the commentary and the final spliced reel was projected for LeMay. It met with his approval, as it later did Kepner's and an edited print was made for me to take to the States.

Much of my time was spent at 'Ajax' and I was able to see something of the planning of fighter operations in conjunction with the bomber missions. The weather forecast was good enough for a mission to Wilhelmshaven on 3 November and I was delighted to see the 56th credited with four more victories and only sorry not to have been along. Next afternoon I learned there was going to be a Ramrod to Munster if the weather held on the 5th and here was I kicking my heels. The temptation was too much to resist. After making myself thoroughly familiar with the flight plan and mission requirements for the 56th I got to bed. Early next morning, a P-47 borrowed from Bovingdon strapped to my parachute, I headed for Halesworth, arriving at the briefing room just as Schilling was about to ascend the podium to commence the session. As I entered through the door I called the 'troops' to attention. Poor Dave could hardly believe his ears and eyes as I marched up onto the podium and told him I was taking the mission. His protests were countered with a reminder of rank. I went on to say I had been instrumental in persuading the 'Ajax' fabricators of the field order to place the 56th to cover the particular air bomber task force heading for an area where opposition was the next thing to assured. As Bob Landry would be flying an element lead — it would be some time before he had the experience to lead the group — we could not have too many 'wheels' on the show and I therefore grounded Dave for the day. No doubt he spent the next few hours cursing that son-of-a-bitch Zemke!

So off we went. Our rendezvous point with B-24s we were to escort was to the east of the Zuider Zee. With eight fighter groups available it had been possible for 'Ajax' to provide near continuous cover for the bombers by a relay system. Using our successful technique of placing the one squadron to cover the vulnerable rear box of bombers, while Gabby and I took the 61st and 63rd forward to position on either flank of the leading Liberators, we proceeded for some minutes without any action. As we went deeper into enemy air space we began to encounter small formations of enemy fighters which we were able to drive off. Near the target someone called in bandits approaching from the north. There were approximately thirty FW 190s divided into an assault and top cover sections; all appeared to be making for a point well ahead of the bombers to commence head-on attacks. Calling Gabby to cross over and provide direct support to the 63rd, with the sun behind me, I commenced a long diving attack on the FW 190s flying top cover. We maintained the element of surprise and shot two out of the sky on this initial pass. One fell to my guns; its cockpit canopy coming away and narrowly missing my aircraft. The enemy immediately broke only to be hit by Postgate Red, my second flight, who caused further dispersal as they followed them down. Meanwhile Gabby and the 61st went for the assault FW 190s seen to be armed with rockets. These enemy fighters also broke up in trying to evade the bounce.

The Luftwaffe outfit was by no means a novice for they had plenty of aggression and attempted to get our people into turning fights. Every time any of them managed to get into an advantageous position, P-47s in our top cover sections dove to drive them off. In five minutes the FW 190 Gruppen had been completely scattered and no longer threatened the bombers. It was an excellent example of proficiency in teamwork that the 56th had attained and, as a result, only one B-24 was lost to fighter attack. Back at Halesworth there was some excitement to see if we had obtained the four victories necessary to make the century. Debriefing soon revealed we had bagged six and that a fired-up red-head named George Hall had the honour of shooting down number 100 when he attacked a lone Me 210.

A rousing bachelor party ensued in the Officers' Mess that evening as an extra allotment of hard liquor and beers was authorised to celebrate the attainment of our vow. If a few .45 calibre pistol holes appeared in the metal roof I wasn't one to put in a complaint this time. What had been achieved was a justification of all we had striven for over the past months of training and operations. From being the green sprogs who took some pretty rough handling from the Luftwaffe, we had emerged the leading group in England with nearly twice as many victories to our credit as any other; cubs that had become a seasoned wolfpack. Through developing the right tactics for using the P-47 in the particular air combat environment in which we were placed, constant training, the acceptance of air discipline and teamwork and promotion of the aggression so necessary to successful fighter pilots, we had proved the Luftwaffe could be beaten over its home ground. The 56th Fighter Group had shown the way and the other groups would catch on fast. We now had six rated aces —

Gerald Johnson, Bob Johnson, Walker Mahurin, Frank McCauley, Schilling and myself, with several more hot-rods on the verge. Here was the spirit with which victory is achieved. Perhaps another, softer generation yet unborn might be appalled that we could celebrate actions which had extinguished many lives of young men just like ourselves. But as we saw it then, the pilots of the Focke-Wulfs and Messerschmitts were not like us; they were the hated enemy who gave no quarter and had to be defeated. No doubt the Luftwaffe pilots were similarly motivated. Such is war.

Next day was Sadie Hawkins Day. Dave Schilling demanded to drive me to the local railroad station, insisting that he was going to make damn sure I caught the train to London. 'Sorry to do that to you Dave,' I said, 'but I couldn't leave without one more crack at those bastards.' We shook hands, joked and said farewell. As the cramped little English train puffed away, I realised that the past few months had been the most exhilarating of my whole life. I wouldn't be happy until I was back again.

10

STATESIDE INTERLUDE

In the late autumn of 1943 the US 8th Air Force was under severe strain. Its heavy bombers had taken near prohibitive losses during the series of long range missions in October, with the result that even the most ardent exponent of the bombers providing their own defence against enemy interceptors had come to accept the advantages of fighter escort. The strength of the enemy defences and unsuitable weather for precision attacks had set back the bombing programme against priority targets in Germany. There were some signs of lack of confidence in the campaign in Washington and part of the new forces scheduled for England were instead diverted to Italy to form another bombing arm. This, and the lobbying of those who supported more forces for the war with Japan, motivated General Eaker — always appreciative of public relations — into assembling a team of experts who would put the case for continued and increased support of the USAAF's operations from the UK. Eaker picked his best men for what he considered a vitally important mission to influence and convert opinion in the USAAF hierarchy.

Hub Zemke was selected because he was in both Eaker's and Kepner's opinion the best fighter leader in England. Through discipline and training he had moulded his group into an efficient and aggressive team. He had assessed their tool of trade, the P-47, and had developed tactics to employ it repeatedly in successful actions. The 56th Fighter Group was indeed showing the way and while Hub might demur and say it was due to the team spirit, he was nonetheless both catalyst and driving force. A lecture tour was not something Hub desired to participate in, for although articulate he was not at ease in such situations. The prospect of seeing his home country and family after the austerity of Britain was a pleasant inducement to this assignment as he finalised his presentation with the team assembled at 'Widewing'.

★   ★   ★

After a few days we were alerted to move. A train took us to Prestwick, the big trans-Atlantic air terminal in south-west Scotland from where we were to wing westwards. On our arrival we were informed that the weather along the route via Iceland and Greenland was now too bad for the proposed trip by B-17. Instead we were rushed to Greenock where the *Queen Mary* was about to set sail. Anchor was drawn on 15 November and I left Britain as I had arrived, under cold grey skies.

Unlike my previous trip on the *Queen Elizabeth* when the ship was overflowing with GIs bound for the UK, there could not have been more than fifty or so passengers aboard. Although the vessel's interior had been transformed for troop carrying and all the niceties of a luxury liner vanished, a few suites had been retained for VIP passage and these were available to us. We ate at the Captain's table and there was little to do but take a hearty tour of the outer deck before each meal, talk shop and play cards. I discovered that General LeMay enjoyed cards and there ensued penny-a-point sessions of gin rummy for much of the five days at sea. When LeMay got his mind set on something he ground his teeth and really worked on it and his card playing was no exception. Luck or skill — I know not — I did most of the winning. As we played we talked and I was able to appreciate something of why this man was such a determined and successful commander. Most people judged him by his curt, gruff manner; but he had a sense of humour and a deep interest in a wide range of subjects. One topic of which we both never tired was hunting and hunting guns. LeMay was not the man to loose and didn't like it when he did, yet he lived up to every part of his obligations in life and when we reached New York he paid me out the $10.23c that the score card showed I had won. This was the second occasion the little upstart fighter pilot had marred his fun, although he had probably long forgotten the business of the skeet ammunition at Langley. Needless to say, my ill gotten gains did not last long with buying a few rounds of American beer on the train from New York to Washington.

Our first presentation was to the Combined Chiefs of Staff in Washington. In addition to LeMay and myself, the team consisted of Glenn Nye, who commanded a B-26 group and lectured on the part played by the medium bombers, and Group Captain J.R.Robinson, a senior RAF intelligence officer who gave an account of the overall air-war scene in Europe. This eloquent man was also a British Member of Parliament. After two further presentations to Washington dignatories, a B-24 was provided us and we toured the whole country putting on our show for senior officers at major USAAF bases. One of the first stops was my one-time haunt, Mitchel Field, New York, Headquarters of 1st Air Force. Here my old boss in VIIIth Fighter Command held roost as commander, Major General Frank Hunter. He greeted me cordially and was present during our presentation to his officers, many of whom were in training to lead new fighter units to Europe before the next spring. We spent the best part of a month on our tour of bases. General LeMay saw to it that we never over or under played the time allotted to us wherever we went, and the show was generally well received.

We had been told that following completion of our assignment a week's leave would be forthcoming before assembling in Washington, D.C. for return to Europe. I caught a ride back to Montana to see my wife and family. The Missoula Rotary Club asked me to address them and my father came along. He didn't let his guard drop but I knew that he was secretly proud that his son had finally had some success. Neither my mother nor my wife hid their concern for my safety. As must be the case with all women whose sons and husbands were at war, theirs was a miserable existence living in fear of that telegram from the War Department.

The New Year found me on my way to Washington to join the others for return to England. I reported to the appropriate office in the Pentagon and received the disconcerting news that my orders had been changed. Further enquiries from a staff officer friend revealed that orders were being promulgated to have me re-assigned from the 8th Air Force to the 1st Air Force in New York. This turn of events could hardly have been more devastating. Despite my having stood up to General Hunter and incurred his displeasure on a couple of occasions in England, after the presentation at Mitchel Field he had obviously decided that combat-experienced Zemke would make a useful addition to his current command. Exactly what position I was to fulfill was not known so a long distance telephone call was initiated to Hunter at his headquarters. I was told that I was being placed in the Directorate of Operations at 1st Air Force. A man with combat experience was needed to lead-up the command operations which had the major task of preparing new units for overseas service. I told him that I had been promised I would be returned to the combat theatre and given back command of my group but Hunter insisted that my orders had now been changed. Having learned the worst I did not prolong the conversation; I needed time to think — and quickly.

The thought of being confined to a staff desk apalled me. I had no desire to work directly under Monk Hunter. In England it had been my view that he was out of touch with the situation in his command — and General Eaker had apparently come to this conclusion too. Perhaps Hunter cut a swathe with his old time Air Corps buddies, but in my book the social set at the London Savoy or the New York Granery Park was not where raging battles at 25,000 feet were won. I visualised that with a string of ribbons on my tunic I would help decorate and add interest to his Mitchel Field headquarters. Perhaps some officers would have considered this a great posting but I could not have felt more gloomy if I was destined for Alcatraz.

Quick action was needed to counter this demoralising prospect. As yet I had not actually received formal written orders. Before they were forthcoming there was one escape route; I still had the travel papers and original orders for return to the UK. Without saying where I was going I took my duffel bag and went to nearby Andrews Field from whence Air Transport Command commenced many of its worldwide flights. On presenting my papers at the traffic desk the clerk said a seat could be found on one of the new Douglas C-54 transports leaving for the UK that afternoon. I could not get on the plane quickly enough. There was to be an intermediate stop at La Guardia airport, New York, before leaving the States and during this first hop I was given to thinking deeply about the step being taken. No doubt Hunter would see this as a case of a Colonel going AWOL (Absent Without Leave) but I felt that once back in England I could prevail upon Kepner to honour his verbal promise.

Even so, my misgivings were such that it was decided to make one more plea to Monk Hunter to change his mind after the C-54 put down at La Guardia. It was around eleven in the evening when I was connected to Hunter's quarters at Mitchel. I apologised for the lateness of my call and put my case. Hunter was adamant; no, he would not change the orders which he had arranged by a personal request to General Arnold. There was no mistaking I'd struck an impasse. I politely wished him good-night, hung up and walked back to the transport. Hunter probably thought I was still in Washington as I had been careful not to disclose from where I was calling. Hunter's request to his old friend was small potatoes to Hap Arnold but with such endorsement I was going to be in a hot spot if I didn't get the backing hoped for in the UK.

The C-54 reached Iceland the next morning and then flew on to Prestwick. My apprehension that military police might be on hand to meet the aircraft to detain an AWOL Colonel proved unfounded and I could relax a little. By nightfall I was on my way by train to London. Leaving the wheezing steam engines I was once again in the hustle of service uniforms from the many allied nations, the air raid wardens and bobbies, the bomb-scarred buildings and blackout. Strangely, I had a feeling of elation just to be back in this drab foreign country; it was a little like coming home.

After getting to Bushey Hall and finding a cot for the night, I was up and into the Chief of Staff's office as soon as Colonel Francis 'Butch' Griswold was behind his desk. He was unmistakably surprised to see me. 'What are you doing here? I understood you had been retained on Monk Hunter's staff.' 'No Sir, my written orders were to report back to my group after the lecture tour in the States.' I had known Butch when he was a squadron commander at Langley; he was no fool and quickly sized up the situation. He questioned me further about written orders and I repeated that I had not received any — which was the truth. Butch could sense trouble: 'I think you better see General Kepner immediately. Go into his office and I'll notify him.'

What I had not known until arriving back in the UK was that General Eaker, who did not see eye to eye with Hunter and might support my action, was no longer boss of the Eighth. He had been given to overall command in the Mediterranean theatre and his place in England taken by Jimmy Doolittle with Carl Spaatz as the supremo of all US airpower stacked against Hitler. I was sitting turning the pages of a magazine and pondering my fate when General Kepner came in. He listened to my story and questioned me about orders to stay in the States. I told him I had heard rumours of such orders but had not actually received them. Kepner too had a good idea that I knew more than I was telling. I pressed the point about his promise that I should get my group back and that I knew he was a man of integrity. Bill Kepner was as sharp as a needle and could see the ramifications of my action. Happily I sensed he was on my side even if he was not going to openly condone what, at the least, amounted to a snub to a senior officer. He said this business was something that would have to be referred to Doolittle and Spaatz and while it was sorted out suggested I take myself out of the way for a few days.

Thus heartened I went off to Scotland, but before leaving 'Ajax' a call was made to Dave Schilling at Halesworth to warn of my impending return. Dave, ever the joker, protested that once again his schemes to bury me had flopped, although there was probably a true touch of disappointment, he being heir apparent to command of the 56th when Landry pulled out.

For seven days I fretted in Edinburgh and had my fill of castles and kilts. A fine city not seen at its best in cold January weather. I couldn't wait to return to 'Ajax'. With trepidation I entered Kepner's office: 'Get back to Halesworth.' he said. What actually happened was never told to me: General Spaatz must have put in a good word with Hap Arnold. My conduct probably marred chances of higher promotion but that was of no concern to me at the time. At heart I was only a fighter pilot; all I wanted was to be back in the air leading the 56th. I couldn't get to Halesworth fast enough.

11
GREAT DAYS

My two month absence from the air war scene in England had seen a lot of changes. The number of fighter groups in action had trebled and more were arriving every few weeks. Most of these were P-47 equipped and assigned to the 9th Air Force which was forming in the UK to support the cross-Channel invasion planned for the spring. The primary mission of these groups would be the support of the ground forces but for the present they were available to fly escort for the Eighth's bombers. A few of the Ninth's fighter groups were equipped with North American P-51B Mustangs, a new development of a fighter originally produced for the RAF. The P-51B used a Packard-built version of the powerful Rolls-Royce Merlin that gave the aircraft a far better performance than any other American fighter plane. More important, it was superior to the main enemy types, except in rate of climb. However, the major attraction of the Mustang was its range. On the internal tankage alone it could fly more than 700 miles; with drop tanks just about anywhere the B-17s and B-24s could go. To me it looked just the fighter we needed to seek out the Luftwaffe in its lair. The 8th Air Force had already made arrangements that in future P-51s came to them and not the 9th, although the machinations of Materiel Command in the States would make this a long drawn out programme.

Unfortunately, but perhaps understandably, Bob Landry and the 56th Headquarters preferred to remain loyal to the Thunderbolt and didn't recognise the potential of the Mustang. VIIIth Fighter Command was scheduled to receive a total of fifteen fighter groups and although only twelve were in place at this time, a plan for converting six from P-47s to P-51s was already approved. Had I been around the 56th would have been one of them.

Because of their better range, the sole Mustang outfit already operational and the two P-38 Lightning groups that had joined VIIIth Fighter Command missions at the back end of the old year, were given the target area support for the heavies. Mechanically, the P-38 was not up to conditions prevailing in the north-west European winter, particularly its Allison engines with which the extreme cold and damp played havoc.

While range remained the chief limiting factor in our P-47 operations, the 56th had continued to foster means of conserving fuel by retarding throttle and turbo settings to obtain optimum economy consumption. Using the 108 gallon drop tanks, endurance was regularly pushed out to three hours and occasionally to three hours fifteen minutes, although involvement in prolonged air fighting would drastically reduce endurance. An interesting development was the provision of shackles under wings to carry a tank below each and further extend our range. These were currently being installed and there was some trouble with the tanks oscillating on the racks, a problem that had to be overcome before we could use them.

Two other technical advances coming into use around the time of my return greatly improved the Thunderbolt's performance. The first of these was water injection equipment on the engine to allow extra power to be drawn from it for short intervals. Provision for this equipment had been built into the P-47 since the autumn but lack of kits of parts and other work at depots had delayed the introduction of this aid until December. The other innovation was a wide blade propeller which took a much bigger bite of air and improved climb at low altitudes. Several P-47s at Halesworth had these 'paddle props' when I resumed command. With both these fitments the speed was increased by about ten miles per hour but the improvement in rate of climb was quite dramatic, around another 600 feet a minute at low altitude, and we could now top 30,000 feet in about thirteen minutes instead of twenty. Of course, this was with a 'clean', light loaded 'plane.

While I was away from Halesworth the 56th had consolidated its position as the leading fighter group in England. The boys had knocked down another eighty Jerries for the loss of twenty of their own and, while it was sad to see some familiar faces were no longer around, such success could not be bought without cost. The group's best day had been 26 November when Schilling led a show which netted 23 victories for an ETO record.

Beginning in November, the group's aircraft complement had been increased from 75 to 108 to meet a new 'Ajax' requirement for two formations to be sent out on each mission. Sufficient additional pilots and mechanics to enable use to be made of these extra P-47s were slow in arriving. The 56th was the second group to have the ranks thus swollen and the first 'double mission' had been despatched a few days before my return. This became the norm from then on, with the two forces, known as A and B groups, supporting different parts of the bomber stream or going out at different times. With A and B group formations, squadrons usually consisted of only three four-plane flights instead of four.

Before my departure there had been some consideration about using P-47s for bombing and some experimental missions had been run with our neighbours, the 353rd. The Metfield group had, in fact, pioneered dive-bombing with the Thunderbolt, carrying a single 500 pounder on the belly shackles. Not without cost for on one mission McCollom's plane was hit by ground fire and went down. Mac baled out and became a PoW.

Landry had certainly tightened up around the base and merged the headquarters of the 33rd Service Group with that of the 56th to improve administration. He also caught on well in the air and had led several missions. When I turned up unannounced at 'Ajax' one of the first moves Kepner and Doolittle made was to transfer Landry to 8th Air Force Headquarters. Schilling then assumed temporary command for a week although Bob Landry, who must have become addicted to a fighter pilot's life, hung around until the end of January and flew a few more missions before taking up his post at 'Widewing'. When notice of Landry's departure was received, Schilling brought Gabreski into Headquarters from the 61st Squadron and placed Major James Stewart in command of that unit. When I arrived, on the 19th, Dave resumed Flying Executive duties and I made Gabby a Deputy Flying Exec' and Operations Officer as group headquarters needed the extra leaders now that we flew the A and B group set-up. On returning to operational flying I chose to let Schilling, Gabby and the others continue to lead the group while I flew with one of the squadrons. I needed to re-orientate myself in the various procedures and become thoroughly familiar with any new developments. Having acquired a new P-47D with paddle-blade prop', I decided to place it in the care of the 63rd Squadron, having previously used the 62nd and before that the 61st. This was in pursuit of my policy of avoiding squadron favouritism. Tech Sergeant Damon Itza had crewed Bob Landry's plane and, when Landry left, he took charge of my aircraft.

Coincidental with my return to combat was a major policy change by 8th Air Force and VIIIth Fighter Command. General Eaker's brief had been that our first objective was to bring back the bombers and our second to shoot down enemy aircraft. Now General Doolittle told us to pursue the enemy when and wherever we could; we were now permitted to follow him down and no longer had to break off attacks. At lower altitudes the P-47 would have to be wary of getting into dogfights, but apparently our generals believed that there were now sufficient P-47s to warrant the risk of it keeping the pressure on the now hard-pressed Luftwaffe fighter arm. It also meant official recognition of what I had long advocated; getting way out ahead to bounce the enemy fighters before they had a chance to make their attacks on the bombers. With the enormous number of Allied fighters now regularly roaming over Holland, Belgium and northern France, the Luftwaffe was even more anxious to avoid contact and unnecessary attrition. For this reason and the reduced number of operations due to winter weather, the 56th did not have the opportunity for many air fights in January. Even so, we were able to gain our 200th air victory on the 30th, a success dedicated to the President, whose birthday anniversary it was. Of the seventeen downed by the group that day, one was credited to Bud Mahurin, his 15th, keeping him just ahead of the 353rd's Walt Beckham as the 8th's leading ace. Bob Johnson claimed two to raise his score to fourteen, level with Beckham. Gabby Gabreski also got a double, pulling up next in line with a total of eleven. Mike Quirk and Stan Morrill achieved acehood this day to make a dozen in our group — Joe Powers, Walt Cook and Leroy Schreiber had made the grade while I was in the States. Several other pilots had three or four victories and many one or two. On the day the 56th reached 200 victories the 4th Group passed the 100 mark in second place.

While around forty pilots had destroyed an enemy aircraft there were some who had not had a chance to fire their guns even, though having flown seventy or eighty missions. Most were wingmen whose job was to follow and protect their element leader who did the shooting — but many were not. Even squadron commanders, eager to prove themselves to their men, couldn't find enough opportunities. Horace Craig, CO of the 62nd, was a good example. On 3 February he became the first man in the group to complete 200 hours' combat flying, the total required to finish a tour and be rotated to the States. I rated Pappy a steady dependable leader who made the right decisions. He was a modest, pleasant fellow who knew and performed his job well but only had one confirmed victory in all that time. He had fired his guns several times. Perhaps he was out of range, or his opponent just saw him coming in time to break, or whatever. He had been in a few tight corners but no Hun pilot ever put bullets in his crate. A few days later, when Pappy left us, I put Leroy Schreiber to head the 62nd. This former flying school instructor had come to us in England as a casual and proved to be an exceptional fighter pilot who was going to go far. There were many others among the original pilots heading for the 200 hours mark. I foresaw a time when we could have a crisis situation through lack of experienced commanders. Representations were made to 'Ajax' to give pilots a fifty-hour extension option so that if some asked to continue on ops they could. This was eventually agreed and later pilots were given the opportunity of thirty days' rest and recuperation back in the States with a return to their old unit. This went a long way to solving the problem.

For the time being it looked as if we might run into a situation where we would be short of experienced pilots. This must have been discussed at one of our headquarters bull sessions for Gabby, who still had contacts with the RAF Polish fighter boys he had flown with, brought along Squadron Leader T. Andersz and Flight Lieutenant Michael Gladych. These men had flown against the Germans when Poland was invaded, escaped to fly with the French, and when that country was over-run joined the RAF. After amassing a considerable number of operational hours and several victories, the RAF decided they needed a rest. This was not these officers' opinion and now they were offering their services to us. Impressed, particularly by the gangling, quick-talking Mike, I cleared it with Kepner and put them in P-47s and didn't regret it. In time word got around to other 'resting' RAF Polish fliers and we ended up with enough to fill a whole flight in Gabby's squadron. These were a wild, verbose bunch but they had one thing in common; a burning hatred for the enemy who occupied their homeland and an overwhelming desire to shoot down his aircraft. These people had RAF ranks, wore RAF uniforms and were paid by that service. The situation wasn't in the rule book so high command condoned it.

A major difficulty following a bounce or break in air fighting was reforming a flight or section. This was normally achieved by radioed directions to form over a prominent landmark — if the ground was visible — or by a bearing reference to the bombers we were supporting. Even so, until pulling into a position where the letters on the next P-47 could be clearly seen it was often a matter of luck if one was joining the correct slot. Mulling this over at one of our bull sessions, the idea was put forward than an aid to squadron recognition at a distance would be distinctive coloured engine cowlings. There was another angle to this. From our earliest clashes with the Me 109s and FW 190s we were aware that the various Staffeln were identified by bright nose colours. In contrast, all P-47s had the type identification white cowling and if we painted them with bright colours the enemy fighters might be fooled into thinking we were friends when they saw us at a distance.

I telephoned General Kepner to obtain his permission to reintroduce the squadron cowling colours used when the 56th was at Bridgeport — red for the 61st, yellow for the 62nd and blue for the 63rd. After some discussion this was approved and in one night all white paint was removed from our P-47s' noses and the appropriate squadron colours applied. We first flew with this bright paintwork on 6 February and on this and subsequent missions the recognition benefit was proven. We were able to engage and destroy a few enemy planes which through their tardiness in evasive action may have been fooled by our new look. However, it did not take long for the Luftwaffe to cotton on to this change. Our distinctive markings also bestowed a morale factor in identifying us as the elite unit among the many American fighter groups then operational.

I took out my first group lead since returning to the 56th on 8th February with a Ramrod to Frankfurt. Both A and B groups only managed a single claim between them. The directive was notable in that for the first time we were officially permitted to shoot up enemy planes on the ground. Three days later I again led A Group to support Big Friends going to Frankfurt and had no opportunity to engage the Luftwaffe. The apparent dearth of enemy fighters and the relaxed attitude of 'Ajax' to engagements at low altitude brought me to consider strafing enemy airfields. At this time strafing of enemy airfields had only been carried out on a couple of occasions by a few P-

47s when returning from operations. I knew that Luftwaffe airfields were heavily defended with light automatic weapons and that low-level attacks could be a dangerous business. Although cautious I determined to have a go at the first opportunity.

On 11 February it was my turn to lead a group in support of a raid by the Big Friends on Frankfurt. We made landfall through layers of broken clouds over Walcheren Island at around 23,000 feet and continued a slow climb to rendezvous with the bombers. Contrails to the east were called in and drawing closer to these bogies I gave orders for the 62nd Squadron to give back-up support while I took the 61st to make an interception. At the same time the 63rd Squadron was directed to continue to meet the bombers at the appointed time. As now so often happened, the enemy fighters, probably briefed to go for the bombers, did not want to engage us and fled in to the protective cover of the clouds. One Me 109, not quick enough, was shot down by one of our pilots. In this action we consumed more of our fuel than I had anticipated and on reforming the squadrons to try and catch the bombers, I realised we would soon have to turn back.

Reducing altitude as we flew westward over France, soon a large airfield was glimpsed off my wing. Even at our high altitude the shapes of parked aircraft could be distinguished. An instantaneous decision was made: we would undertake our first ground strafing. Telling the 62nd Squadron to follow in a long circling dive to the east, I took my flight, the only one of the 61st to reform after the brush with the '109s, down to the deck to make a firing pass in line afront. Picking out a prominent bunch of trees on the east of the airfield as a reference point, I dropped down to low level some distance from the target in the hope that the anti-aircraft gunners had not seen us. Swinging round towards my reference point the low level descent was continued until the clump of trees dropped below my horizon. Now keeping true on that bearing, the four Thunderbolts raced across the French countryside, full throttle, hedge-hopping at around 340 mph. Fields, trees, houses, flashed past the nose of my aircraft and before really recognising it the airfield was below. Almost directly ahead some Me109s reposed outside a hangar. I fired and saw dirt fly short of my selected target. Instantly lifting the nose I ran the stream of bullets into the aircraft. The next moment I was over and past my target. A flick of the rudder pedals to skid the P-47 allowed a short burst at another parked fighter but I was conscious of the need to avoid varying my flight too much lest I get into the fire of following aircraft.

Another burst into a hangar and the airfield was gone.

As I pulled up to clear boundary trees a quick glance in the mirror revealed the '109 hit first was on fire under a plume of smoke. My only intention then was to get the hell out of the territory because the explosions and tracer seen out of the corner of my eye told me flak was coming up thick and fast. Having pulled well away from the airfield, I led a circling climb to around 10,000 feet and made haste for home. Listening to the radio crackle and the comforting steady rumble of the R2800 engine up front, I mused over in my mind that casual ground attacks of this nature could seriously reduce fighter pilots' longevity, thoughts no doubt shared with the other pilots in the homeward bound formation. More knowledge of the disposition and strength of flak defences at enemy airfields was essential as was the development of special tactics if losses were to be kept low.

Back at Halesworth we established that the airfield strafed was Juvincourt near Rheims. Eight of our pilots put in claims but after analysis of gun camera film by 'Ajax' mine was the only destroyed credit for the 56th's introduction to ground attack. Somehow all our aircraft had come through this rather clumsy assault on a heavily defended airfield. I had seen enough to know that hitting the Luftwaffe on its home bases was going to be a task few, if any, of us would relish.

For more than a week winter clouds blanketed most of western Europe and apart from a few raids on the V-weapon sites just across the Channel the bombers stayed home. The 56th was not called to escort any of these minor raids. With this brief respite from operations I took the opportunity to do a little duck shooting down on the nearby coastal marshes.

Pilots tended to become absorbed in their own world and forget their dependence on the men on the ground. The non-combatants were vital to the success of our missions and it had always been my policy to regularly monitor their performance. The men who serviced the planes often had a miserable task working in the exposed winter weather. The English climate was not extreme but many Americans could not acclimatise to the penetrating damp cold of the winter which made for a miserable existence and seemed to foster respiratory infections. Despite the often foul working conditions, mechanical malfunctions on our aircraft were few.

In the latter half of February 1944, General Spaatz got what he had been waiting for; a large high pressure area over central Europe

allowing him to launch 8th Air Force bombers from England and those of the 15th Air Force from Italy on a series of raids aimed at crippling German aircraft production. Neutralising the Luftwaffe was a pre-requisite of the impending cross-Channel invasion, and destruction of engine and airframe plants was reckoned a major step in this direction. What occurred in those late February days is known as 'Big Week', the most intensive period of operations up to that time for 8th Air Force. Its ranks had now grown so much that for the first time more than a thousand aircraft could be despatched.

The first major mission in this series of attacks took place on the 20th. As usual, we put up A and B group formations with three squadrons of three flights each. For Major Sy Burke, CO of the 63rd, this was to be his last mission, needing just over three hours time to pass the 200 hour mark to complete his tour. To honour the occasion Sy Burke was given the lead of the A Group, even though Gabby, the Deputy Flying Executive, would be along heading the 61st Squadron. B Group, led by Schilling, with Gil Meyers (once a compatriot at Mitchel and now CO of the 9th Air Force's newly arrived 368th Group), flying as his wingman on an operational initiation, was to leave 23 minutes after A group and take another relay section of the bomber stream.

This mission was also notable for being the first time we had used the 150 gallon capacity belly tanks. Locally made from sheet metal, these had a broad section to gain capacity without fouling the ground under the fuselage of the P-47. With the extra fuel adding at least another fifteen minutes' flying time we were enabled to reach the Hanover area, 350 miles from Halesworth. Not long after crossing the German border, Gabby's 61st A Squadron spotted two Stafflen of Me 110s, undoubtedly waiting to be vectored in when the German ground controllers found an unescorted bomber box. Gabby, leading his boys down out of the sun, caught them by surprise. The decimation of these Me 110s resulted in credits of eight destroyed, one probable and ten damaged. However, records of the Luftwaffe unit involved, III/ZG26, suggest that practically all the Me 110s claimed damaged went down. The B group also did some successful shooting with a 6-1-8 score, the cool, calculating Captain Schreiber bringing down three Me 109s. The total for the day was fourteen credits of the total 61 made by US fighters. Prior to the change of policy a few weeks earlier, the Luftwaffe could assemble its forces at lower altitudes knowing the Allied escort would remain up above with the bombers. Now they were finding out the hard way that this no longer held true. In most cases the enemy fighters hadn't seen what hit them this day and, even more satisfactory, we didn't suffer a single loss.

Next day it was my turn to lead and I took the A group to central Germany. A lone Me 110 was spotted early in the trip to be knocked down by Johnny Vogt and, apart from another inconclusive attempt to nail another Me 110, we were unable to find the Luftwaffe. Schreiber took the B group out about an hour after us. Tasked to bring the bombers home, they found several single-engined enemy fighters ganging up to attack the rear formations. In a number of diving interceptions, twelve FW 190s and Me 109s were shot down, two by our one-man Polish Air Force, Mike Gladych. Again without loss; reflecting the polish and precision of our tactics and aggression. There was now much evidence of the effect these battles were having on the Luftwaffe's fighter arm, notably the declining quality of our adversaries, many of whom displayed a decided lack of experience judging by their poor tactics. Too many German pilots attempted to evade our attacks by trying to dive away, usually a fatal move as a P-47 could soon overhaul them. Enemy formations were also showing a marked lack of co-ordination. We did not know it at the time but this was often due to pilots refueling away from home base and joining with others from different units for second sorties against the bombers.

Our winning streak continued. On the 22nd Gabby led A group and Jim Stewart B on another Ramrod into that area of west central Germany we now dubbed The Happy Hunting Ground. Both groups saw action, ringing up a combined total of fifteen victories. This mission saw the 61st Fighter Squadron become the first American squadron fighting Hitler's Luftwaffe to destroy 100 enemy aircraft in air combat. Back in the States the 61st had seemed to do everything wrong. It had definitely untangled itself in England and had a flush of aces. To date, 25 of its pilots had scored one or more victories. The 61st certainly lived up to its nickname of the Avenger Squadron — adopted after loosing three pilots in one of our early hidings from the Luftwaffe.

For the third day in a row we had bested the Luftwaffe without loss. The bombers sat on their hardstands on the 23rd but next day the campaign was on again with Schweinfurt as their principal objective. My turn to lead the group on penetration support going with the bombers to Herford where they were to turn south-east and

P-51s would take over. The lead B-17s called that they were under attack before we made rendezvous over Holland. We opened up to reach them and on arriving I picked out a flight of FW 190s below flying wide, line abreast. 'This is Yardstick. It looks as if there are about four of them at 18,000 going in. Keep your peckers up!' With this call for each man in my small force to attack, I rolled over and dove. Going down I saw the FW 190 selected had a wingman several hundred yards to the rear. This fellow was evidently more intent on protecting his leader than saving his own skin, for I suddenly saw time-fuzed cannon shells exploding around my plane. He must have opened up as I dived on his leader and let me fly through the fire. My own wingman, Archie Robey, then clobbered him and relieved me of considerable embarrassment.

Continuing my attack, I was about to close and fire when I noticed the gunsight light was out and thus inoperable.. Instantly my aim was transferred to the simple post and ring back-up sight. I fired and the '190 rolled over into a diving curve. Chopping the throttle, I followed, having no difficulty in staying behind him although his turning only allowed deflection shots. For some reason he clung to his drop tank which must have checked his manoeuvrability. All the same, down and around we went and I would try another short burst until finally we were almost on the tree tops. Since having unleashed more than 300 rounds and never registering a hit using the auxiliary sight, I decided it was now prudent to break off and try another day.

Until once more safely on the ground at Halesworth, I did not know this aerial duel had been conducted with cannon shell perforations in my P-47's flaps and an elevator. The fourth occasion Mrs Zemke's son little Hubert had returned with evidence that somebody was trying hard to eliminate him.

This day A group came home with five scalps and B group with three. Once more we had no losses through air combat but on their way home Lieutenant Fred Christensen and his wingman, Wilbur Kelly, strafed an airfield. Ground fire hit Kelly's P-47 and he never returned, being later reported killed. Since I initiated these strafing attacks several pilots had shot up enemy airfields on the way home. Our first loss underlined just how dangerous this casual strafing could be.

Pressing their campaign, the bombers went to Augsburg on the 25th and we went to meet them but only pulled off two victories. Thereafter the clouds came back to protect German targets from precision attack and brought the curtain down on 'Big Week'. It had provided the 56th Group with its most successful period of intensive fighting and during February we had credits for the destruction of 72 enemy aircraft against the loss of only two of our own. An interesting angle on our success was that over half the battle damage sustained by our P-47s was caused by particles from enemy aircraft they had destroyed. The loss figure was all the more remarkable in that flight over long distances and often through heavy layers of cloud was in itself a risky business for single-seat, single engine fighters. After combat pilots were often scattered far and wide and came home in ones and twos. Radio stations we called for a home bearing were frequently our lifelines in such circumstances. A year before, even our own air planners did not foresee their single-engine fighters regularly flying into western Germany; the Luftwaffe certainly didn't. An hour and a half was looked upon as about the maximum time one could expect a pilot to be cooped up in a small cockpit, which about matched the maximum fighter endurance of those days.

12
MORE GREAT DAYS

Consolidating our position as the leading American fighter outfit in Europe brought us considerable publicity which, in my view, was unwanted. As a nation we Americans are awfully vain, we have to shout about our successes and wave the flag. We must have heroes to worship. The ball game star fills this need in peacetime; in World War 2 the fighter ace was one of the main recipients of this kind of adoration. In contrast to the British who were tight-lipped over everything lest they gave useful information away to the enemy, our air force command placed little restriction on the release of pilots' names by the press, and while drawing the line at the mention of actual unit designations, there was no objection to their being identified by the commander's name. In this way newspapers, and in particular the US Forces daily, *The Stars and Stripes*, made frequent mention of the Zemke group and its pilots. An almost daily box score of fighter aces and their victories was published just as if it was some sort of sporting event.

Apart from meeting the public's need for heroes, high command thought this publicity encouraged competition between fighter groups and made the pilots more aggressive. This publicity annoyed me because it reduced the bloody business we were engaged in to the level of a ball game. Just to up their scores some pilots were going to take unnecessary risks. We didn't lack aggressiveness and I could not have been more intent on knocking hell out of the Luftwaffe and seeing the 56th remain champion. But we could do without the unnecessary pressure imposed by a continual stream of press people to our base whose attitudes were often akin to those of a sports reporter's. They got in your hair and I tried to avoid interviews, fending them off onto people who didn't mind indulging in verbosity. Even so, my real concern was that someone would let slip some tactical information that could be of advantage to the Germans. Unless directly involved, our own personnel were not allowed to attend mission briefing, yet high command gave reporters permission to do so! That said, with hindsight, perhaps the 56th should be grateful to the press for promoting the name which caught the public's imagination and gave us a place in the folklore of air fighting: 'The Wolfpack'.

On our last mission in February we took the bombers to Brunswick and for the first time the Luftwaffe made no attempt to intercept the bombers. The attrition wrought by the American fighter groups was really beginning to tell. We saw little of the Luftwaffe during the first two missions in March. On the 4th the bombers were set to make their first daylight attack on Berlin and in anticipation that the enemy would rise to protect his capital I had high hopes of action. The weather forecasters were wrong in their prognosis and we climbed through layers of cloud to find the Big Friends turning back when their way was barred by towering cumulus. Lieutenant Irvin Valenta didn't show up back at base. Notwithstanding his experience, it is believed he became disorientated in the clouds, suffered vertigo and spun in.

Two days later, 6 March 1944, the heavies made their first really successful strike on the enemy capital and, as we had anticipated, the Luftwaffe rose to give battle as probably never before. The air battles over the Continent were of epic proportions, resulting in the 8th Air Force's heaviest loss of the war, 69 B-17s and B-24s and eleven fighters. Claims against the enemy were 97 by bombers and 81 by fighters. His true losses were later established at around seventy and our fighter claims were not far from the mark.

I led A group off from Halesworth at 10:13 hours and Gerry Johnson, who had taken command of the 63rd when Burke left, headed the B group which departed twenty minutes later. Our job was to shepherd the bombers through the Happy Hunting Ground until relieved by P-51s. The route was more or less straight and climbing out we made landfall over Egmond while at around 22,000 feet. We passed one formation after another of the Big Friends until we established our rendezvous with the leading box near Lingen at 11:28 hours. So far the enemy had not shown his hand. The familiar shape of Dummer Lake passed below, a landmark we knew the Luftwaffe used to assemble its formations for attacking the bombers. 'Tackline', our fighter wing ground control, gave me the coded warning that a large formation of enemy aircraft was somewhere ahead to our north. Shortly afterwards Jim Stewart called that he was engaging a large enemy formation, an estimated 75 to 100 planes! The 61st Squadron was about fifteen miles north-west of the 63rd which I was leading. 'Yardstick here: Postgate Squadron follow me.' Throttle and boost to maximum we cut through the icy air with the tense commands of men in combat coming over the radio. All eyes in my squadron scanned the horizon for sight of combats. But where were they? After five minutes the radio calls ceased and it was evident that the battle was over. We finally saw parachutes and burning aircraft further to the west; we had arrived too late.

Then I caught sight of a lone FW 190 around 3,000 feet below diving towards one of the Fortress formations. Calling my flight to follow, I did a fast wing over and went down. The '190 was lining up to attack one of the trailing B-17s so I gave the engine water injection, but my rate of closure was still not fast enough to catch the Focke Wulf before he opened up on the Fort. After strafing the bomber he immediately banked left, enabling me to cut across behind his tail. When he filled the 300 yard graticule marks on my sight I gave him a burst of about fifty rounds before a quick evasive manoeuvre had to be made to avoid a collision. As I glanced back I saw the '190 going down in a steep dive trailing flame and smoke.

While starting to regain altitude an Me 109 was glimpsed to the south. Turning towards it in a shallow dive, speed was increased to catch him. Again when about 300 yards behind my quarry, but being slightly to one side twenty degrees deflection was allowed, I fingered the fire trigger. At first no hits were seen, then many strikes on his right wing, whereupon the pilot put the '109 into a dive. My superior speed quickly carried me into close range and another burst brought hits all over my victim causing it to burst into flames and go into a spin.

I called Postgate White flight to circle up to 20,000 feet and reform. As we climbed, yet another lone enemy fighter was seen, soon identified as an Me 109. 'Postgate White Flight: follow me.' Power was increased to bring him into range but the pilot saw us coming in time and pulled the old familiar escape routine of split-S and dive. An advance of boost and rpm and a wing over to follow him. He was diving vertically. Then suddenly the '109 burst into flames and went tumbling and spinning down. My immediate reaction was that some eager beaver in my flight had got there first, but no, they were all to my rear with no other fighters in the vicinity. The dying Messerschmitt continued its fiery descent and was almost consumed with flame when it finally hit the ground. Its demise was to remain a mystery, for back at Halesworth it was confirmed no other member of my flight had fired a shot. Other members of the A group had seen action and with red lights blinking many touched down on home plate after near three hours forty minutes in the air. B group also returned with a few victories and our standing for the day was ten in the air for one missing. Not until many years after the war did I learn that the Me 109 that so mysteriously ignited had been badly damaged in a fight with 78th Group P-47s and as we attacked its pilot baled out, unseen by us, opening his parachute at lower altitude.

After a day's respite the bombers again set out for Berlin. We were given the job of penetration support with B group following out right behind A group. While Schilling and Gabreski led, it was my turn to sit home and miss out on what was up to that time our biggest victory and severest loss, but making us also the first group to claim 300 enemy aircraft destroyed in the air.

In the Happy Hunting Ground things didn't go well at first. Near Dummer Lake the contrails of enemy fighters were seen at about 30,000 feet headed for the bombers and Dave Schilling started to climb his group towards them. What nobody saw was another large flock of enemy single-seaters below contrail level and while our pilots concentrated on the contrails ahead the Luftwaffe struck. We lost three planes and pilots in short order and some tough fighting ensued. Gabby's group was also bounced but their only loss in this melee was Tony Carcione. Somehow he became separated and cornered by enemy fighters. He immediately began screaming for help over the R/T. His panic calls prevented anyone getting a word in edgeways to find out his position to come to the rescue. Instead our people had to listen to his terrified yelling until his radio abruptly fell silent and they knew some Luftwaffe pilot had put the finger on him. One of the original pilots, Tony had made ace status and had only a few missions left to complete his tour. Time and again he had been told to cut his radio chatter but his nervous disposition always got the better of him. In the end it had been the downfall of this lively and likeable individual.

After fighting to break up Luftwaffe attacks on the bombers both our groups went to lower altitude to try and catch enemy fighters returning to their bases. This worked beautifully and most of the total 27 victories were obtained in this way; more than a third of all VIIIth Fighter Command claims this day. Once again the Jerries were caught off guard, having for so long enjoyed comparative immunity at lower altitudes, it was taking them a long while to catch on to our complete change of tactics. In short, they were now the people being hunted wherever they were; and the '*Wolfpack*' was in the fore. Our other missing pilot this day was Lieutenant Caleb Reeder, who baled out after being hit by flak at low altitude. Reeder was in the first bunch of replacement pilots we received back at Horsham. Among the successful combatants this day, Captain John Bennett and Major Walker Mahurin both made triple credits. Bud Mahurin had knocked down an FW 190 on the previous mission and had now run his score to twenty, which made him the first American ace in the ETO to reach the twenty mark. His old rival, Walt Beckham of the 353rd, had been shot down by ground fire a few days earlier. Our wild Pole was so busy chasing Germans he didn't watch his fuel gauges and only just made England, having to bale out when the tanks ran dry.

The bombers went to Berlin again next day and while we were hopeful of further success the Luftwaffe chose not to penetrate the overcast and no one in our two groups set eyes on an enemy aircraft.

The weather, which had been particularly nasty around this time with snow flurries and biting east winds, took a turn for the worse in that towering and extensive cloud hung over north-west Europe and restricted the few bombers sent out on radar-guided attacks. We stayed home and did housekeeping. We had done well but I was surprised that it warranted a visit by the top brass of the Eighth when unexpectedly told they would descend on us during the afternoon of Tuesday, 14 March — which happened to be thirtieth birthday. There wasn't much time to lay on anything special but we arranged a reception party and warned people to be properly attired. To have Spaatz, Doolittle, Kepner and Auton all in one go was an over-whelming honour. After the tour of inspection I was truly surprised to be asked to step forward and have General Spaatz pin a Distinguished Service Cross on my tunic. The citation attributed my performance in our first enemy airfield strafing and on the first big Berlin raid as the reason for this award. In truth this was nothing extrordinary and they were obviously hard put to cobble up something to justify my being given the Army's second highest decoration. This is not affecting modesty, for our pilots were doing the same sort of thing on most missions. That said, several pilots at Halesworth were deservedly wearing the deep blue ribbon with red and white edging on their tunics.

Our winning streak continued. On 15 March the bombers went to Brunswick and in the Happy Hunting Ground some fierce engagements netted us 24 for one. Bob Johnson downed three to raise his score to 22 and pass Mahurin. Next day I led A and Gabby B to support Fortresses on their way to Friedrichshafen. Soon after rendezvous with the B-17s we were able to break up a bunch of enemy fighters ahead of them and in tackling a number of fights we added another eleven scalps, Gabby getting two as did Fred Christensen, who had joined the 62nd Squadron as a replacement in the late summer of 1943. Everyone returned home which was particularly pleasing, enhancing our eight to one ratio of aerial victories to losses; by far the best in VIIIth Fighter Command.

The noses of all our P-47s were now painted bright red and for the remainder of hostilities this would be the distinguishing mark of the 56th amongst 8th Air Force groups. Following our idea to paint the noses of each squadron's planes in different colours, other units had besieged 'Ajax' for permission to use bright markings on their aircraft. Kepner decided to bring some sort of order to the scene by using coloured noses to identify individual groups and this was ordered on 13 March. I still figured we needed some high visibility markings for our squadrons and received permission to paint the rudders of 61st and 62nd aircraft red and yellow respectively. We were the only group to do this until late in 1944 when 'Ajax' adopted the idea for all its squadrons.

We did not know it at the time, but the late February to early March period of 1944 was to be our heyday as far as air fighting went. From now on the Luftwaffe would be more difficult to encounter. Already the P-51 Mustang equipped groups with the advantage of greater endurance than our P-47s were regularly running up substantial scores. The fitting of shackles under each wing of a P-47 allowed two 100 gallon drop tanks to be carried and offered better range. When the heavies went back to Berlin on 22 March we made use of this capability and for the first time pushed our endurance to over four hours.

This date we sent out three group formations on one mission, the C group being made up with aircraft not having the wing racks. I led A group and penetrated as far as Hagenow near Bremen. The Luftwaffe was not to be seen. In frustration I led my squadron down to shoot up locomotives and freight cars on the German railroad on the way home. B group, led by Schreiber, also went to town shooting up railroads and enemy shipping. Four pilots of the 61st in B group never came home. Three, all members of the same flight, were last seen entering the overcast. They either collided or were caught in violent turbulence and presumably crashed into the sea. The fourth, who became a PoW, was another loss to ground fire. What the Luftwaffe pilots could now rarely achieve, the flak gunner did with a vengeance. They were about to follow this left hook with a straight right that had me reeling.

On the 27th the bombers flew to southern France where the forecasters predicted weather clear enough for bombing Luftwaffe airfields. We didn't expect much in the way of air action and knew there would be some strafing. When the boys returned four were missing including two of our most experienced aces — Gerry Johnson and Bud Mahurin. The resourceful Gerry Johnson had picked up small-arms fire while strafing a column of military trucks. He bellied his P-47 in and was seen to get out of the cockpit. Lieutenant Robey, his number 3, thought he might be able to land and pick up Johnson. He called Gabby — who was leading A group — and received an affirmative to try. Then Robey found he had sustained battle damage to his aircraft as the flaps would not lower. The third member of the flight, Lieutenant Everet Everett, then attempted a landing but on approach his wing struck a tree. Barely managing to keep airborne, Everett headed for the coast and a little later apparently attempted a ditching in the sea. The Air Sea Rescue searched the area in vain.

Mahurin and his flight had come across a lone Dornier 217 bomber near Chartres which they promptly despatched. Its rear gunner was evidently a good marksman for his shooting hit Bud's plane, setting it afire. He baled out and was last seen running into a wood. Bud was a highly popular member of the group and long an inspiration to other pilots. Despite the attention he had received from newsmen on becoming the leading ace, he remained the same self-effacing character. His reaction on being shown a couple of articles describing his achievements was: 'Gee, I hope my mother doesn't see them — she'll worry herself sick.' It was genuine concern.

Around a quarter to eleven on the morning of 29 March I was in operations preparing for a mission to Brunswick when there was a sharp rending noise followed by screaming engines and a dull thud. Two B-24s from the nearby base at Hardwick had collided while forming up and crashed about four miles from our base. Fire fighters and ambulances were despatched to the scene immediately. About three quarters of an hour later there was a violent explosion which shook the building I was in. Outside a cloud of smoke, looking blue in the morning haze, wafted into the sky. My worst fears were more than realised: besides the B-24 crews, six people from our station were killed and 33 wounded, although I did not know the full extent of the casualties until after returning from the mission. Among the men killed was Stan Morrill, one of the best pilots in the 62nd with ten victories to his credit. Only two days before, he had belly-landed his badly shot-up Thunderbolt. Morrill had gone to the crash site with a bunch of helpers and apparently was trying to assist some of the medics when the explosion occurred. I would not detract from his courage in helping at the crash, but to me it was an unnecessary death. When there were people trained and equipped for rescue work it was no place for a valuable pilot to be. A deal of time and expense went into training fighter pilots for one basic purpose; to destroy the enemy. In performing that duty we put our lives on the line. Writing letters of condolence was a job I disliked; when for a life lost unnecessarily it sickened me.

On the day of the crash tragedy, in the hope of coming upon German fighters forming up to attack the bombers, I took a section of 63rd Squadron out ten minutes ahead of our main formation. At first, the only fighters seen were friendly, but later we spotted a small formation approaching which on investigation turned out to be a Staffel of Me 109s. We turned in behind them and saw that several other P-47 and P-51 formations had also seen them and were beginning to box them in. It was then they must have figured that if they were going to get out they'd better go now. So, individually or in pairs they peeled off to make vertical dives for clouds some 10,000 feet below. Finally the leader and three others were the only ones left and I began to catch up with them as they wriggled back and forth trying to find a place to go down. The leader finally turned broadside to me and I gave him a short burst with deflection in the hope of making him break downwards. Sure enough he rolled and down he went in an endeavour to gain the safety of a cumulus cloud. This fellow held it straight down for 10,000 feet while I followed and fired before finally deciding to let him go. In the pull out I completely blacked out, recovering to see my wingman, Lieutenant Archie Robey, still chasing the '109 in an almost vertical dive into the tops of clouds. The German was either a mighty brave man or extremely scared. Robey recovered and soon we were back together again and following along the bomber track.

In April we saw less and less air fighting and more and more ground strafing. When we did make claims for combat it was usually only in small numbers, whereas the P-51 groups, and in particular our old rivals the 4th Group, saw most of the air fighting and made the big scores. The ability to haul two wing drop tanks had given us only marginally more endurance in that once these were released we still had to rely on the internal fuel supply to get us home. As the most we could squeeze out of internal tankage was around an hour and a half's flying time, this became the restricting factor. We had been promised an extra capacity tank built into the P-47 but, like many things promised, it had yet to materialise.

The 56th was probably the genesis of more organisational and tactical developments than any other unit in the command. Everyone was encouraged to bend my ear and put up something new. My subordinates provided 95 per cent or more of the ideas that were adopted. The final decision on their worth may have been mine but the ideas usually came from someone else. We had given a lot of thought and discussion to the problems of ground strafing and came to the conclusion that better results and fewer losses could be obtained if we were thoroughly familiar with the topography in the area of our objectives. This was only possible if every group was assigned a specific limited area within which to operate, so that pilots could reasonably study and absorb a mental picture of the ground features and landmarks. I put the suggestion to 'Ajax'. Initially there was no response, probably because my past frank exchanges with Colonel Bobby Burns, the Operations chief, didn't help when I needed a sympathetic ear. However, I did have a good rapport with Colonel Larry Calahan who headed the Intelligence Section. He was quite enthusiastic and probably instrumental in getting the scheme adopted. As a result we were assigned Schleswig-Holstein, the German-Danish peninsular. Around 360 miles from our base, it was at extreme range and not the area I hoped we would get.

A great wad of maps and other material was sent down from 'Ajax' and some intensive study ensued until we could have drawn our assigned hunting ground blindfold. To improve our attack technique I flew over to the 355th Group at Steeple Morden to talk to Jonesey. Nobody seemed to use his real name — Szaniawski — because it was such a mouthful. Jonesey had recently achieved spectacular success leading his squadron in the impromptu strafing of an airfield and I was able to pick up some useful tips.

The first of these planned airfield strafing missions, involving around 450 fighters, was set up for 5 April. The low overcast may have offered us protection but visibility was bad enough to frustrate our effort. A few of the P-51 groups did have a field day. The second planned strafing mission, under the code word 'Jackpot II', was run on 15 April. Only the fighters went out that day and 600 of them ranged over specified areas of the Continent shooting up airfields. Total claims for all groups that day were forty enemy aircraft destroyed on their bases, another thirty damaged, and eighteen shot down. The losses were some of the heaviest ever sustained by US fighters; 33 missing in action.

The 56th was given airfields in the Elmshorn and Rendsburg areas. Taking the 24 P-47s of A group I climbed through the overcast and found only low broken cloud in the briefed locality. Not seeing anything on Hunsum airfield we proceeded north to Flensburg where several He 111s were parked. Heavy guns opened up and after moving away I descended with the 63rd Squadron to 8,000 feet to take a better look. About five miles from the airfield we dropped down to low level but losing my reference point on the airfield, I had to abort the pass.

After a diversion peppering a train, my wingman and I took another higher level look at the airfield then again came down to make a pass. Just as I approached the first of four Heinkels on a ladder-type dispersal, I noticed several aircraft bunched together on the left. Transferring my attention to this better target I opened fire only to quickly realise I was shooting up wrecks in the airfield boneyard! There was just enough time to turn back on my original targets, three of which were left blazing as I sped away low over the countryside to escape the flak. This and other passes by the group left a dozen Heinkels burning.

Another six enemy airfields were strafed by the other squadrons and our day's bag was five in the air and twelve on the ground with sixteen damaged. The cost of braving the heavy defences on these airfields was high. During the strike on Flensburg, Leroy Schreiber, leading the 62nd, took a direct hit. His P-47 was seen to climb to about 700 feet as if he were attempting to gain height to bale out. If so, he never made it for his aircraft stalled and spun in. Captain Dick Mudge was hit at another airfield but managed to bale out successfully. Captain Charles Harrison was shot down by FW 190s encountered. He was thought to have baled out but apparently was killed. Dick Mudge and Charlie Harrison were both original members of the 56th and near to the end of their tours. Schreiber, an outstanding pilot, tenacious, aggressive and competent, showed all the makings of an exceptional air leader. With fourteen victories he was one of our leading aces. Had he lived I would have expected him to go far in the service. We had done our duty but to lose such good men, who had done so well in air combat, to ground fire tinged my sadness with anger. The reliable Pete Dade was taken out of headquarters to fill the post of 62nd CO created by Schreiber's loss. I was concerned that if such attrition continued we would soon be short of good leaders.

Coupled with the Mustang's success, I noticed that the 56th was now being given slots in the bomber escort relay that were unlikely to provide opportunities of seeing combat. I was frequently voicing my displeasure to Colonel Bobby Burns at 'Ajax' until I must have become a constant thorn in his side. No doubt he viewed the irascible Zemke's protests as pique but it was not vanity that motivated me. The 56th had proved itself the most competent and accomplished fighter outfit in the command and it made sense to use us to advantage in knocking the hell out of Jerry. I was not above a little subterfuge. Jim Stewart had reached his 200 hours and I had word that 'Ajax' was looking for an experienced man to fill a vacant slot in their operations section. Jim was suggested and accepted. My hope was that he would look after the old firm in his new duties. This meant I had to find a new CO for the 61st and it was decided that Gabby could again shoulder the mantle as well as his duties as a deputy flying executive.

Early in April we had received notice that we would shortly have to move base. Halesworth was at last required for a B-24 group expected from the States in a few days and we were to move south to Boxted in Essex county. Boxted, like Halesworth, was built for bombers and had similar facilities and layout. However, it had been occupied for some time and was complete, its current tenants being the 354th Fighter Group, the 9th Air Force outfit which had introduced the Mustang to combat. They were going south to a sod strip in preparation for the cross-Channel invasion which we believed was imminent. We moved south on 18 April and around the same time our neighbours and friends, the 353rd, moved out of Metfield to end up just north of Boxted at Raydon. This was our fourth move while the other two older timers in VIIIth Fighter Command, the 4th and the 78th, remained snug in their centrally heated country clubs at Debden and Duxford. Still, Boxted was not as remote as Halesworth, being just outside the large town of Colchester and right beside a main highway to London. For all its discomforts, most of us must have had a touch of regret on leaving Halesworth that spring for it was here the 56th had experienced its great days.

13
DOGDAYS

The move to Boxted was completed in three days and without a break in operations. The squadrons flew down on the evening of the 18th after returning to Halesworth from a mission. I led the first operation from our new home the following morning. War waits for no man.

The group soon settled in and found the location had several advantages, not least that the soil when wet did not become the glue-like substance encountered at Halesworth. Like most wartime airfields in eastern England, Boxted had been prime farmland and the old farmhouse, Langham Lodge, stood close to the technical and operations site. Finding this to be substantially built and in fair order, it was earmarked for headquarters staff. There were six bedrooms which were allocated to myself, Schilling and the senior ground officers. My staff car driver did the housekeeping, cooking and running around for us. Relative to Halesworth, it was a comfortable billet and, predictably, soon known as the Wheel House to the troops.

With the change of base came new call signs for the group and squadrons. I was now Fairbank instead of Yardstick. The homing call of the Boxted control tower was Dogday. Instead of Keyworth, Woodfire and Postgate, the squadrons were now Whippet, Platform and Daily.

Around the time of our move to Boxted, Dave Schilling and several other pilots completed their tours and went home to the States on a month's leave. The imminent crisis caused by our surviving original pilot complement all reaching the 200 hour mark was temporarily avoided by allowing pilots to volunteer for a fifty hour extension and 25 more after that. Alternatively, men completing a tour could take a few weeks rest and recouperation in the States and then return to us, which several were doing. In the meantime we had a fairly rapid turnover in squadron commanders and other leadership appointments. This was one reason why I was pleased to take on board the RAF Poles with all their experience.

Around this time I received a 'phone call from General Curtis LeMay, who had returned to take up his command of the 3rd Bomb Division after our lecture tour in the States. As was expected, he came straight to the point. He had a Lieutenant Colonel Preston Piper in his command, a lead bomber pilot who had flown some pretty rough missions. Coming back from the shuttle to Africa back in August, Piper's B-17 had been forced to ditch. The crew got into a raft and spent a stormy night at sea during which two men were lost. The British rescue service fished the survivors out next day. As a result of this experience Piper developed an anxiety complex; not for his own safety, but for his men. He could no longer mentally shoulder the responsibility of his crew's lives. The answer was to put him in an aircraft where he had no crew; a fighter. Could I help? Yes, I was pleased to. Piper arrived soon after and shaped up well piloting a P-47.

We knew that sometime in the coming weeks the long talked of 'Second Front', the invasion of continental Europe from the UK, would take place. Just when was a matter of constant speculation. One thing was sure; when it did occur the Luftwaffe was unlikely to be a threat for in the past few months Allied fighters had established air supremacy over those areas within their range. Anyone reading the daily newspapers or listening to radio news bulletins might be given to thinking that Allied airpower was a continual presence over enemy territory. The truth was that our offensive operations only affected certain areas of the enemy's domain for perhaps a few hours at a time. He still enjoyed plenty of respite to lick his wounds, especially on days when the weather kept us on the ground. Happily, the spring weather was improving and we flew most days and often performed a second sweep or ground attack mission after a Ramrod. As the Luftwaffe now rarely put in an appearance within our range most escort missions were terminated by impromptu strafing of airfields or rail, road and water transport.

Since we commenced attacking his airfields, the enemy had built

After repair, following the battle damage of 2 September, my personal P-47 was transferred to the 63rd Squadron and became UN:S. I continued to fly it on most missions until my return to the States. To my knowledge, ten Luftwaffe aircraft fell to its guns. It was a good and trusty steed.

On 18 October 1943 the British awarded decorations to a number of USAAF officers, myself included. Wing Commander Al Deere, an RAF 'ace' who had given lectures on tactics to 56th pilots while we were in the States, was on hand to admire my DFC. One can see I had the cigarette habit bad!

Curtis LeMay, the most successful bomber commander of the war. We had a common interest in sporting guns.

'Schilling's Acres'. The abandoned farmhouse and outbuildings on Halesworth airfield resurrected by Dave Schilling and his men for the 62nd Fighter Squadron HQ and crew rooms.

Early in February 1944 our 'Bud' Mahurin (left) and the 353rd's Walter Beckham were running neck and neck as leading 8th Air Force aces with 15 air victories apiece. The P.R. people made much of this and both pilots were invited to Buckingham Palace to take tea with the young princesses.

Entertained by the English aristocracy on the occasion of a dinner party at Heveningham Hall. The attractive Mrs. Van Eck stands between Major Wilbur Watson and myself. Andrew Van Eck has his arm round Dave Schilling.

As a Flying Executive, Lieutenant Colonel Francis Gabreski led many missions and began to build an impressive score of victories. A good natured guy, Gabby was an all-round competent pilot and air leader. He is seen here with his Crew Chief, Staff Sergeant Ralph Safford.

My aircraft in the Service Group hangar at Halesworth for patching of the shell splinter holes collected on 24 February in the flaps and an elevator.

Major General Bill Kepner, cigar in hand, talking with Bob Johnson (centre), 'Bunny' Comstock (behind Bob) and me in the Halesworth Officers' Club on 14 March. The nose and cigarette clasping hands belong to Dave Schilling.

I never saw General Spaatz in a really relaxed mood. He wasn't the sort of man you tried to joke with. He tended to listen rather than speak and if he asked a question it was because he really wanted an answer. This photo shows me trying hard to give the right one during the 14 March visit.

This is what fire did on 16 March to my first UN:Z and wrote off a $100,000 airplane.

To lose two of our most successful pilots on the same day was a demoralising blow. Walker 'Bud' Mahurin, a 133 pound, unsophisticated, unaffected young man and a great fighter (left).

Gerald Johnson (right) was a darn nice guy and an excellent shot. 'Bud' had 21 victories when he went down and 'Gerry' 18.

Robert S. Johnson, probably the most aggressive fighter ace of the bunch. During an air fight on the first Berlin raid, Bob's squadron leader thought one of his flight fired at him by mistake. He asked Bob if he was responsible. Bob's calm reply was: 'Sir, if I opened my guns on you, you wouldn't be here asking the question.' It was said as a joke but it was true.

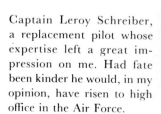

Captain Leroy Schreiber, a replacement pilot whose expertise left a great impression on me. Had fate been kinder he would, in my opinion, have risen to high office in the Air Force.

Gun camera film stills of the pass along the refuelling lines at Hunsun/
Flensberg airfield on 15 April 1944. The first He-111 was well hit but my angle
of attack was a bit steep. This aircraft caught fire as I passed over. The second
frame shows the second Heinkel catching fire and frame 3 my fire going into
the third aircraft as the second explodes. My wingman flew right through the
fireball to shoot the fourth Heinkel.

At Boxted Bob Johnson was reassigned to the 62nd Squadron to put in extra combat hours. On 8 May he claimed his last two victories as top ace in the ETO. Here he poses for the picture boys with Crew Chief Penrod.

Robert Rankin who knocked down five Me-109s — the last off my tail — during the 12 May battle.

up defences and improved dispersal of aircraft, so much caution was now required to achieve worthwhile destruction and keep losses low. As part of the pre-invasion programme, the heavy bombers pounded many airfields in France. We found that directly after the bombing we could often dive down and strafe aircraft or buildings still intact without much trouble from the anti-aircraft defences, the gunners still having their heads down. When the heavies plastered an airfield at Metz on 25 April, I took my flight down across the airfield as soon as the last bombs of the first wave had exploded. After the last wave of bombing another pass was made although then I appeared to be alone. As a result two Ju 88s that escaped the bombs were destroyed.

In pursuing this campaign to neutralise enemy airfields, 'Ajax' made increasing use of its fighters, particularly in a bombing role. On the 28th I led our first attempt at dive-bombing when mid-afternoon sixteen P-47s set out from Boxted each carrying a cluster of a dozen twenty-pound fragmentation bombs, while another eight aircraft provided top cover. Our objective was Orleans-Bricy airfield, south of Paris. As we flew across the Channel clouds thickened and the weather gradually deteriorated to a point where I decided to turn back. North-east of Paris, however, in the vicinity of Soissons, we found several breaks in the clouds and saw an unidentified airfield down below. The order to attack was given at which time the squadrons were flying at from 11,000 feet to 13,000 feet. The dives at the target were made at angles between 45 and 60 degrees, pointing our noses at the airfield and diving about three or four thousand feet before releasing the bombs and pulling up. Results were difficult to assess but if we did no more than put holes in the landing ground we were giving the hard-pressed enemy repair work.

During the early spring of 1944 the Luftwaffe had developed a tactic that proved highly successful in bringing down large numbers of our heavy bombers. It involved an assault group — called a Sturmgruppe — of heavily armed and armoured FW 190s which made a mass attack on a bomber formation, saturating the defensive fire. These assault Focke-Wulfs, being extra weighty, were very vulnerable if bounced by our fighters so the Germans provided a strong force of Me 109s to fly top cover to protect them. Together these formations could be composed of anything from fifty to over a hundred planes, requiring time to assemble and shrewd work by German ground control to keep them clear of our roving fighters. Since returning from the States I had often tried to persuade Colonel

Bobby Burns at 'Ajax' to send out a sweep ahead of the bombers to catch enemy fighters assembling to intercept. We knew from experience that Luftwaffe ground controllers directed assembly of the fighter units over prominent landmarks, notably Dummer and Steinhuder lakes if the bombers went into north-central Germany. I reasoned that a force of our fighters, arriving at such locations fifteen or twenty minutes before the bombers, could disrupt assembling Luftwaffe formations to such an extent that they would be unable to reform in time to meet the Forts and Libs. Following a few devastating Sturmgruppe attacks on our bombers, this suggestion was finally accepted for the mission to Berlin on 8 May.

Our A Group was scheduled to fly out to the Brunswick-Dummer Lake-Celle area and patrol until the bombers turned up. Gabby led and arrived in the assigned area on schedule but was unable to spot the enemy. The German ground controllers, with the aid of radar, were undoubtedly able to monitor our planes and keep their own out of the way. My pilots could only depend on their eyesight, which had its limitations. Not until the bombers droned into view did the Messerschmitts and Focke-Wulfs appear, mostly too far away from the Wolfpack to be caught before they disappeared into the abundant cloud. Gabby and the boys did manage some successful engagements, though, claiming six victories for the loss of one. Two of the enemy fell to the guns of Captain Robert S. Johnson elevating his personal score to 27 air victories. Bob had recently completed 200 hours' combat time and had asked for an extension. He was moved from the 61st to the 62nd Squadron which was currently short on experienced leaders.

America's top scoring fighter ace in World War I was Eddie Rickenbacker who attained 26 aerial victories on the Western Front. The newspapers had resurrected this figure for an American World War 2 ace to better and aroused much speculation as to who this would be. Don Gentile, a Mustang pilot of the 4th Group, had passed this figure but his total included a half dozen ground victories. Bob Johnson was the first in the ETO to surpass Rickenbacker with air victories and, at the time, it was thought in the whole USAAF. Later we learned that Richard Bong, flying in the South West Pacific against the Japanese, had run his victories' total past Rickenbacker's nearly a month before Bob Johnson. While not belittling Bong's achievement, he had started his score some seven months before Bob went into action.

Bob was cool, confident and a deadly shot. He learned his trade the hard way, having had some narrow scrapes in the early days, partly due to his lack of adherence to the rudiments of air discipline. The newsmen tried to present him as some sort of super warrior but Bob had the right philosophy. I once heard him counter their questions on what it took to knock a record number of enemy planes out of the sky and not end up as a number in a German ace's score with: 'You need good eyes and a good neck to survive. If you haven't those — you're a gonner!' Later, in some writings, it was said that I had deliberately placed Johnson in favourable positions on missions where enemy aircraft were likely to be encountered so that he stood a greater chance of enhancing his score, achieving more victories. This was not true. Bob Johnson, like other experienced pilots, flew flight and squadron leads but took his turn like all the others. Bob was a tenacious fighter pilot and needed no help from me. Such suggestions were an insult to his ability.

The Air Force was intent on obtaining the maximum publicity for air power through Bob's achievement and he received an immediate reassignment back to the States. We were sorry to lose him but he had played his part and it was my policy not to ask a man to chance his luck with a further tour unless he so wanted. As it happened Bob ended up in the clutches of Monk Hunter's 1st Air Force, where no doubt his experience proved invaluable.

At the time of Bob Johnson's ultimate victories good news came of another great Wolfpack ace Walker Mahurin, who had been shot down in late March and evaded capture, and was now back in London. A day or so later he arrived at Boxted, well and with a few extra pounds on his lean self. The French underground movement had hidden him on a farm until the RAF collected him one night from a secret landing strip and flew him back to England. Bud would have liked to return to operations and I was in need of men of his experience. This was not to be, for the authorities had a strict rule that any evader who came out via the escape organisations in occupied Europe could not fly combat again in the theatre. The ruling was sound for if the man had been unfortunate enough to be shot down again and captured, he might give information under interrogation that could endanger the lives of those who helped his escape. Mahurin stayed around for a couple of weeks until finally the expected orders came sending him back to the States. Like Bob Johnson, Bud never returned to Europe. After leave he went out to the South Pacific and added a Japanese scalp to his victory belt before the end of hostilities.

Having identified the problems that denied us greater contact with the enemy on 8 May, a good amount of thought was put to ways to improve our chances. I reasoned that to confuse the enemy ground controllers we required to break up our formation into individual flights to cover a far greater area of sky, and this would also give better chances of somebody sighting the enemy aircraft. A plan was devised whereby we would fly to a designated area as a group and, having reached that point, the various flights would fan out over a 180-degree arc. An extra section would be maintained in the centre so that if one flight called in enemy fighters this section could move out to help. If we went out well in advance of the bombers and employed these tactics we stood a good chance of picking up some of the Luftwaffe units assembling for a mass attack and would be able to break them up.

I flew down to put the idea to Burns and Kepner, believing personal approach the better to sell the idea to them. On this occasion they were quite receptive and approved what they termed 'The Zemke Fan'. As it happened, a vital mission was coming up next day, the first 8th Air Force bombing of Hitler's vital oil supplies, when substantial enemy reaction was anticipated. I flew back to Boxted to work out the finer details of the plan, knowing that of late when considerable Luftwaffe reaction was forecast it didn't materialise. As it transpired high command was right and the Zemke Fan proved successful. In fact, a bit too successful for my liking.

When the teletype machines chattered out the Field Order in the small hours of 12 May, Group Operations learned that the bombers' targets lay in south central Germany involving deep penetration. We were to go out twenty minutes before the bombers and sweep the Frankfurt area. We arranged for an A group consisting of three eight-plane squadrons to fly to a prominent bend in the River Rhein some 35 miles south of Coblenz, where the three squadrons would then fan out. Five minutes behind would come B Group, also composed of three eight-plane squadrons, who would sweep round in the Koblenz-Frankfurt area and come to the assistance of A Group if called. I would lead A Group and Gabby B.

The day dawned fine and at 09:46 hours I was on my way leading the eight P-47s of the 63rd Squadron which made up the first section. Lieutenant Willard Johnson flew as my wingman in Daily White flight with Lieutenant Colonel Preston Piper leading the second element and Lieutenant John McDonnell as his wingman. Piper, the bomber leader sent to me by LeMay, had previously flown six trips with us and was shaping up well. As we climbed out towards the Continent to make landfall over the prominent coastal estuary near Knocke, my attention was drawn to McDonnell's aircraft. He was experiencing some sort of mechanical trouble and with a waggle of his wingtips peeled off and turned back. Piper would now have to operate as a second wingman to me. We continued our cruise climb to conserve fuel, making 22,000 feet by the time the bend in the Rhine appeared below, the point at which the 61st Squadron flights turned north towards Marburg, the 62nd's south for Mannhiem, while I took the 63rd ahead in the direction of Giessen, White Flight fanning out to the north and Red to the south.

After some 40 miles I turned to begin a north-south patrol. All three of us scanned the hazy horizons of the blue void, periodically dropping a wing to get a better view below where we hoped to spot enemy aircraft forming up. No moving specks observed, I flipped the radio switch to the Bomber-Fighter channel for word of action elsewhere. Nothing. Flipping the switch back I just caught the electrifying alarm: 'Fairbank, Break Left.' The instinctive reaction was violent movement of stick and rudder pedals. As the Thunderbolt skidded round I was conscious of the all-too familiar white puffs — time-fuzed cannon shells exploding. In the next fraction of a second I glimpsed the shape of an Me 109 and then others above. Throttle to the firewall; cut in water injection. 'Fairbank to Daily White Flight. Turn in trail, make a Lufbery.'

Obviously outnumbered, until I had time to size up the situation the protective turning circle with each of us covering the man ahead's rear was my reaction. It was a mistake; we were picking up speed too slowly and I could now see there were seven Me 109s about 5,000 feet above waiting to pick us off. They had advantages in altitude and speed and periodically launched an element of two to come down, shoot at us and then recover; the same tactics as we so often pulled on some unsuspecting Luftwaffe outfit. As we turned I made repeated calls for assistance hoping another of our flights was near. Suddenly a single Me 109 cut across our circle and took a deflection shot at Johnson's plane. Flames enveloped the fuselage and the Thunderbolt turned over and disappeared from view. Where was help? I called again. Piper and I tightened our circle.

Desperation rather than fear gripped me as I looked for an opening to escape. If we attempted to dive our initial acceleration would be sluggish and they could nail us before we built up sufficient speed. Then the lone Me 109 repeated its previous act: diving down across our circle he opened up with a deflection shot on Piper. Again, out of the corner of my eye, I saw smoke and flame erupt. Two down, one to go. Fear took hold, in that racing jumble of thought the prospect of death spun by. Is this the exit for Mrs Zemke's little 'Hoo-bart'?

Perhaps my dread would have been all the greater had I known that the pilot I had just seen despatch Johnson and Piper was the third ranking ace of the Luftwaffe, Major Gunther Rall, commanding II/JG11, with more than 200 victories to his credit. The fact is, there is no time for such conjecture when one instinctively knows termination of life is possibly but seconds away. And it was only a matter of time before an enemy slipped in behind my violently turning Thunderbolt to claim the final scalp. With a shouted oath to spur myself into action, I took the only possible course to escape. With violent movement of the controls, I rolled UN-Z over with a fast aileron flip and headed vertically for the ground, barrel rolling as I went to make a difficult target for my pursuers. Down, full power, into the realms of compressibility. By the time the altimeter had unwound a couple of times and the airspeed indicator had hit the peg, the Thunderbolt was rumbling and vibrating so much I expected it to fly apart. It was time to start recovery; cutting power, centralising the stick to stop the barrel roll, and starting a long and gentle pull back to bottom out at around 5,000 feet. A quick glance over each shoulder and a buck to clear my tail. To my relief no frontal view of a Messerschmitt in hot pursuit or blinking cannon. Perhaps they couldn't catch me; perhaps they thought I was out of control.

Shaken and damp with sweat, I turned the faithful UN-Z westward, putting on altitude again as rapidly as I could and oscillating my head as it had never turned before. I was now conscious that the R/T was filled with the staccato calls of combat; the rest of the group must also be seeing plenty of action. Near Wiesbaden, just as I had passed 12,000 feet, the adrenalin surged. I caught sight of four Me 109s coming in on my tail. Again, vicious action with the stick and the P-47 skidded round to meet them in good time. The '109s flashed past. Full throttle, water injection and into a barrel roll, heading for the ground in a steep dive. Once more this tactic appeared to work for, when pulling out a few thousand feet above the fields there was no sign of my assailants. This was quite enough activity for one day and a 290 degree magnetic course was set for England, climbing to gain altitude as fast as possible and twisting my neck as never before. I had just topped 20,000 feet when a quick glance down as I crossed the Rhine south of Coblenz, picked up four '109s circling about 5,000 feet below me. The aggressive mood was quick to assert itself: the plan was a quick bounce from my superior altitude and a fast dive away for home.

I started to circle to make the attack when another glance revealed several more aircraft assembling on the original four. Caution reigned as I continued to circle and watched more fighters join the formation down below. I had wound up directly above a Luftwaffe assembly point, just what we had been seeking to do in developing the Zemke Fan — but instead of a sizeable bunch of Wolfpack eager beavers poised for the kill there was, ironically, only the lone originator of the scheme. My throttle hand depressed the radio microphone switch: 'Fairbank Leader to all Fairbank and Subway ships. I need help fast. Angels 20. South Coblenz.' I continued to call for help as the force below me grew to an estimated thirty in number, a whole fighter Gruppe. With each orbit they gained altitude and as they went up so did I, to maintain my advantage. For more than fifteen minutes I continued to circle, climbing and calling for assistance. Eventually I topped 29,000 feet and contrails began to stream back from the Thunderbolt. They should have given me away to the Jerry formation but the contrails did enable two 61st Squadron pilots, Lieutenants Rankin and Thornton, to spot me and radio their presence.

As soon as the two red-nosed P-47s appeared below and around a half mile away, I told them to give me top cover while making my bounce. So, wing over and down into a fairly steep dive, picking out a lonesome Me 109 on the outer portion of the enemy formation. By the time I was behind in firing position it presented a sixty to ninety degree deflection shot and over two rings of lead were laid off in the sight before squeezing the trigger. From the tracers my aim was seen to be too far ahead of my target so I continued firing, letting the '109 fly right through my bullet pattern. Strikes were seen along the fuselage before superior speed necessitated an abrupt pull back on the stick to avoid ramming my victim. Zooming up in a climbing turn, a quick peep over the shoulder revealed the '109 in flames and the pilot baling out. Foolishly I let elation momentarily take charge: 'I got him,' I yelled into the radio, only to hear an abrupt 'Fairbank, Break Left'.

The senses reeled from elation to fear as once more instantaneous movement of the controls brought me round to find four Me 109s coming straight towards me. Turning a half roll to the west with full power and a dive, I was ready to outrun them if they pursued. A squint back revealed I was again alone. Looking at the fuel gauge, it revealed 125 gallons of gasoline for the 340 miles to the safety of England. An hour and a quarter trip; it would be close. Boost and throttle settings were adjusted for optimum economy; while there could be no relaxation of neck muscles across Belgium although a further encounter with the enemy was unlikely. It was past two o'clock in the afternoon when the wheels of my P-47 touched the runway at 'Dogday', some four hours and twenty minutes since leaving. It was a tired, shaken group commander who gave his interrogation report. Afterwards, probably for the first time in my life, I took refuge in really drinking alcohol; I went to London, took a room at the Dorchester and got stupid drunk.

The Zemke Fan had certainly brought the action we sought for both A and B groups had seen plenty to claim, in all eighteen victories for three losses. Bob Rankin, our pint-sized pilot, had made group history by shooting down five of the enemy on one mission, the fifth from my tail. The principal error had been in using only flight strength forces at an altitude where they were vulnerable to attack from above. Despite our high claims the loss of two wingmen was not easily dismissed from my mind, for I believed both to be dead. Happily, we eventually learned that all three 56th pilots that went down that day had survived. Also unknown at that time, Major Gunther Rall, who had disposed of my wingmen and was probably poised to take me, was later pursued and shot down by Captain Joe Powers and Flight Officer Vitale of the 62nd Squadron. A bullet severed Rall's left thumb but by a remarkable piece of airmanship he managed to parachute from his crippled Messerschmitt at low altitude. Despite his serious injury, this distinguished pilot returned to the cockpit of a fighter before the end of hostilities.

'As far as I am aware, Lieutenant Colonel Preston Piper was the first of many 8th Air Force bomber pilots to change to fighters. He was by no means the last. Following General LeMay's request that we take Piper, it occurred to me that volunteer tour-expired bomber pilots could be useful in view of the current dearth of replacement fighter pilots from the States. This was proposed and apparently approved by Kepner and Doolittle. We were allowed to recruit an experimental cadre of six to see how they fared. There was no lack of recruits when the B-17 and B-24 bases were circulated; presumably the idea of dealing out some punishment to the Luftwaffe after having been on the receiving end appealed to many bomber men and there was no lack of volunteers.

Interviewing and making the final selection was a time-consuming job, nor did I appreciate how much effort had to be devoted to training these men in fighter formations, tactics and gunnery. In fact, we didn't have the time to fully train them at Boxted. Of those first six pilots received in May, five were soon lost. Many other ex-bomber pilots transferred to fighters during the final year of hostilities and their loss rate continued to be much higher than that of men trained in fighters from the outset. To hazard a guess why, I would say that it was the difficulty in taking the step from the comparatively slow sit and take it philosophy of the bomber cockpit to the instant gut reaction necessary to survive in the world of fighters.

We next had an opportunity to try the Zemke Fan on 22 May. The heavies were going to Kiel and we were to sweep ahead in the Munster area to try and catch the Luftwaffe Gruppen in the act of assembling. This time we flew to Dummer Lake and split up into three sixteen-plane squadrons with each having a section flying high as top cover. The 61st went north towards Bremen, the 63rd southeast to Paderborn, while I led the 62nd to Hanover. This time my squadron encountered no enemy fighters so we made our way home, livening up the German railroad system and perforating a number of barges. Back at Boxted I learned that the 61st Squadron had been involved in extensive combat having come across a force of German fighters that had just risen from an airfield. Led by Gabby there had been some stiff fighting with two of our men shot down against claims of twelve. Gabby had accounted for three FW 190s and Jim Carter and Evan McMinn two each. Gabreski now had 22 air victories and was at the top of the ace tree. Until now, this efficient, deadly operator had been quietly working away for months just outside the limelight that was accorded the top aces.

No sooner had we been interrogated than many pilots were required at briefing for a fighter-bomber raid against an important bridge at Hasselt in Holland. The operation was basically experimental, to discover the best method of hitting bridges. Each P-47 carried two 500 pound bombs. One section flew across the target at heights varying from 100 to 1,500 feet releasing in level flight. The next section tried glide-bombing, coming down in gentle angle dives and unloading at 8,000 feet while the third tried vertical dive-bombing from 10,000 feet, releasing and pulling out after 4,000 feet. We all missed.

For this mission I had my new Superbolt, the name we gave to the P-47D-25 model incorporating two significant changes. The first, giving the Thunderbolt a completely different profile, was a one-piece, clear cockpit canopy. It provided excellent all round visibility and helped cut down the fatigue in neck twisting. The only drawback was that the rear fuselage cockpit fairing had been removed, affecting the directional stability of the aircraft. The other welcome change was an enlarged internal fuel tank providing an extra 65 gallons. This allowed us to take the maximum advantage of our external tanks for we could push much further into Germany and still be able to return on internally held fuel. For the moment, however, we had only three Superbolts assigned.

Fighter-bombing became an increasing mission requirement as May drew to a close. The accuracy of our attacks was generally poor and there was much discussion on how this could be improved. I still favoured the medium altitude formation bombing technique used by the true bombers. While I was back in the States the group had tried this, flying behind a Liberator whose bombardier sighted for them. The heavy bomber was so slow it made it difficult to keep in formation, apart from providing a good target for flak gunners. Cass Hough and his team at Bovingdon decided that the technique could be successfully used by fighters if a faster aircraft was used to carry the bombsight. They set about removing the guns from the nose of a P-38 Lightning to provide a compartment for a bombardier. Known as a Droopsnoot, some success had been achieved with these special P-38s leading bomb carrying normal Lightnings in raids on airfields. I figured we could obtain a better bomb pattern with a tight-knit formation of P-47s behind a Droopsnoot and requests were sanctioned by 'Ajax'. I was ultimately allowed to borrow a Droopsnoot from the 20th Group together with its bombardier, Lieutenant 'Easy' Ezzel. Having a little P-38 experience I was the pilot and on the afternoon of 30 May we set out with 24 bomb-decked P-47s following to try and take out a rail bridge at Creil, east of Paris.

The bomb load was too heavy; we should have had 500 not 1,000 pounders as the climb out was too slow and the P-47s wallowed around trying to keep close. Our target was identified and we began our run from the north. We were immediately met with a host of exploding shells, too close for comfort. The formation started to disperse so I gave orders to abandon the run. Further down the same rail line we picked out another bridge, around five miles from the first at Chantilly. 'Easy' mastered the Norden sight and 32 1,000 pounders went down from 12,000 feet on his signal with direct hits and the destruction of three spans of the bridge. The flak didn't reach us here. On this showing I was eager to retain the Droopsnoot, but the 20th wanted it back urgently.

The following morning the heavies continued their disruption of marshalling yards in north-west Europe and I led the 56th as part of their escort. Having no contacts in the air we went down to look for strafing targets and found Gutersloh airfield loaded with enemy aircraft and only light flak opposition. Back at Boxted a 'phone call to Colonel Burns and to our friends next door, the 353rd Group, resulted in a return to Gutersloh that evening to finish what we had started. It was anticipated that the Luftwaffe would not expect to see American fighters over its bases again that day which proved the case. After we had finished dive bombing, Colonel Duncan took the 353rd down. Flying at 21,000 feet with the 62nd Squadron as top cover, I heard Gabby warn his squadron there were bogies coming in from the south-east. He had mistaken us for enemy: I called and told him my twelve planes were south-east of him. Very pointedly he assured me he was looking at a lot more than twelve.

With the rest of my squadron I began to peer around in the haze: nothing. So we continued to circle over Gutersloh. Then I happened to look over my left shoulder and saw thirty plus bogies two miles in the back of us at our level. The order was given to step up the power and investigate. The squadron was only halfway through a turn to meet them before part of the gaggle peeled off to attack the 63rd which was climbing at around 14,000 feet after bombing. This squadron was in a very vulnerable position and could have taken heavy losses but for atrocious shooting by the enemy and the presence of heavy haze that enabled them to run and be hidden.

Calling repeatedly to the 353rd Group below to scatter, Platform White Flight was taken into a steep left climb in an endeavour to pull an attack on the enemy from above. The main enemy formation, still fairly well bunched, also began to climb and moved rapidly ahead of us. Then the flak batteries opened up on them but they avoided this and began to turn back towards Gutersloh. During our pursuit I continually called out the position of the FW 190s in the hope that other squadrons would join up to help box these Jerries in. Gabby radioed that he did not have enough fuel and the 353rd apparently didn't hear me. The decision was taken to attack with my lone flight and at least break up the enemy formation.

We were now at 26,000 feet, just above and behind them and in a good position to launch an attack. A straggling weaver on the left flank was picked out and I closed to 300 yards. The concentration of my fire hit him with a hell of a jar, and pouring smoke, the Focke-Wulf fell away into an uncontrolled spin. The rest of the formation continued on its way, obviously unaware of the danger behind them. Slipping my aim onto another FW 190 nearby, I gave it a lengthy burst and smoke began to appear. At that moment I realised I was over-running an FW 190 to my right which would endanger my own position. Thus I transferred my attention and fire to this enemy. A long burst and he started to come apart and fell off burning. A fourth Focke Wulf ahead was brought into my sight but surprise was now lost and this one began to turn into me as I closed spraying bullets around him.

The warning flow of tracers from my guns told me ammunition was exhausted so I rolled away to the right and did not see what happened to my last target. On looking round all that was to be seen were specks in the distance and several flak bursts. This combat had taken place in the space of two minutes, during a single pass in which 1,789 rounds of ammunition had been delivered from the guns of my Superbolt — which couldn't have helped barrel life. When my flight reformed we took another look at Gutersloh. We left the scene with hangars and a fuel store on fire. A highly successful outing.

Our strafing and bombing of airfields had highlighted the inadequacy of the intelligence with which we were supplied by higher headquarters. The Luftwaffe continually moved its units from airfield to airfield in an effort to avoid losses to air attack and our intelligence data was frequently out of date. Often the target information sheets received were weeks old and only good for papering the walls of the briefing room. On most missions we could not hang around to study airfields we passed over, to say little of the fallibility of human eyesight and memory regarding what was on them. Sometimes we couldn't even identify the airfield location. The answer was clear: cameras, so that we could generate our own up-to-the-minute intelligence. With photographs our own headquarters staff could assess potential targets, identify them positively and pinpoint anti-aircraft defences.

Once again we called on Cass Hough's Bovingdon boys and they soon came up with a K-25 model camera fixed to the back of the armour plate in my Superbolt — which was ideal because of the unrestricted one-piece canopy. The camera had a powerful lense and took 3½ by 4½ inch size negatives. Operation was by a control button placed on the stick. To take photos it was necessary to bank the aircraft to ninety degrees and it must have mystified many German watchers on the ground to see a P-47 detach itself from a formation, dive down and fly on its side for a half mile or so before climbing back to join its pals.

14
D-DAY — AND A DILEMMA

After returning from an uneventful sweep over the Pas de Calais on the afternoon of 5 June, a message was received from 'Ajax' summoning me to a group commanders' meeting at 16:00 hours. The caller emphasized that I was to come by staff car and not fly. Normally I would take a P-47 and go to Bovingdon and from there by staff car to Bushey Hall, a far less time-consuming way to go. A week previously a similar summons had come in to go to 'Ajax' by car and on that occasion nothing unusual had come up at the group commanders' meeting. After dinner we had returned to our bases without receiving any explanation for the requirement to travel by road. My driver and I tootled off in the staff car along the widening roads to Watford.

Immediately on entering Bushey Hall I sensed something was up; security was tight with guards posted. This was it, tomorrow D-Day, the long talked-of cross-Channel invasion. Excitement was high; our briefing thorough. The 56th was assigned to patrol an area from Boulogne to the north of the Seine, a squadron mission at a time, all day long. Torpedo planes were expected to be brought down from Norway and we must watch for these. The reason for the insistence on road transportation was now plain: each group commander was provided with a large quantity of plans. No risk could be taken with these in the air lest someone got lost in bad weather and ended up across the other side. The previous trip to 'Ajax' had obviously been a trial run. No cocktails and dinner this time.

It was around 11 o'clock when I got back to Boxted. Robby and the other intelligence officers were called to the briefing room and the door locked. The base became as tight as a prison with guards posted and no one allowed out. I never went to bed that night and I doubt if anyone got much sleep. The maintenance crews had received orders to paint black and white stripes on the planes in the late afternoon and must have guessed something special was coming. Those in the know were tight-lipped but I guess most everyone had a good idea what it was. That night the noise of aircraft engines was never-ending. Red, green and yellow flares were scattered in the darkness by bombers grinding round in assembly. Gabby led our first mission off soon after 03:30 hrs. Group commanders were not allowed to fly during the initial stages of the landing as we knew too much about the operation, so I had to sit around and watch our squadrons come and go. We expected the whole of the Luftwaffe in the west to be thrown into the battle but as the day wore on it was clear that was not to be. As Eisenhower had prophesied, the planes over the invasion beaches were ours.

So that pilots could catch some sleep we erected cots in the Squadron Ready Rooms and arranged for meals to be served to them there. The mess halls were set up for 24 hour service to let ground crews feed whenever they had a chance: the whole station worked round the clock. After daybreak I managed to catch a few hours sleep.

It was evening before I was off the hook and could fly on operations. The seventh and last mission of the day was coming up, a fighter-bomber Type 16 where we would be under radar control. I led 31 aircraft of the 61st and 62nd Squadrons off at 18:45 hrs, skirted round the invasion beachhead to Rouen and Evreux where the 61st dive-bombed the airstrip at Fanville. The controller then gave us a vector towards Bernay where enemy aircraft were supposed to be. We found none so swept east towards Dreux. Soon we came across blue-nosed Mustangs of the 352nd Group strafing a parked ammunition convoy. We joined the party which was later interrupted by some FW 190s. Two Mustangs were seen to go down. As we climbed our P-47s to gain advantage I saw a single FW 190 trying to sneak up on one of our lower elements. Turning right and down to attack him, he saw me coming, changed his mind and fled to the west. Because of my superior altitude I rapidly overtook him in the dive. The Focke-Wulf pilot then broke right to engage me and as I came in behind him he tightened his turn, suddenly losing control and spinning down straight into the ground. I never fired a shot.

Reforming my flight, we headed back towards the area of the air battle. Another lone FW 190 was seen ahead and as I began to race for position on him a P-51 came slicing out of the blue to fire on the enemy at close range. The Focke-Wulf immediately burst into flames and the pilot baled out. He was a half mile ahead when his 'chute opened and I could see his clothes were afire and flames licking round his head. Fixing the descending pilot in my sight I opened fire to end his pain and misery. Had I been in that dreadful situation I would have wanted the same deliverance. On this mission the 56th suffered its only loss of D-Day when Flight Officer McMinn was brought down while strafing the road convoy.

The group flew even more missions on the 7th, patrolling and fighter-bombing in its assigned area. The danger in ground attack was again made plain, for all four of the planes lost that day went down while bombing or strafing. There was also more Luftwaffe activity and in various combats we claimed twelve without loss. I went out with the 61st Squadron in the late afternoon and dive-bombed the rail yards at Gournai. Afterwards we wandered south-west in the quest of enemy road and rail activities. While at 10,000 feet, just north of the Seine, I thought I saw a truck convoy on a road. Instructing Bob Rankin to provide top cover with his section, I told mine to follow me down to investigate. My convoy proved to be large heaps of stones piled at intervals along the road! As we were climbing back through some low cloud Rankin called in bandits. They hit us from above and everyone broke to meet them as fast as possible. I fired at a couple of FW 190s, more to make them break than hit them, and immediately had to perform some fancy evasive action to escape an Me 109 who was firing at me.

Recovering, six aircraft were seen two or three miles to the west so I continued to hold full power and climb in their direction. Checking my tail I saw my wingman was missing — I would learn later he had been shot up during the encounter. Although gaining altitude in my pursuit of the six bandits, I was gradually falling further behind until only two could be seen some ten miles ahead. Just as I considered abandoning the chase these two suddenly executed a turn and started to fly south-east towards Paris. This allowed a corner-cutting manoeuvre to bring me closer and to again pick up the other four aircraft, which were about five miles ahead of the trailing two. With the advantage of altitude my attack was launched from the rear on the two stragglers. In the dive to position behind their tails the familiar shapes of P-47s with red noses were recognised; I was bouncing my own men who had been chasing the four Germans. Over the radio orders were given for the P-47s' pilots to join with me and together pursue the four aircraft ahead. Resuming the climb I turned to find the P-47s had disappeared; I could only think they had misinterpreted my instructions.

Consideration was given to abandoning the chase for the supposed bandits were now specks in the blue, besides which I was one lone Thunderbolt deep in hostile airspace. Then it was noticed that the specks were climbing and figuring this would slow their speed, I succumbed to the temptation to see if a sneak kill could be made. South of Paris the four aircraft turned right onto a westerly heading enabling me to cut off considerable distance. Now around 7,000 feet higher I was still some distance behind. They flew in the same wide company front formation as we did but I was now pretty sure they were FW 190s. Very conveniently, near Chartres, they performed a 180 degree turn and headed east; probably on patrol looking for Allied aircraft and so far unaware of one busily stalking them.

Having established they were definitely FW 190s, my plan was to drop down to their level — 22,000 feet — pick off one and evade by diving if the others turned to pick a fight. When a little over a mile to the rear in my closing dive, the leader did a 45 degree turn south-east and the others started crossing over to reform on him. Picking out the last man, I hit him squarely with about fifty rounds and he went spinning down in flames.

To my amazement the rest of the formation completed their turn as if nothing had happened. Evidently they hadn't seen their comrade go. I was now about 300 to 400 yards behind the element leader of the fellow just shot down. As I was preparing to despatch him similarly he suddenly started rocking his wing tips; he thought I was his wingman! To keep him thinking that way, I gave a brief rock of my own wings in return. I could imagine this fellow shouting into his radio mike: 'Hans, you bastard, move up in line abreast and stop flying in back of me.'

Opening up on the Focke-Wulf, I fired a long burst until it nosed over and went straight down. Unbelievably the other two '190s still continued merrily on their way. Sliding over behind the lead flight leader I fired. My tracers showed just as I hit him — the warning that ammunition is about to run out — and the game was up. He kicked his rudder and rolled over into a dive. As I swung over to shoot at the last man he too rolled away down. Climbing for more altitude and safety I could see both the survivors diving away at full speed.

This had been another classic example of unwary pilots who never saw what hit them. Surprise was frequently the major success factor in air fights. Without surprise, if he saw you coming, he could usually evade and live to fight another day.

Arriving back at Boxted I found Captain Zbigniew Janicki orbiting the field. His aircraft was shot up in the original mêlée and he could not lower his landing gear. I flew alongside him around the base as he tried to shake it down. It wouldn't budge so I radioed for him to belly in by the Dogday tower. This big blond handsome Pole disappeared on another dive-bombing mission a few days later. Calling in that his engine was running rough, he bid adieu to his comrades and said he was going to land. That was the last we saw or heard of him and his fate remains a mystery. I carry an inward feeling that Janicki's war didn't end with his descent into France. Knowing the hatred these Poles had for the Nazis, he was the sort of individual who would have tried to carry on the war on the ground.

My admiration grew for our little band of Poles who were ever eager to have a crack at the Jerries and could be relied upon to fly and fight well. My only real confrontation with them was over their habit of excitedly reverting to Polish in the heat of battle and jabbering away among themselves as if the radio channel was solely their domain. Some strong language was needed to drive the point home to stick to English and that they must not jam up the radio channel. Thereafter we still had a few lapses in the heat of battle when the odd Polish oath would float through on the radio waves, although nothing we couldn't live with.

In the weeks following D-Day we continued to act as flying artillery on the majority of our missions, dive bombing marshalling yards, bridges and communication checkpoints in France. Sometimes we returned to the same target again and again, notably at Argentan. There was a lumber yard beside the tracks and we hit that so often the timber must have been matchsticks. The pace of activity immediately before and after D-Day was tremendous; in June alone the 56th went out on fifty combat missions. Only really bad weather kept us on the ground. We lost ten pilots during the month, most, but not all, to light flak. One pilot was so low his plane was engulfed in flame from the ammunition railcar his bombs exploded. Another couldn't clear a wooded hill after making a strafing pass, and a third, who had come safely through the flak thrown up during a dive bombing mission, carelessly pulled up into the prop' of another P-47 while in the circuit to land.

I was not above a dash of foolishness myself. The group was dive-bombing La Perthe airfield, just south of Paris. As the new P-47 I was flying did not have wing shackles fitted I wasn't carrying bombs and stayed upstairs to direct the show and give top cover. Me 109s had been seen landing just before our attack so after the bombing I dropped down to investigate. Just as I approached the end of the field in a fast dive the engine faltered and cut. The immediate thought was that flak had finally done for me. Calling over the radio something to the effect that I'd had it, I prepared to crash-land on the other side of the field. Momentarily I looked down at the fuel switch: it was still turned to the auxiliary supply. A quick flip followed by a few coughs from the trusty Pratt & Whitney up front and it thundered back to life. Loss of speed and this clumsy approach found my P-47 accelerating away above the tree tops and out of range of the ground fire my act had attracted. Orbiting over the field I had forgotten to check my fuel gauges and switch from the drop tank to the main tank, the former draining dry as I had started my run on the airfield. It scared the hell out of me and this lapse probably generated some amusement in the Officers' Mess that night.'

Flight Lieutenant Witold 'Lanny' Lanowski was one of the two Polish pilots who remained with the 56th Fighter Group until the end of the war (the other was Squadron Leader Michael Gladych). Lanny's keen eyesight and considerable experience in air fighting was frequently utilised in the leading elements of the 56th Fighter Group. He found the organisation much to his liking:

'When I arrived at Boxted I quickly became aware that Zemke's Wolfpack was something special. There was an atmosphere about the place; you quickly became aware you were part of an elite organisation. We never saw much of Hub Zemke in the Officers' Club. When he wasn't in his office working or inspecting some part of his organisation he would disappear. Quite often he would be lying on his bunk quietly thinking. He was alway thinking up ways and means to improve the group's performance. On the other hand, he was always receptive to ideas from others. If the newest Second Lieutenant in the outfit thought up something, Hub would give it as much consideration as if it came from an old hand.

'Zemke was strict; he kept a tight rein. This was part of his success. If someone fouled up or did something foolish, Zemke fined him, hard, whoever he was. But he applied the same rule to himself. On one operation he led things went wrong. Afterwards, at the critique, he got up before all the pilots and announced: "I made a mess of that, fellows. I'm fining myself £5." In all my long experience in the military he is the only commander I have ever heard publicly admit he made a mistake.'

★   ★   ★

Early in July the group had a four day run of successes in the air, the most fruitful days for several weeks. After a slow start the Luftwaffe had brought several Gruppen of fighters and fighter bombers into France, the first to harass our fighter-bombers and the second to attack our ground forces. They were still overwhelmingly outnumbered in the air but they could cause some hurt. To make life more difficult for them, a regular pounding of their airfields was carried out. We were sent to disrupt rail traffic in France on the afternoon of Independence Day but because of weather Ground Control told us to look for targets of opportunity. Cumulus was piled high over Boxted and, with each of the 48 planes lugging two 250-pound bombs and a 150-gallon drop tank, a slow orbit through the clouds was necessary until we could break out and get into formation at 10,000 feet. The billowing undercast extended over France to our target area and we were eventually forced to seek places where the cloud was broken and go down to attack targets on the railroads, a squadron at a time. When I sent the 62nd Squadron down, Conches airfield was found in the clear with some thirty enemy aircraft seen flying low in the vicinity, plus top cover several thousand feet above. Battle ensued. The low flying Me 109s appeared to be fighter bombers and were heavily bounced by our P-47s. Dogfights ranged all over the sky, only I couldn't participate, having exhausted just about all my ammo strafing. We came home with twenty victories for the loss of one. It put us past the 500 mark in air victories and gave us our 38th ace — Captain James Carter.

Next day Gabby led the group to meet a force of B-17s returning to the UK from Italy following a shuttle bombing trip to Russia. The Wolfpack came home with eleven destroyed claims, one of which was Gabby's 28th, making him the ETO ace of aces. In fact, no other American pilot flying against the Germans would top his score. Francis Gabreski had long proved himself to be an excellent all-round fighter pilot. Additionally, he was a good leader and had conducted many of the group's most successful missions. Occasionally Gabby's natural exuberance got the better of him. For example, one day I was off base and returned to Boxted unexpectedly to find P-47s diving down and rocketing up. Gabby was leading a buzzing party. He and the other offenders were duly fined for there were no exceptions in my rule book. Flying Executives could buy the farm just as easily as sprog 2nd Lieutenants if something went wrong.

An early morning low-level bombing and strafing mission was set up for 6 July; I flew with the 62nd Squadron. Crossing in at Dieppe we swept to Bernay. We had just turned east towards Beaumont, flying at 14,000 feet, when someone called in bandits coming towards us, about 4,000 feet above. One look told me we were obviously about to be bounced. There was nothing for it but to jettison sixty odd bombs and thirty drop tanks over the French countryside and try to counter the threat. I radioed for the 63rd Squadron to do a 360 degree manoeuvre, and for the 61st to pull out to one side as cover while I went up to attack: 'Daily squadron, follow me.' With full power and a climbing left turn we tried to meet the attack. While climbing I kept my eyes on the high elements of the enemy formation; my goal.

Suddenly out of the corner of my eye were white puffs — there and gone. Crump! The aircraft shook. Violent movement of the stick; round and down. Just a quick glimpse of my assailant, an Me 109. Looking at the left wing I saw an enormous hole at the ammunition compartment door. I tried the controls. No response from the left aileron; the cannon shell hit had taken out the control wires. After a descent of about 3,000 feet, with the stick way over in the right hand corner, the Thunderbolt gradually recovered. A look round: the comforting view of two P-47s alongside, George Bostwick my Number 3 and his wingman. No sign of Lieutenant Steven Murray, my Number 2. He had given no call to break. Had he been shot down? 'Fairbank to Daily White 3. I've taken a hit in the left wing. Give me cover back to England.' We reached the emergency base at Manston where I decided to go on for home plate as reasonable control could be maintained. The landing at Boxted was tricky but safe.

To my surprise Lieutenant Murray was there. What I learned from Bostwick and the others did not please me. When the enemy fighters above us had launched their attack, Murray broke away down and fled without even giving a radio warning. As I began my climb there was no wingman to watch my rear and an Me 109 had detached itself and come down in on my tail. But for Bostwick's prompt action in quickly opening fire and shooting it down, I might not be safely back at Boxted. My immediate reaction was to have

Murray transferred. Once a man breaks under duress no one is going to trust him again. Some of the kinder hearts in headquarters reminded me that others who once panicked, had later proved their worth. So I relented although Murray never flew as my wingman again.

The following day the group supported heavies going to Leipzig, about the longest trip to date — over five hours. Since the stalemate at the bridgehead, 8th Air Force had occasionally been allowed to pursue its campaign against strategic targets and we were given a few Ramrods. On this occasion the group came home with ten claims, six by Fred Christensen. He and his flight had seen a string of Ju 52 transports in the circuit at Garddegen airfield. What followed was a turkey shoot for Chris; the only escape for the big lumbering transports was to run. This bag elevated Christensen's personal score to 22 but, unfairly, there were some snide comments in some quarters about a score built on shooting down helpless transports. To my mind transports were helping the enemy's war effort as much, if not more so, than any Me 109 or FW 190. Besides, the rest of Chris's victories were fighters bested in some hard fighting. He had come to us as a replacement in August 1943 and built up a good reputation. A blond, good looking fellow of Scandinavian background, he had that essential quality of any successful fighter, an aggressive nature.

Chris was coming to the end of his tour at this time. So was 'Goody' Goodfleisch. He turned up 300 hours on 11 July and said goodbye. At this time Joe Egan arrived back from leave in the States for a second tour and I gave him the command of the 63rd which Goody had vacated. Egan, at six feet three inches, was probably the tallest pilot in the 56th. A hell of a nice guy. His father was president of Western Union, one of the top ranking corporations in the US at that time. Two days after Egan took over the 63rd he went on a Ramrod in support of bombers going to Augsburg. Joe took his flight down to shoot up an enemy airfield. No flak was seen on the first pass so he came back for a second and all hell broke loose. As he went across the field his plane took a 20 mm shell hit near the cockpit. It probably stunned or killed him for his P-47 did a slow roll and smashed into the ground. It did not burn. A few days later 'Bunny' Comstock, also just back from leave in the States, was given the 63rd.

Another returnee I was pleased to see was Dave Schilling, who had lost none of his zest for living and fighting. In this land of austerity and the unobtainable, Dave was always proving otherwise. He had only been back a few days and we had a refrigerator in the 'Wheel House', and ice cream became a regular attraction when he found an old ice cream plant and trucked it half across England. My old Flying Executive took his first mission out on the 19th, the day Egan was killed. The perils of airfield strafing were once more underlined boldly next day. Gabby went down. It was hard to take; that grinning face had seemed almost a permanent part of the Wolfpack. But the good news was that the chances were that Gabby was alive. While strafing Bassenheim airfield near Coblenz, he had flown too low in avoiding a welter of tracer and his prop' struck a small rise on the far side of the airfield. He bellied in and ran. Francis Gabreski, the greatest American ace from the war in Europe, did survive to fight again in another air war, Korea.

Three of the 8th's four P-38 Lightning groups had converted to the P-51 Mustang during July and I learned that there was a good chance of acquiring one of their cast-off Droopsnoots. My request was granted by 'Ajax' and with the memory of our successful use of this type of aircraft in May, I had high hopes we could do similar good work. The Droopsnoot was painted up in our colours and the services of a bombardier, Lieutenant Arthur Scroggins, acquired. On the late afternoon of 25 July we put it to work.

Earlier that day, while returning from a dive bombing mission, I had noticed four Ju 88s being pushed under some trees at Montdidier airfield, north of Paris. Reaching Boxted, I ordered the Droopsnoot made ready with a 500 pound bomb under each wing. Tieing in with the next P-47 mission, which Schilling was leading, Scroggins and I tagged along behind until just north of Abbeville where I broke away to seek Montdidier. There was no difficulty in locating my objective and the Droopsnoot was lined up at 12,000 feet for a one minute run. At the same instant the count-down reached zero and Scroggins released our bombs, there were four violent explosions and the aircraft fell into a right-hand spiral. Looking out I saw that the propeller, spinner and part of the right engine had disappeared! With concerted effort the Droopsnoot was righted and headed north to escape the flak. On the way home, an ever enlarging oil slick appeared along the cowling of the good engine. This concentrated the mind wonderfully. I suspected we had taken a piece of flak in the oil tank — which proved to be the case. After landing, the brakes failed and we hurtled off the end of the runway into a field. It would be no exaggeration to say that pilot and bombardier were very relieved when they finally climbed out of that kite. This was to be the one and only mission with our own Droopsnoot. We did not have the facilities to repair it, nor the experienced ground crew to conduct maintenance. On top of that I was now convinced that flying straight and level at 12,000 feet with a close formation in trail tended towards the suicidal. So we decided to persevere with dive bombing and strafing and saw plenty of it during the next few days as the ground forces finally broke free of the Normandy bridgehead and swept across France.

The volume of light flak and small-arms fire we encountered seemed to grow with each passing day. To survive you learned to keep high enough for it not to reach you or low enough so they didn't see you coming in time to draw an accurate bead. More often it was the latter. Several times Thunderbolts came back to Dogday with damage caused by trees. Fred McIntosh must have flown through a forest judging by the branches embedded in both wings. After jumping down from my plane one day I noticed slashes in the fuselage and found a considerable length of telephone wire wound round my prop' boss. But we couldn't escape all the fire and more than once I heard the clunk, clunk of shell splinters or bullets smashing into my P-47.

Blocking the enemy railways to prevent movement of troops and materials was a frequent task. We had a field day in the Strasbourg area on 3 August, shooting up 31 locomotives in the course of a near five hour mission. 'Ajax' liked us to classify locomotives as destroyed or damaged. In my view very few were truly destroyed because perforating the boiler and firebox to bring one to a spectacular steam-cloud halt didn't destroy the loco. I'm sure most were soon towed away and repaired. On this mission each P-47 carried a single 250 pound GP bomb on the belly shackles and two drop tanks under the wings.

Following a railroad between Saareburg and Luneville I spotted a cement factory. Instructions were radioed to the three 63rd Squadron flights I was leading to unload their ordnance on it, hoping to make more difficulties for the Germans in repairing airfield runways. There were some rail cars loaded with vehicles nearby and I made a couple of firing passes at these and then pulled up to orbit the scene at about 4,000 feet. Then a slow moving freight train was seen further down the line and I went after it. Dropping down, I was just getting into position to strafe when: 'Fairbank. Break Left,' stung my ears. A fast manipulation of the stick and pedals skidded the P-47 round; trees, track and fields below disappeared as the nose came up above the horizon. With no height to dive away, it was water to the cylinders and into a full power climb to gain altitude as quickly as possible. Swivel neck; no sign of an enemy plane, just a parachute descending over Saareburg. By the time my altimeter showed 5,000 feet, a radio message came in that the enemy aircraft had gone. So back to strafing the railroad.

Not until interrogation at Boxted did I discover what happened. Lieutenant Richard Anderson, my wingman, had seen an FW 190 curve round behind me as I dived to strafe. The German pilot obviously didn't see Anderson flying some distance to the rear and about a thousand feet above his leader. Anderson immediately called a warning, pulled in behind the '190 and fired. The Focke-Wulf had started to fire at me but now broke left to try and save his own skin. Anderson's aim was good. The '190 straightened out, the canopy flew off and the pilot baled out. All I'd seen was the German floating down to fight again! This was a perfect example of what the wingman's job was all about, to protect his leader. And here was a guy who knew his job. After incidents like this no plaudits were too great for someone who had probably saved your life. But the Group CO never dropped his guard; it was retain the stiff upper lip and a simple, 'Good show, Anderson'.

Next day, following a Ramrod to northern Germany, we got together for a voluntary show with our good neighbours, the 353rd Group at Raydon. This was another result of co-operation between the respective intelligence officers, our Dave Robinson and their Hank Bjorkman. The 353rd had for some weeks scouted and plotted the developments at airfield Plantlunne, east of Nordhorn, and earlier that day had seen it was well stocked with aircraft. We were invited to participate in giving this place a working over. Setting out in the late afternoon with a combined force of 69 P-47s, most lugging two 250-pound bombs, the Luftwaffe was caught off guard. Leading the show, the 353rd did some excellent strafing of defences, allowing the 56th to follow up with dive bombing. We then strafed every aircraft and military installation to be seen. The known flak positions were silenced on the first pass and, as others were found, individual pilots would silence them. When we had finished there were between 25 and thirty aircraft burning on the field and the whole place was covered in a pall of smoke. It was the finest exhibition of saturation strafing I ever witnessed and a model for how such an attack should be carried out. My greatest difficulty in this race-track to strafe was to stay out of the way of other P-47s and their fire.

As the ground forces pushed through France, so our area of operations receded. The amount of time we could spend in hostile airspace was reduced and three and a half- to four-hour missions became the norm. The increased internal fuel capacity that came with the P-47D-25 and subsequent models helped a great deal but as yet only a third of our complement were Superbolts, as the boys called them. The attrition after D-Day, especially with the 9th Air Force P-47 groups which did most of the direct ground support for the US armies, was such that there was now a great shortage of fighter aircraft. Replacements were slow coming through and our squadron complements had gradually dropped from around 36 at the beginning of the year to under 25.

Our attrition was nothing compared to the hammering the Luftwaffe had taken. Despite the large numbers of his planes shot down and shot up, plus the bombing of his aircraft factories, Jerry still seemed to have plenty of fighters. What he couldn't replace was the experienced fliers who fell in battle. Since the early spring we had noticed a general deterioration in the quality of the fighter pilots we met and this became more pronounced as the weeks went by. A great many showed poor airmanship, pathetic gunnery and lack of tactics, all indicative of insufficient training, which proved to be the case. The P-51 groups, with their range and endurance, had some spectacular turkey shoots at this time, intercepting huge enemy formations where the majority of pilots seemed to blindly follow the formation leader and make only clumsy attempts to avoid the attack. This was in marked contrast to the high calibre of the average German fighter pilot when we had arrived on the scene the previous summer.

We missed out on most of the big air fights over Germany in the late summer of 1944, primarily because our P-47s didn't have the necessary endurance. With two drop tanks we could be gone five hours but if we were bounced on penetration and had to release the tanks our range was immedietely cut. For this reason 'Ajax' gave most of the long-range escort to the P-51s. I was often burning Bobby Burns' ear with pleas that our experience be used out in front where it would count, only to be brushed off with short-range slots in the escort relay. It became increasingly frustrating to see the Mustang groups get most of the choice pitches. There were now ten P-51 groups in VIIIth Fighter Command and the plan was to convert the others

before the end of the year with the 56th last in line. We figured that
the way things were going the war would be over by then. I expected
that we would move to the continent which would put us nearer to our
area of operations. General Spaatz, however, decided that this would
only impose unnecessary logistic problems and that his strategic air
force could fulfil all its duties quite satisfactorily from permanent
bases in the UK. And so the lot of the four P-47 groups was mostly
fighter-bombing and strafing for which we were better suited than the
more flak-vulnerable P-51s. Occasionally we were given a Type 16
sweep where we would be directed to any enemy aircraft by radar
control, but this was rarely fruitful.

Following an uneventful Type 16 sweep of the Chartres area on 11
August — the sky was too clear for any Huns to venture up — I
reported to Robby for interrogation and was told General Griswold
had 'phoned from 'Ajax'. Would I call him back? 'Butch' Griswold
had taken over the helm of the Fighter Command at the beginning of
the month when General Kepner moved to command the 2nd Bomb
Division. I told the base operator to get a connection to 'Ajax' and
finally Griswold came on the phone. At first he asked about the
mission and made a few general comments. I knew immediately this
wasn't a courtesy call; he wanted something. You could tell; that
special intonation in his voice. 'Hub, I want you to do me a favour.'
It wasn't a directive and I knew him well enough by now to know
what was coming was going to be a very big favour indeed. 'We lost
Kyle Riddle yesterday and I need another commander for the 479th.
As you know, it's the youngest group in the command and they don't
have anyone with the necessary experience to take over. You've had
Dave Schilling a long time. It's time he had a command of his own.
I'd like him to take the 479th.'

There was a brief silence at my end; it was a surprise. I guess I
thought Dave was sacrosanct. But he certainly deserved a command
of his own and was more than able to handle it. 'Okay, General. I'll
talk to Schilling and call you back. He's off base now and I may not be
able to come back 'till the morning.' Griswold purred and hung up
the phone. Word was left at Headquarters that Dave was to be sent
along to my quarters in the 'Wheel House' when he arrived back. He
wasn't scheduled to fly early next day and didn't show up until next
morning. I don't know where he'd been; probably pursuing one of his
amorous adventures. I left word that he be told to report to my office.

'I've got a group for you.' Dave's face sparkled. 'The 479th,' I continued. 'Riddle went down.' There was an abrupt change of attitude: 'Hell no, not P-38s.' I told him they were about to transition to P-51s but his disquiet at the prospect of commanding the 479th was expressed in a few choice four-letter words. This was the response I had anticipated. 'Okay, Dave, I'll tell you what we'll do. You take the 56th and I'll go to the 479th.' He was incredulous. Twice it seemed command of the Wolfpack was his, only to have it snatched away, and now here was Zemke handing it to him on a plate. Sure he would take over.

I called 'Ajax' and spoke to Griswold. 'Dave prefers to stay with the 56th at Boxted but I would be delighted to go to the 479th at Wattisham.' Griswold didn't even query it. 'Fine. How soon can you get over there?' 'This afternoon,' I replied. And that was that.

After Griswold's first phone call I had done a bit of thinking. There was only one group Schilling wanted to command and deserved to command. And for me there was need of a new challenge, a new purpose. My total combat hours since returning from the States were creeping near to the 300 hour mark and I didn't want to be pensioned off to some desk job. The change would probably stave off the order to quit for a few more weeks. Perhaps this war would be over by then, judging by the way things were going. Command of the 56th had been near to an obsession with me; now perhaps I was stale and the group should have a different regime. In making the decision to leave I felt like a parent who feels the child is grown up and can go its own way.

Watson was called in, told of my decision and asked to get as many of the station complement that could be spared into No 1 hangar around 4 o'clock that afternoon. I got up on the podium, erected for a Glenn Miller concert a few nights before, and expressed my thanks and good wishes for the future. Most seemed bemused by the announcement that I was moving on. My belongings were collected from the 'Wheel House', hands shaken, goodbyes said, and then into the staff car. I was driven down to the main gate, past the scarlet-nosed Thunderbolts on dispersal. Behind me was the greatest command of my service life.'

15

WATTISHAM WEEKS

The news that The Hub, the Old Man, had departed of his own volition was at first greeted with surprised disbelief by the majority of men at Boxted. There were, no doubt, those individuals with experience of the Colonel's discipline who were not sorry to see him go, but even they had long believed Hub Zemke and the 56th Fighter Group inseparable. After all, it *was* Zemke's Wolfpack; while others might come and go it seemed nothing short of a German bullet would separate their dedicated leader from his command — and with his record of near misses and narrow escapes few could conceive that happening. Although the group could look forward to a lighter rule under the popular Dave Schilling, most men would admit they were a little uncertain about life without Zemke.

Regardless of his popularity rating with individuals, he was the centre stone of the foundation on which the group's success had been built. However, the foundations had been well formed and laid and the 56th's position as the leading fighter group in the European Theatre of Operations was maintained under Dave Schilling and, when he was finally grounded, by the level-headed Pete Dade. Although operating P-47s until the end of hostilities, being last with them in the 8th Air Force, and so denied the opportunities afforded the long ranging P-51s groups, it still ended up with more air victories than any other USAAF fighter group fighting the Luftwaffe. As an acknowledgement of its contribution to victory, the 56th was instructed to prepare one of its aircraft for exhibition beneath the Eiffel Tower. The group chose to dedicate it to the one man who had been their prime driving force; emblazoned along the fuselage was the slogan "ZEMKE'S WOLFPACK".

For Hub, having made the decision to go, there was no regret. He had reasoned a change would benefit both the 56th and himself. He was eager to meet the new challenge.

★　　★　　★

Wattisham lay about twelve miles due north of Boxted, but it appeared to entail twice that distance to reach along the narrow winding roads in this part of England. The base, of similar vintage to Horsham St Faith, was built just before the war for the RAF and fitted out with centrally heated brick-built barracks and what were termed permanent facilities. Bombed during the Battle of Britain, one of the hangars was still without a roof. I was already familiar with Wattisham as a large air depot had been constructed on the south side of the field which handled all the major fighter overhauls for VIIIth Fighter Command. The 479th Fighter Group occupied the northern side with the original hangars and the old camp. I didn't know a great deal about the 479th other than it was the last fighter outfit to join the 8th Air Force, that it flew P-38 Lightnings and had taken some pretty heavy losses.

My immediate task was to obtain quarters and make myself known to the senior establishment in the group. Obviously it would take time to gain acceptance but from the outset I found all the headquarters people friendly and willing to go with my ways. In particular I took an immediate liking to the Intelligence Officer, Major Evans Pillsbury, who proved to be both genial and industrious. It was necessary to introduce myself around the base and try to pick up as much information as I could to be able to evaluate the efficiency and weaknesses of the various departments.

A careful look at the 479th's operational record was a first step. The group had come to England in May and had set a record by going operational in eleven days, although I suspected it might have been hustled so as to have some missions under its belt by D-Day. In two and a half months the group had shot down ten enemy aircraft while losing some 35 of its own pilots killed or missing. True, most of the combat losses had been to ground fire during strafing raids. Even so, they appeared excessively high and I suspected a weakness in technique and general leadership.

A contributory factor to these high losses was the type of aircraft. The Lockheed P-38 Lightning was heralded as a wonder fighter when it first appeared in 1939, faster than anything else in the sky, very manoeuvrable and with good firepower. It transpired that the design had some inherent weaknesses that were never fully overcome. The most serious was tail buffeting in high speed dives which led to restrictions that were a handicap in combat. Due to the peculiarities of the design aerodynamics, at very high speeds air flow over the cockpit and wing centre section became turbulent and hammered round the tailplane linking the two fuselage booms. Lockheed and the

Air Force tried in vein to cure this: they never succeeded as far as I know.

A large plane for a fighter, the P-38 could turn as well as most single-engine interceptors at low altitudes and it had good speed. In the Pacific our people developed a successful technique of employing it against Japanese fighters with great success. It was popular there by virtue of its range being superior to other American pursuits available during the early war years and, with plenty of over-water flying, two engines were a comfort. The same should have applied in Europe but the operational circumstances and climatic conditions were different. Here the P-38 was a big flop, although the Air Force would never admit it as they believed their own propaganda.

The Allison engines were the main trouble. At low and medium altitudes they were fine, at high altitude they were hopeless. The design just couldn't take the combination of extreme cold and high humidity that characterised flight over Europe, especially in winter. Engine failure had been rife during the winter of 1943-44 when the P-38s really began to see action. The position had improved, but they still were not 100 per cent. There was a standing joke that the P-38 was designed with two engines so you could come back on one. A P-38 mechanic's life was not easy, the type demanded a hefty maintenance load.

There were several good points about the type. Without doubt it was an excellent gun platform. All five guns — four 50s and a 20 mm cannon — were in the nose compartment ahead of the pilot. This made the estimation of range much less critical as, unlike the P-47 and P-51 with their wing mounted guns, the fire didn't converge.

Although I had a little time in P-38s I needed to become really familiar with the type before leading a mission. So one of my first priorities was to get in some flying hours so that the operation of flaps, gear and other controls became near automatic. I didn't anticipate having to fly many missions with P-38s because the 479th was about to convert to P-51s. There were two or three war-weary Mustangs on the base assigned for pilot conversion. Enquiring about the delivery of combat models I learned that there was currently an acute shortage of P-51s and it might be some weeks before any were delivered.

Time was required to identify weaknesses and impose changes, so I began by setting up a number of lectures and discussions on tactics in order to better appraise the pilots and operations personnel. The deputy group commander was Lieutenant Colonel Sydney Woods who, having flown a tour on P-40s in the Pacific, had been assigned to the 479th in Stateside training to provide operational experience. I soon found Syd Woods to be an able officer and my estimation of him grew as the days went by. In fact, I wondered why Griswold had not given him the group when Riddle went down. Nearly all the officers were strangers to me, most being youngsters not long out of flying school. I was surprised to find that one tall, broad-shouldered ball of energy was Robin Olds, who I think I had last seen in the pool at Langley when he was a young teenager and his dad commanded the 2nd Bomb Group. Robin got himself mixed up with a flock of Focke-Wulfs a couple of days after I arrived at Wattisham, and claimed two.

A commander needs to gain the confidence of his subordinates and the quickest way to do this is to undertake some action to bring the unit success. Not something that can be set up like a ball game, so I had to scan the Field Orders for anything promising. On the morning of 18 August I spotted a likely opportunity. We received an assignment to fly escort for a small force of Libs sent to blast the enemy airfield at Nancy-Essey, immediately east of the town of Nancy in France. The 56th had taken some photos of it in past weeks, so I had our intelligence people run over to Boxted to pick up some prints. I chose to make this my first group lead. At briefing, I informed the pilots that there might be an opportunity to carry out some strafing. In my experience gunners who manned airfield defences usually kept their heads down when being bombed and afterwards there was a good chance we would find little flak to contend with. I went through the various ramifications of how we would strafe after I had gone down and tested the defences.

We took off from Wattisham mid-afternoon. A pleasant day with some clouds scattered around the sky. Our fifty P-38s made rendezvous with the B-24s at the coast near Bayeux, went south of Paris and then headed to eastern France. As planned, two squadrons of the 479th — the 434th and 436th — took up positions on either flank of the bomber formations while I led the other squadron, the 435th, to scout ahead. On reaching a point near St Dizier, I took the freelance squadron well ahead to sweep across the target area with the specific intention of scouting what was on the airfield. So as not to alert suspicions down below we maintained our course eastward but as we went by I was pleased to see the field was well stocked with twin-engined planes.

The bombers had an unobstructed run on the target and their aim

The 'Wheel House', Boxted. Langham Lodge farmhouse served as residence for the Group CO, his air and ground executives, group operations and intelligence officers and the three squadron COs. Here Dade, Watson and Zemke prepare to board our Ford staff car with 'Red' my driver (on left).

63rd Squadron Flight Chief, Tech Sergeant Jack R. Jackson, and Staff Sergeant Damon Itza, the Crew Chief of my second UN:Z, on their way to chow. This was the aircraft in which I led the first 'Fan'.

One of the Me-109s assembling between Frankfurt and Wiesbaden on 12 May. He had just gone into a climbing left turn. Giving a couple of rings lead at between 250 and 300 yards, he was allowed to fly through two seconds of fire from the P-47's eight guns.

Joe H. Powers. The last of his 15 victories — shared with his wingman — was the Luftwaffe's No 3 ace, Major Gunther Rall.

Major Gunther Rall nurses a thumbless left hand a few days after the first Zemke Fan. But for my hasty exit from the scene of battle his score of victories would now stand at 276 and not the 275 that makes him the No 3 Luftwaffe ace. We have since become friends — even though one of my boys was responsible for Rall's wound that May day.

Itza shows me the damage caused by a 20mm shell in the supercharger ducting of my UN:Z after strafing at Celle airfield. My eighth 'near thing'.

In D-Day dress, the first 'bubble canopy' P-47D at Boxted. This 'Superbolt' was a presentation aircraft 'bought' with savings bonds in Oregon and inscribed 'Oregons Britannia' [sic]. The aircraft served me well.

Long shadows cast by poplars on the evening of D-Day point to the burning remains of the FW 190 whose pilot lost control in countering my attacks. Another K-25 shot from UN:Z.

The 61st Squadron Poles gathered around Gabby in front of 'Silver Lady', our first bare metal finish P-47. (Left to right) Squadron Leader Michael Gladych, Flight Lieutenant Sawicz, Gabby, Flight Lieutenants Janicki, Andersz and Lanowski. Janicki later went MIA. Gladych and Lanowski stayed with the 56th until the end of the war.

Fred Christensen at Boxted a few days after he shot down six transports and raised his score to 22. Fred was a first rate fighter in the air but his aggression sometimes spilled over on the ground.

Once more the Colonel nearly 'had it'. Examining the mess a 20mm shell made of my left ammunition door after the mission where my wingman cut and ran.

Gabby and his ground crew pose in front of HV:A a day or two before he went down. (Left to right) Sergeant Ralph Safford, Corporal Felix Schacki and Sergeant Joe DiFranza.

Captain James R. Carter came to the UK with the 56th and flew two tours, commanding the 61st Fighter Squadron at the war's end. He is seen here in 'Silver Lady' with crew chief Joe Gibson.

◀ Smile the cameraman said. A welcoming handshake for the legendary Glenn Miller when he brought his band to play at Boxted in August 1944.

▼ 'Zemke Wolfpack'. The P-47M named in my honour and exhibited under the Eiffel Tower at the end of the war.

The new CO, in relaxed mood talks to an assembly of 479th personnel on the afternoon of 12 August 1944. Wattisham had been a permanent RAF base; the rose-clad brick-built barracks in the background being in sharp contrast to the damp Nissens at Boxted and Halesworth.

The CO and his P-38J Lightning in the August sunshine. It was assigned to
the 435th Fighter Squadron and carried my identification letter Z.

The great shoot out at Nancy/Essay, 18 August 1944. A frame from Lieutenant H. F. Grenning's combat film shows his bullets raising dust round an
He-111. His element leader's P-38 can be seen pulling away over a hangar.
The shot of burning aircraft and clouds of smoke came from the gun camera
of one of the most successful 479th pilots, Captain C. A. P. Duffie.

The CO and his P-51D. While with the 56th, I moved my personal aircraft from squadron to squadron to show no favouritism. The Mustang was handled by the 436th Fighter Squadron and carried the identification 9B:Z.

Lieutenant Robin Olds. One of the bright stars of the 479th.

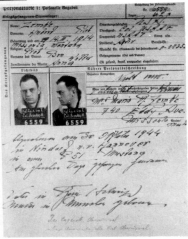

The Luftwaffe record on Kriegsgefangner 6559. With a swollen cheek and unco-operative frown he looks the real 'Terror Flieger'.

A photo taken in Dulag-Luft on 21 November 1944 shows a bit of fooling between bomber and fighter types. On left Major A. C. James and Lieutenant C. G. Cille frame up to Zemke and Colonel Charles Stark, the Senior Allied Officer. The cartoon murals were contributed by PoWs to brighten up the small mess hall. I wear the navy blue sweater that eventually ended its days as darning wool.

was good. While we orbited and waited for the smoke and dust to clear, I radioed Major Jules Biscayart, the 436th leader, to escort the bombers back. Not very happy about being denied an opportunity for action, he did not leave without protest. Before the smoke and dust of the bomber strike could settle, two flights were taken down in a steep frontal attack to test the flak and try and destroy some of the aircraft parked in the vicinity of the hangars. Just as I opened fire, out of the corner of one eye a P-38 was seen rapidly converging on mine. With a violent evasive turn the mid-air collision was averted — but only just. Angered by the other pilot's lack of attention, a few curt commands were radioed to the squadrons as I climbed to rejoin them. Having emphasised the need for air discipline, another fast diving attack was launched and this time my bullets ignited a twin-engine aircraft, a fact which was called out over the radio to obtain confirmation from other pilots.

No flak was seen, and after hearing from others in my squadron that they had seen none, I called the rest of the group down to start a traffic pattern for strafing. On a rough estimation there were a good seventy aircraft dispersed around the field, most of which appeared to have escaped damage during the bombing. The majority were He 111 bombers and by the time we had finished just about every one was afire. Wave after wave of P-38s swept over the field for around 25 minutes until the pall of smoke from the burning aircraft was so large and dense that to continue would have put our people at risk through collision. A re-assembly was called at 8,000 feet. One of our number who didn't make it had been seen to crash into the town of Nancy. There were only a few reports of shooting from the ground but perhaps he caught some of this.

Climbing out of my aircraft back at Wattisham I was confronted with P-38s skimming along only a few feet above the grass, doing victory rolls and generally buzzing the place. No doubt I was going to be labelled a sourpuss for stamping on this show of exuberance but to me it was unnecessary and dangerous. Names of the offenders were obtained from the tower, and they were later summoned to my office and fined a half month's pay.

Pillsbury and his staff were handed one colossal headache in trying to sort out all the claims which at first added up to more than a hundred. As this was around thirty more than reconnaissance photos showed on the field a lot of people had been shooting at the same targets. It took a number of discussions and evaluation sessions with

VIIIth Fighter Command to settle for a more realistic figure. Eventually, I was given the instructions to distribute 43 destroyed and 28 damaged credits amont the 32 claimants, taking into consideration combat films and pilot reports. So that nobody missed out I decided to forego my own claim. It was enough to be told by the boys that this was the most successful and rewarding mission the group had so far undertaken. Some of the pilots seemed to think all was to do with Old Man Zemke conjuring up a little magic. In reality I knew we were just fortunate that so good a target presented itself: weeks or months might have gone by before finding such pickings.

The opinions of Kermit Brickson, an Operations Clerk in the 434th Fighter Squadron, were typical of 479th men who came into contact with the new CO.

The group commander's office was in our Operations Building. When Colonel Riddle went missing his name plate on the door was replaced with that of Colonel Hubert Zemke. However, Zemke had them put up another sign underneath his name which read: "I AM A SON-OF-A-BITCH TOO, LET'S SEE YOU SALUTE". It was typical of his way of maintaining military order while at the same time letting you know he was a regular guy. People soon knew who was boss for he was firm on things he thought important. Usually he had a twinkle in his eye and an easy manner. He came to us with quite a record but it wasn't only that which made people respect him. The pilots knew on the days Zemke led if there was an opportunity to see some real good action then he would find it. It was probably that he had been around the sky of western Europe so long he knew it like the back of his hand and had developed an intuition of where the Luftwaffe would appear and what they would do. Most of us considered him a real gentleman and a hell of a leader.'

★   ★   ★

Following the laying waste of Nancy-Essey there were some pretty lean missions. An exception was 25 August when one of the squadrons on an escort way out near the Baltic coast ran into a gaggle of Me 109s, apparently from an operational training unit, and shot down five. Robin Olds claimed three of these to become the 479th's first ace. A one-time All-American football star, Olds proved to be a talented fellow with a great sense of humour which he employed in drawing cartoons that caused much amusement in the Officers' Club.

On the same mission I experienced one of the P-38's known problems. We had just arrived above the B-24s we were to support when a small gaggle of Me 109s was seen below. Pressing the R/T button and giving my flight the order to follow me, an abrupt roll into a dive was made and as the speed built up the throttles retarded so as not to exceed the given dive limitations for the aircraft. To my astonishment both engines cut out. Thrusting the throttles open brought them to life again only to produce engine over-speeding. As I wrestled with the power settings the revolutions on one and then the other engine fluctuated wildly. All consideration of engaging the enemy in combat was given up as attempts were made to master the bucking Lightning. It took a great deal of sky and a much lower and warmer altitude to effect stability. What had happened was that the oil in the hydraulically controlled turbo-supercharger regulators had jellified in the low temperatures, the sluggish operation leading to imbalance. A not uncommon happening with P-38s in high-altitude operations over Europe. I wasn't the only member of my group to fly home streaming blue smoke that day — the air was blue inside my cockpit too.

Around the beginning of September we finally began to receive brand new P-51Ds. I took one of these gleaming Spamcans — as they were irreverently dubbed — as my personal machine and gave it the markings 9B-Z. The 479th's first mission with the Mustang was on 13 September but thereafter the supply dried up again and the group was forced to fly several operations with a mixed force of P-38s and P-51s.

With the staging of the airborne operations to secure bridges in Holland and thus provide the Allied armies with a passage over the Rhine and into Germany, our P-38s were used to patrol over the landing sites, where the unmistakable shape of the Lightning ensured a friendly identification to the trigger-happy Allied gunners below. To cover the operation a 9th Air Force P-38 group, the 370th, was sent to operate from our field which made the place pretty crowded for a few days. Around this time there was a marked deterioration in the weather, with cloud, fog and rain. The British said this was one of the wettest autumns on record and I can believe them. Time and again we had to penetrate many thousand feet of overcast before breaking out into the sunlight. On 21 September it was particularly nasty, great walls of cloud welled up to 28,000 feet or more and I had to go through it with the squadron of P-51s. It was so turbulent that the formations soon became separated and scattered and most of us wound up having to land at bases in liberated France or Belgium.

The 479th was handed a radar-vectored patrol east of the Nijmegen and Arnhem battle area on 26 September. I led the dozen

P-51s of the 435th out ahead while the 31 P-38s of the other two squadrons stacked up as top cover. For around ninety minutes we patrolled, making bounces on everything seen, only to have them turn out to be friendly aircraft. Finally I decided to move deeper into Germany to escape the congestion. Taking a due east heading over Wesel on the Rhine we set off along the northern extremity of the Ruhr. Near Haltern I squinted down over the edge of my right wing to check a small grass airdrome in case there were parked aircraft deserving a strafing pass. We were at 13,000 feet — two and a half miles above the ground. As my eye picked up the field I saw an aircraft speck fly directly over it on a westerly heading. 'This is Highway. A bogie below. Lakeside aircraft follow me.' Wing over and into a long steep dive.

Visibility was good and as we descended I picked up other aircraft around the first flying a four-ship flight line abreast. Would they see us coming and break? Were they Me 109s or P-51s? I wasn't sure. I could now see several flights flying around 2,000 feet above the countryside. Reaching fire range I still wasn't sure. Better safe than sorry: I pulled up sharply to the left, rolled the Mustang onto its back and saw black crosses on the upper surface of their wings. A quick movement of the stick to right the Mustang; jettison the drop tanks. I then saw we had lost the element of surprise for the '109s were also dropping their tanks while breaking to the right. Picking out one of the centre machines I opened fire at about 500 yards. One short burst, another and again as he tightened his turn, all apparently without any hits. I gave another burst when he was at an angle of about forty degrees to me and saw strikes on the top surfaces of the wings and fuselage. He didn't appear to be hard hit but the Messerschmitt immediately flopped over onto its back and the pilot baled out. I then remembered I had forgotten to use the ranging device on my throttle handle to control the gunsight.

By this time the whole group was mixing it up, P-38s, P-51s and Me 109s going everywhere. I picked out another '109 who, seeing me headed his way, hopped into a nearby cloud. I went over the top to meet him coming out whereupon he promptly turned back in. This time I went under the cloud to catch him the other side. Again he saw me and ducked into the mists. I pulled up above to wait for him to appear but somehow he gave me the slip. Taking a quick glance in my rear-view mirror I was alarmed to see a fighter bearing down on me. Violent evasive action followed, break down and round. He was still there. Again a severe break round and down. Lost him; so into a climbing turn. But no; he was still there! More violent manoeuvres but dammit the fellow hung on like a leech. Then as I broke again I clearly saw it was a P-51 not an Me 109! I had been trying to escape from my own wingman!

At this moment another Me 109 was seen turning under me and heading for the clouds to the south. Sweeping round to the right I managed to hit him with two long range bursts just before he disappeared into the vapours. Looking around, P-38s were turning with the enemy about a mile away. A lone Me 109 broke away from this mêlée and headed down. He must have seen me diving after him for he started skidding and slipping long before I closed to good range. At 400 yards with a 20-30 degree deflection I gave him a burst hitting the fuselage. Immediately his canopy flew off and he baled out. The Messerschmitt plunged down into a field and exploded just as I took a photograph with the K-25 camera fixed to my headrest armour. Now there was little sign of other aircraft except my faithful wingman, 2nd Lieutenant Billy Means. We called it a day and headed home.

Back at Wattisham I found a lot of excited people. The group had had a spectacular success with 29 destroyed claims, one probably destroyed and eight damaged for the loss of one P-38 and pilot. This was some sort of 8th Air Force record at the time. We had started with around even numbers and scattered the Germans in about fifteen minutes. These people were obviously little experienced, judging by their lack of tactics and the disintegration when we attacked. Some seemed more interested in running than fighting. I could not help drawing a comparison between these people and our accomplished adversaries of the previous year. Five 479th pilots had shot down two enemy aircraft each and Jim Herren, CO of the 434th Squadron, and George Gleason of the same outfit, brought down three each. Once again better-trained pilots, imbued with an aggressive spirit, had won the day.

Some of the success could also be attributed to the K-14 gunsight. This gyroscopic instrument, based on a British design, produced remarkable accuracy in deflection shooting. In fact, it allowed shots which previously would not have been attempted. Ten of the victims had fallen to the guns of the twelve P-51s and my enthusiasm for this fighter increased. While not having the firepower of the P-38 or P-47, it was superior on nearly every other count. The P-51 probably couldn't outclimb a '109 or '190 but it could outdive and outrun them at any altitude. It could usually out-turn these opponents too. The all-round view from the cockpit was excellent — and that was of major importance to a fighter pilot. Best of all, with that large built-in tankage and moderate appetite we did not have to sweat over fuel gauges as had been the case with the P-47 and, to a certain degree, with the P-38. In making the transition from P-38s, pilots found take-off and landing the most difficult thing to master. The Lightning, with its two contra-rotating props, was as steady as a rock on take-offs. The P-51 with that damn great Merlin out front, tremored and had terrific yaw when the power was poured on. If you didn't watch the directional control you could be way off the runway in a second. One of our pilots was killed on his first mission when he went off the hard into the mud during take-off.

★   ★   ★

Robin Olds became a leading ace in the 479th Group and more than twenty years on earned fame in the air fighting over South-East Asia. He attributes much to Zemke's influence.

"Prior to Hub's arrival we had tasted success in small measure, we had been blooded in large measure; we were learning both to survive and to cope. But what we really wanted was to achieve, to succeed, to earn the respect of the older units in VIIIth Fighter Command; but we were frustrated in all this. We wanted a bigger piece of the action; someone to get us there. We Lieutenants were beginning to find any excuse to get separated during a mission, to sneak off and 'do our own thing'. A bad situation that could only get worse.

"Then came The Hub. You could feel things changing; a presence, a leader. Soon after he arrived I shot down my first two FW 190s. I really thought I was going to get a royal ass chewing for barging off on my own; but I sensed Colonel Zemke knew why I did it, was tolerant of my frustration, inwardly amused at my attempt to hide my elation, and pleased that the two victories were confirmed — all the while looking at me with wise steely eyes that made me inwardly squirm and vow to myself not to push this man.

"On 18 August we escorted a bunch of B-24s to Nancy/Essey airdrome. They bombed, then Zemke took our squadrons down for a little strafing action. What a show! Burning aircraft everywhere. But the best thing, we had pleased the Boss. Though he remained stern we could tell he was more than just a little proud of us. Exactly a week later my wingman and I tackled some fifty Me 109s near Rostock. Hub had led us there, a member of my flight spotted them, two of us attacked, I knocked down three and my wingman two. This time Hub was really proud but put out too because I was so green, so excited, I couldn't give clear readings on location, heading and altitude. Only one or two others in the whole group managed to tangle with Jerry. I learned tremendously from that; elation, education and chagrin; I had both pleased and frustrated the man we damned near worshipped.

"Hub was respected at high command too, and as a consequence we were accorded better and better positions on the daily mission frag. Our admiration for the man kept soaring, as did our morale. He challenged us to do better, to study (literally) and gave us the rope needed to put it into practice. We tried our best to live up to what he expected of us and earning his respect was the reward we sought."

★　　★　　★

At the end of September we finally received enough P-51s to convert the other two squadrons and the last mission with P-38s was flown on 3 October. By then the Arnhem adventure had turned to disaster with the Allied armies checked at the Rhine. The war, which a few weeks ago we were expecting to be over by Christmas, now looked set to drag through another winter. For my career there had been another development. Kyle Riddle, the 479th's original commander, had evaded capture in France and been liberated as our armies swept the German forces back. A pilot who had once been helped by the French escape organisation was not allowed to fly against the Germans again, but as France had now been liberated this rule no longer applied. Riddle returned to Wattisham in late September and became my deputy. I was surprised when Jesse Auton, the Fighter Wing commander, informed me that Riddle was on his way back because I had recommended that Syd Woods take over the 479th when the time came for me to go. It would have been kinder to hold Riddle at Fighter Wing headquarters rather than return him to Wattisham as my deputy for he must, naturally, have resented taking orders from me. Kyle Riddle was an intelligent man, small of stature and rather quiet. If he harboured a dislike for me it certainly did not show and we rubbed along pretty well.

In mid-September the three fighter wings and their groups had been taken away from VIIIth Fighter Command and placed under the three Divisions which, in effect, then became little air forces within an air force. Our wing, the 65th, went to the 2nd Bomb Division so at least we were back under Kepner's rule again. The new set-up gave the fighter wing headquarters more status in the scheme of things. However, I had never been greatly impressed with Jesse Auton's staff and felt this business with Riddle could have been handled better. Wrongly or rightly, I always had the impression that Jesse Auton favoured the 4th Group which was on his doorstep. This view was reinforced by his plucking good men out of other groups to assign to Debden. My recommendation of Syd Woods' ability apparently was not overlooked because, later in the year, Auton pulled him from the 479th for transfer to the 4th.

I knew that it would be only a matter of time before Auton or Kepner pulled me out and gave the 479th back to Riddle, for I had been reminded that my total of combat hours demanded a rest. The prospect of a staff job in Auton's headquarters had no appeal; I was not burned out and wanted to keep flying. So some preliminary scheming resulted in an eye and an ear open for any commander vacancies in other fighter groups in England. Meanwhile I was intent on getting as much experience in the P-51 as possible before that desk job became a reality.

The 479th shepherded the bombers over Berlin on 6 October and the Luftwaffe staged mass formation attacks. Many of these people were experienced and fought us in the old style, breaking to meet our head-on passes time and again and not running for the clouds, as so often happened now when we arrived on the scene. Next day we flew an escort to Brux in Czechoslovakia. There was a low undercast over parts of the continent and some very high cirrus at near 30,000 feet. In between the two visibility was good. There is great beauty in a cloud-decked sky but a fighter pilot cannot afford to be a romantic. Somehow we couldn't locate the combat wing we were assigned to protect and flew back along the trail of bomber formations to try and find it. Failing to see the markings we wanted on any B-17s, I decided to take my people on towards the target area.

As we moved forward again, past one bomber formation after another, someone reported a formation of single-engine fighters approaching from the north at a fast rate. At first I thought they were another P-51 outfit but their formation was much closer than that usually held by US fighters. They were around ten miles ahead, too far for positive identification. Suspicious, I radioed our boys to step up power as we were going to investigate. The bogies began to curve round towards the rear of a B-17 combat wing about four miles in front of us. My suspicions were quickly confirmed as the sky ahead erupted with detonating cannon shells, tracers and exploding bombers. Drop tanks away and full throttle. The Luftwaffe assault group was now seen to be mostly Me 109s which, having delivered a mass attack to saturate the bombers' defensive fire, were diving away for the deck as hard as they could go.

I picked out two '109s several thousand feet below making a level getaway to the north. A split-S and down on the leader bringing me within firing range without difficulty. I expected the enemy pilot to pull the usual and dive away down but instead he broke hard right to pull round on my tail. Since the deflection was too great to fire and my speed much too high to turn, I pulled up in an almost vertical climb to cut my speed. Falling off on one wing, as the nose of my P-51 came down I saw that my wingman, 2nd Lieutenant Norman Benoit, had made a pass at the '109. When the enemy broke into him, he too went into a climb. Coming down I made a pass at the '109 without results, while Benoit, curving down behind me, attempted to get on his tail.

The enemy pilot was good, the best I had encountered for many a day, for he quickly got into a position of advantage as he and Benoit circled around. I rolled my P-51 over to cut the enemy out of the circle but he saw my intention and dove away down. He must have realised he wasn't getting anywhere fast so he decided to head for very low clouds to the south. As he broke downwards it placed me directly behind him although well out of range. The question was, could I overtake him before he reached the safety of the clouds? With the throttle against the gate, the P-51 began to descend like a bullet, but even so I was hardly closing on the Jerry. A quick glance at the airspeed; the needle was 'off the clock': we must have been doing well over 500 mph. I figured that the '109 pilot would level out just before entering the cloud as the tops were only about 1,500 feet from the ground. This would give me a good chance to really put in a burst. Just as I expected him to commence his pull-out, I was startled to see the left wing of the Messerschmitt suddenly fold back against the fuselage and tail. The whole plane immediately disintegrated, the pieces showering down. I fired at them as they went, to take photos for confirmation. There was no sign of a parachute and I feel certain the pilot was killed in the break-up of his aircraft.

Shortly afterwards we saw another Me 109 in the low clouds and had an inconclusive combat. After shooting up a train near Oschersleben we moved off home. This was the longest mission I had ever flown, as it was for other 479th pilots. By the time I lifted my sore and stiff frame out of the P-51 back at Wattisham, more than six hours had elapsed since take-off.

More long-range escorts followed with little sign of the enemy except the distant trails of one of his new rocket or jet fighters. We hadn't a hope in hell of catching them unless lucky enough to find one heading in to roost. Our intelligence people told us that these "blow jobs" had around a hundred miles per hour advantage over conventional fighters. Even so, a few had been shot down, the first, in fact, back in July by a 479th pilot, Captain Arthur Jeffrey. My first sight of enemy jets was on a hazy day while patrolling east of Arnhem. Two Me 262s were called in above us but were gone as we turned to meet a possible attack. A few weeks later, in a bright clear sky above multiple cloud layers over northern Germany, there was to be a more interesting meeting.

Four of us were wandering home from an escort at around 20,000 feet when a lone Me 262 appeared at 5 o'clock high. There was no mistaking the distinctive twin jet layout and slightly swept wings. Its pilot decided we were fair game, sliding down towards our rear. Calling the flight to prepare to break, I went into a hard right climbing turn just before the jet came into firing range. The next thing his cannons were flashing and he was gone by. Although I had also fired there was little hope of obtaining hits in a head-on meeting, such was the rate of closure.

A glance back revealed my antagonist in a wide climbing turn ready to position for another pass. Calling the other element of the flight, I told the pilots to pull away from me and my wingman and try to gain superior altitude to the jet while we held his attention. Opening up the Merlin to maximum power the Mustang was kept circling inside the jet, but eventually his faster airspeed brought him into a position far enough above and away to initiate another diving attack. Again I turned to meet him head on and exchange fire, involuntarily ducking as his guns blinked light. Again neither pilot found his target.

This cat and mouse play continued for two more frontal passes — and there is no need to say who was made mouse! Meanwhile the detached element had yet to position above the jet. As decoy an added concern was for how much longer would my overheated engine endure running at full power. Whether the enemy pilot saw what we were trying to do or his fuel was low, he suddenly broke away in a fast shallow dive to the east, departing as quickly as he had appeared. I had generated a good sweat, expended several hundred rounds and come near to blowing a good engine during this inconclusive skirmish which clearly demonstrated the superior performance of the jet. On the other hand, it had also shown this advantage was negated in combat by meeting the attacks head-on.

The weather got progressively worse as one storm front after another filled the sky with cloud and rain. Frequently our climb out and descent were through solid overcasts. Coming back from Germany on the 19th and thinking we were over the North Sea, I led the group down to break out of the gloom. We happened to find ourselves over Dunkirk where 'friendly' flak took us to be some Luftwaffe planes attempting to supply the isolated German garrison there. Poor old Gleason's ship got well peppered and he had to bale out, clobbering a leg on the stabiliser as he went. Another of our pilots, Jim Frolking, was hit by fire from a boat in the Scheldt and had to jump. He landed in the water and desperately tried to inflate his dinghy and get aboard. His efforts were unsuccessful and, exhausted, he let himself sink, being somewhat startled — to say nothing of relieved — to find his feet on the bottom just three feet below the surface. He walked out and the Dutch folk hid him until they could get him back to Allied territory.

For the rest of October the weather was so apalling that offensive operations were severely limited. Then came the day when the dreaded order to report to 65th Fighter Wing Headquarters was received. Even the position of Chief of Staff was no attraction; I just didn't want a desk job. The new appointment was to be taken up at the end of the month but I decided to hold on at Wattisham as long as I could in the hope of seeing a few more missions. As the overcast and wet was really set, the group was stood down for 48 hours and I decided to go to London with some of the boys. It seemed I was not going to fly again before Riddle got his command back. After 154 missions and more than 450 hours combat time, there seemed no escape from flying a desk. The usual Zemke protests to superior officers had produced no reprieve. That hadn't stopped me from cultivating connections in another fighter wing where I saw a chance, a vacancy coming along for the command of another group that had not had much luck.'

Wing Commander A.D. Annand, commander of an RAF tactical Mustang squadron, had an unexpected meeting with an old acquaintance one evening towards the end of October 1944.

To make the most of a weekend's leave, with my wife Betty I took a room at the Berkeley Hotel in Piccadilly. When we went down to dinner a small band was playing so we decided to walk across to the floor and dance. Passing a table we heard a firm, strong greeting with an American accent: "Dave, Betty; Hello." We turned to find a grinning Hub Zemke dining with an attractive blonde in a British Red Cross uniform. I had last seen Hub at Old Sarum in 1941 when he was a Lieutenant advising on our use of the Tomahawk. Now he was a full Colonel and a celebrity. He invited us to join him and we spent the next few hours reminiscing. I learned for the first time why he had so mysteriously disappeared on the eve of my wedding (he had been whisked off to Russia), a little of his eventful career as a fighter leader and that, reluctantly, he was about to be grounded. He and his boys were in town as their group had been stood down for a few hours.

The Berkeley closed for service at midnight and Hub insisted that Betty and I went on to a nightclub, a short walk away, where he was to meet with a few of his squadron and flight commanders and their various girl friends. As we walked Hub said to me, earnestly: "Dave, you are not to pay for anything more tonight. I am paid four times more than you to win this war." He was emphatic. On arrival and being introduced to his fellow fighter pilots, a Major asked what we would like to drink. "A couple of small whiskies would be fine, thanks." Up came two tumblers filled to the brim with neat scotch! With a jug of water I made mine last until the small hours of the morning and then finished off Betty's. We finally said goodbye to Hub and his friends around five in the morning and with the effects of the generous American hospitality crowding our heads, staggered back to the Berkeley. We said we would keep in touch but Hub disappeared just as mysteriously as he had done three years before.'

After return from the weekend in London my bags were packed and made ready. However, that morning, the 30th, a Field Order came through for an escort for bombers hitting oil targets in north central Germany. The forecast was good with unlimited visibility at altitude and from ten to fifteen miles at ground level. A cold front had passed through and was scheduled to be over Poland before the mission was launched. One last show. I would lead A group with the 434th Squadron up front. The day didn't look too bad as we took off, only once we were heading out over the sea, cloud started to build up ahead. By the time we had identified the wing of B-24s we were to escort, great stacks of cumulus rose three to four miles high from the ground. Every now and then the Liberators would disappear from view and for safety we had to dodge around or over the mass of clouds. Contrails persisted, the vapours turned to rime ice as we cut through. About 13:15 hours a great front towered up ahead. I didn't like the look of those white billows but it was so high we had little choice other than to plunge through if we were not to lose the bombers.

An order to tighten the Flight formations was given. As soon as my Mustang entered the mists it began to bounce like a cork. The turbulence was violent. 'Highway to Newcross aircraft. Make a 180.' We had to get out; fast. Starting into the turn I suddenly found my aircraft tossed into a violent spin. Automatically my left hand brought the throttle back as the spin and airspeed built up. Recovery from a spin was not difficult, the joystick moved forward and with a rapid kick of the rudder in the direction of the rotation, the P-51 responded like the little champion she was. The spin stopped but the altimeter unwound at an alarming rate. Meanwhile the air speed was increasing in leaps and bounds; by now the gauges showed the Mustang had stabilised but was heading straight down still enshrouded in the mist. I began to gradually pull back on the stick.

What happened next was seemingly a near instantaneous sequence of events. There was a resounding crash, a punishing blow to my right shoulder and head, a rushing blast of air all around me, and my flying helmet, oxygen mask and goggles ripped from my face. The aircraft had gone but here was I still strapped in the cockpit seat! Icy air banished the initial shock to my system. No sense of falling, it was as if I was suspended in a misty void. But that most precious human possession, life, took command with clear, instant action: fingers unlatching the safety belt and feet kicking free of the seat. There was no pondering how far the ground lay below; that same life stream was ahead of reason and had an aching right hand towards the parachute D-ring on my chest; and the left hand there to grasp when the right didn't make it. A flip and a violent jolt. Momentarily dazed I slumped in the harness, then realised the 'chute had opened. Now a feeling of blessed relief flooded through me; I didn't consciously think I had just cheated death. Floating down through the cloud came a fleeting thought of those bags packed and waiting at Wattisham and the desk job at Wing. I didn't intend it this way, but I'd fooled 'em!

Personal Aircraft of Hubert Zemke in the 56th and 479th Fighter Groups

Type	Serial No.	Identification Marking	Squadron Assignment	Period of Use	Crew Chief
P-47B-RE	41-6002	1	61FS	Sep-Nov 42	Sylvester Walker
P-47C-5-RE	41-6330	LM:Z	62FS	Mar-Sep 43	Theron B. Dillon
		UN:S	63FS	Sep-Nov 43	?
P-47D-15-RE	42-75864	UN:Z	63FS	Jan-Mar 44	Damon Itza
P-47D-20-RE	42-76471	UN:Z	63FS	Mar-May 44	Damon Itza
P-47D-25-RE	42-26413	UN:Z	63FS	May-Aug 44	Damon Itza
P-38J-15-LO	43-28823	J2:Z	435FS	Aug-Sep 44	Harlan W. Leachman
P-51D-10-NA	44-14351	9B:Z	436FS	Sep-Oct 44	J. A. Standiford

When his own aircraft was unserviceable Hub Zemke usually flew an aircraft of one of the Group Hq officers or Squadron COs who were not scheduled for the mission.

16

CAPTURE

In response to an enquiry from Hub's wife as to the validity of newspaper reports that he was a prisoner of war, on 5 December 1944 Major General William Kepner wrote the following:

'Dear Missy,
'I have been wanting to write to you for sometime relative to Hub's missing in action. Officially, that is all I can write and say although, as an old friend, I very much wanted to write and give you my personal impressions, but felt it would be better to wait until I had something more definite. I always felt that Hub had gotten away in some fashion or other; while it was only a strong, personal hunch, backed up by my absolute confidence in his ability to take care of himself, I felt that he had either been able to sit his plane down in some isolated spot and, some of these days, I hoped he would walk in as many of the boys do. There just didn't seem that anything else could have occurred, knowing him as well as I do; which is probably more intimately than any other individual combat pilot in this Theater. I had talked with him so much that I felt I knew exactly how he would respond in almost every situation. He had gone through so much and always come out of it that, maybe, I thought of him as I do of the proverbial cat that always lands on its feet no matter how it gets toused about. In fact, it had occurred to him time and again and, generally, it is the fortunes of combat people that they continue to do those very things. Officially, I still do not know anything else about him, and I still have that strong, personal hunch which I shall believe in until I know definitely otherwise. I urge you to take all the courage in the world, which you so much need, and believe the same way. Maybe by telepathy, prayers or other invisible forces, we can bring it to pass.
'Your reported information, which was released in the newspapers, to the effect that he was a Prisoner of War, was and still is a bright spot to all of Zemke's friends over here. In fact, I believe that almost everybody ... that is, his closest personal friends, of which there were dozens and dozens ... have taken your report as being the facts in the case. I certainly hope that it is true and, whether it is wishful thinking or not, there is a world of consolation in it.

'I don't know whether you know any of the facts, but Hub's Group had run into some rather bad weather. As a result of this, Hub's wingman got in difficulty with his plane and had to lose sight of Hub, whom he was following. He said that he thought he had spun and eventually got his ship under control a few thousand feet below, at which time of course he could not rejoin the formation. He stated that the last he saw of Hub, he was flying along, which sounds alright because I would expect him to do exactly that. Another pilot in the next following flight also had trouble and he likewise recovered control of his plane at very low altitude. The leader of that flight, unfortunately, is also missing and I believe that he probably got away in the same fashion that Hub did. Since they would both be flying alone, after going through this weather, they might both have been forced to sit down some place and it would take a long time to hear from them. As I said in the beginning, I feel sure that they will turn up. Obviously, with the much greater experience and superior technique that Hub and this other leader had, they should be able to fly under difficult conditions and get through in a fashion that would enable them to go on with the mission, as they probably did. And, if it be any consolation to you or Hub, I can say freely and without reservation that he was the best Fighter Group Commander I have ever known, and I believe that it was pretty universally recognized by people over here . . . not only General Spaatz and General Doolittle, myself and other Commanders, but by the boys that he led. You don't get the title of "The Big Z", which was Hub's initial, without having evoked beforehand extreme admiration on the part of those you lead. He not only influenced his own Group, but directly influenced the other Groups in the Theater as well. He was frequently quoted when men met together to discuss the intracacies and complex techniques of aerial fighting.

'With my very best and a wish that you can have as happy a Christmas as possible in the belief, unfalteringly, that some day Hub will come walking back to you and your boy, I am

'Sincerely yours,

W.E. Kepner
Major General, USA
Commanding'

This long, closely typed letter was far more than verbose consolation to worried next-of-kin. Kepner was at the time one of the three busy 8th Air Force divisional commanders and, while having a reputation for wordy pronunciations, he obviously considered this a special case. Indeed, his opinion of Hub Zemke is clearly stated. The General may have favoured diplomacy rather than curt command in his dealings with his subordinates but he did not flatter and meant what he said; Hub had been his best fighter group commander. The letter also allows for the possibility that Hub was dead and while promoting hope prepares Missy for the worst. It would be the New Year before the Zemke family received confirmation that Hub had survived. Fortunately, they were spared the knowledge of how narrowly he had again cheated death.

My parachute descent seemed to take ages. The violent wind swung me back and forth causing the silken hemisphere to flap and give me concern that it might collapse. Somewhere I'd read that

pulling on the opposite riser of a parachute would damp this out, so
an attempt was made to pull down on a group of cords. This only
caused a greater collapse of the canopy and I decided to leave well
alone and let the gods have their way. The next thing I knew I had
broken out of the cloud base around 400 feet above the ground. There
was little opportunity to survey the situation. The green blur below
approached so fast there was only time to pull up my knees before,
with a resounding thump, everything came to an abrupt halt.
Consciousness was revived quickly by my desperately gasping for air
and cold water soaking through my clothes. I doubted if I'd ever
before taken a wallop that hard, but fortunately the landing spot
happened to be a shallow marshy area covered with heavy grass and
scrub. The first reaction to the realities of being back on earth caused
me to squirm and struggle to my feet to escape the mud and icy water.
Still half stunned I began to stagger towards a blur of trees, only to
have the billowing parachute canopy snap me off my feet into another
pancake landing. The harness unbuckled, breath recovered, I again
set off to the edge of the marsh.

Although it was not over a hundred yards to where a pine forest
sloped down to the reeds, this first effort to seek safety so exhausted
me I had to sit down on reaching shelter. Sleet fell from the low
hanging clouds and the wind whistled through the treetops, but no
other sound could be heard. From the shock of the past few minutes
another reaction overcame me. A chill ran through my body and I
trembled violently. My teeth even chattered. Being wet probably
didn't help matters. Lighting a cigarette, I tried to ponder on what to
do next. After a few minutes the tremors departed as suddenly as they
had come. The Mustang disintegration had walloped me on the right
side and now my head, shoulder and leg began to throb with pain and
the right eye to close. From where I sat there was nothing to see but
pine forest and the marshy flats from which I had extracted myself.
Wild country, so there was a good chance no one had seen my arrival.
Just in case, it was decided to move further into the forest. The G-suit
was shed and disposed of under a clump of bushes. Returning to the
parachute, a sling for my injured arm was cut from the canopy, plus
an additional piece for future use to improve my travelling attire. The
parachute was then rolled up and crammed under another bush.
Darkness was setting in fast as I returned to the forest to hobble along
for a mile or so before stopping to review a very frustrating situation.

It was concluded that building a fire to dry out must be the next move. Since landing, my teeth had not stopped chattering from the cold. As no one seemed to be searching for me in this fairly deep forest, a fire wouldn't attract attention. The storm had passed and a few dead branches and twigs produced a beautiful blaze. The fire burned well with continued stoking but gave little heat. In the meantime I searched my pockets for anything that might improve my travelling needs. Total assets consisted of a pair of dog tags (metal identification discs) on a neck chain, knife, a still functioning US government wristwatch, a pack of Lucky Strike cigarettes, zippo lighter, and a small escape kit.

While the fire burned and I tried to dry out, the escape pack was opened. A dime-store compass and a silk map were extracted. From the time and the distance covered it could be reckoned that the P-51 had come down somewhere east of Hannover. Belgium or Holland would be a couple of hundred walking miles to the west. Oh, what a happy thought! By the light of the fire, an attempt to reorientate myself with the aid of map and compass only added more frustration. The compass hardly held the cardinal directions; the map certainly couldn't hold the necessary details for a walk in an unknown forest.

The hours were passed drying out socks and mulling over the predicament. Recurring thoughts ran through my mind. My fellow flying comrades were by now returning to home base where there would be a welcoming fire, a drink and a wholesome dinner at the Club. Here the situation was bleak at best. There was only one consolation in all of this, on the morrow I would not have to report at Brigadier General Auton's headquarters to fly a desk.

A miserable night was passed trying to stoke the fire into giving sufficient heat to dry my wet clothing and boots. There were brief lapses of sleep but a bleak morning did finally arrive. Realising that meditating beside a fire would not aid my passage to Allied lines, the few belongings were gathered up and, compass in hand, I set off on a westerly course. Though it wasn't sleeting or raining, bushes, grass and everything I brushed against was wet. An inch or two of mushy snow lay in the open areas. The sky was still sullen with low-lying clouds and a brisk wind whipped through the tops of the firs.

From my flights over enemy territory I knew that German forests were small compared with those in the United States. Most were broken up by tracts of open land and the actual wooded areas were often only a few hundred acres in extent. During that first morning I hobbled in and out of several, moving along the edges, always fearful of being seen. From time to time I sat in a thicket resting and watching for activity in the fields. Apart from some cattle the countryside seemed deserted; which was reassuring in that no-one appeared to be searching for an Allied airman. Again I struck out westward with a knee that ached with every step taken and a right arm swollen like a sausage. Progress was slow at best. In the course of that day no more than a few miles were traversed. Some potatoes were picked up in a field, rubbed and gnawed.

Try as I may I could never orientate myself with the map, it was probably the most disconcerting part of this venture. While quite determined to walk the 200 miles to Allied lines, there was no point in deluding myself. Winter was setting in and there was no hope of 'living off the land'. Further, my injuries made every step painful. I suspected there were fractures, particularly in the arm. Sooner or later help had to be sought. But where in this hostile land? Just before dusk a small wooded plot was entered and after transgressing this covert a small field appeared. Here could be seen a horse and cart with two old people working on their hands and knees, topping freshly turned sugar beet by hand and tossing them into the cart. Neither had seen me so I sat down behind a tree to watch. At evasion briefings back at base we had been told that if people had to be contacted for help it was best to tackle them individually and not when there were more than two. Always approach the individual in an isolated location, do so casually and, if unsuccessful, move off unobtrusively. Having by now concluded that a foot trek to Holland was not exactly on the cards in my condition, a decision was made to approach these two people for assistance.

With the advantage of being acquainted with the German language from my youth there should be no problems of communication. Perhaps they'd give me a break, dry my clothing and check my arm, while some better food could revive my deflated spirit. If they were German there was no reason to believe they would be anything but hostile; on the other hand they might not be sympathetic to the Nazi cause, or even foreign forced labourers.

Even after I had walked a fair way into the field they did not notice me, such was their concentration on the monotonous work of picking up sugar beet, chopping leaves off with a swipe of a large knife before tossing them in the cart. Coming within speaking distance, both looked up with a start as if they beheld the devil. Admittedly, the figure before them was not a pretty sight with torn olive drab flight jacket and GI pants covered in mud, right hand in an improvised sling and displaying a beautiful black eye. When I opened the conversation in German they were even more startled. Although the only thing I said was that I was an American flier seeking a little food and help, the terrified woman took off in great haste towards a distant group of farm buildings.

Fearfully the old man pleaded, on his knees, that he was a Polish forced labourer and could not help me. It didn't take long to realise there would be no assistance here for while these labourers might not have favoured the German cause, both were even more terrified of doing anything to support the Allies. No doubt the old woman would alert the countryside so, with what haste I could muster, the security of woodland was again sought.

Continuing my slow pace to the west, it was not long before the trees thinned and a paved road appeared. Cautiously looking to see if it remained clear in both directions, I started to hobble across to be confronted suddenly by a group of yelling farmers and foresters armed with all sorts of makeshift hunting weapons. Cornered and unable to run, I had no wise option but to give up. These captors made no attempt to search me, nor was I mishandled, although they registered disappointment that I did not carry a pistol that could be confiscated. Incredibly, one actually did say in broken English, 'Fur yoo die var is hover'. Before long every man, woman, child and dog came to look at this 'Terror Flieger'. The procession moved down the road in the waning hours of the day to a forest guesthouse. Here, on entering, they allowed me to sit in a chair in the kitchen while a guard with a shotgun sat nearby. There was some consolation in being here as I was warm if not yet dry. A woman cook who was busy preparing a meal asked if I'd care for a bowl of soup. To this my reply was, 'No thank you, I'm too sick to eat.' No doubt the effects of shock were still with me. Permission was given to wash my face and hands in the sink which was a great relief.

During the course of the next two or three hours a continual chatter concerning the apprehension of the 'Terror Flieger' could be heard issuing from the sitting room of the guest house. I learned that I was in Nindorf, a small village on the Luneburg-Heide moorlands. No one was allowed to come in and see me so I sat in my chair and meditated. Many things passed through my mind. Concern that my family would fear me dead; reaction among my fellow officers in England and trying to figure out just what had happened in that last plunge in the storm. I had been flying my personal Mustang, 9B-Z, the same airplane in which I had executed violent evasive action and exceeded 500 mph in recent fights. Perhaps the wing had been overstrained on those occasions and the attempt at recovery in the storm had been the final straw. I was now fairly certain that the right wing had folded back and struck the cockpit, initiating the disintegration. I had heard about cases of P-51 structural failure but to come through numerous near-misses in combat only to have my airplane come to pieces on my last scheduled mission seemed a darned unlucky break. Then again, I was incredibly fortunate to have been thrown clear and not trapped in the wreckage.

About 11 pm a group of Luftwaffe officers arrived in a small staff car. Their appearance brought a more serious atmosphere to the guesthouse and everyone quietened down immediately. The officers requested only my rank, name and serial number; nothing else. A few questions were asked of the search party whereafter I was whisked into the staff car and driven away. Well after midnight the staff car entered an aerodrome. I was registered in a single room apartment in the station jailhouse, the arrangement being modest with one barred window, a ceiling light that burned constantly, a chair and a bunk bed. While a guard brought a blanket and pillow, an officer told me to remove my clothes, allowing me to retain my long-handle underwear, while the rest of my personal things were removed for the remainder of the night. With a clink, clink the iron door of the cell was locked. Periodically throughout the night the clomp, clomp of a guard's boots could be heard making the rounds of the cells, stopping in front of my door so he could squint through a peep-hole at me. Early the next morning there was a rattle of the key and the open door disclosed a soldier carrying a portion of black bread, a small square of foul-smelling cheese and a quart flask containing some sort of ersatz concoction that passed as coffee.

The jail at this particular aerodrome, Celle, struck me as being about standard for criminal confinement worldwide. It was constructed of mortar stone, with a barred window set too high to look out of, an iron door that looked as if it could easily withstand the attack of a panzer tank, and meagre furnishing which provided just enough accommodation for me to sit or lie down. About the only recreation was to pace the floor or lie on the straw mattress bunk. There being no attempt to interrogate me, about the only break to this solitary confinement came when two meals a day were served. The menu never changed. Breakfast was black bread and ersatz coffee; dinner, which arrived late in the day, consisted of the same solid bread and a plate of soup, the ingredients of which were not known but tasted well enough. Another break in the monotonous routine permitted the prisoner to visit the latrine. By pounding on the iron door the guard's attention could be gained. At least this escorted trip outside the confines of the cell enabled me to see other surroundings in the residence. The remaining cells were mostly vacant but what struck me as being very peculiar was that the other inmates were mostly sixteen and seventeen-year old Germans. None wore prison garb but, rather, normal European work clothes. When I was permitted to go to the latrine they crowded around with all sorts of questions. The guard scattered them with his pistol when they became too blatant. Since none spoke English I feigned not to understand. I can only conclude they must have been delinquents held on minor offences.

My clothing had been returned after the first evening; the flight jacket now had 'Kriegsgefangener' (Prisoner of War) painted across the back in large black letters. Missing from the pockets were the escape kit, GI watch, my knife and cigarette lighter. Instead, a receipt listing the confiscated items was written and given in return. The packet of Lucky Strike was returned but with no means of lighting them there was an opportunity to break the cigarette habit. Needless to say, I was quick to return to this degenerating pastime at the first opportunity. No matches could be provided for PoWs as there was always a possibility they would set fire to the straw-filled mattresses. The guard's explanation as to the confiscation of the lighter was that the Third Reich had the authority vested by the rules of the 1929 Geneva Convention. Since I had never read the Geneva Convention there was little room for rebuttal. Articles taken would be forwarded to the next station for safe keeping, he said. As it turned out, they were never seen again and the paper receipt wore out before my time in Germany had ended.

17

INTERROGATION

Being still partially shocked, most of my time during the next day or so was spent sleeping. On the third evening the grim looking guard unlocked the cell door and motioned me out with a gruff, 'Raus! Ein Offizier mochte mit dir sprechen!' The thought flashed through my mind — now here comes the inquisition, the third degree, be prepared. In the outer office of the jail, a Luftwaffe Major asked, in broken English, for my name, rank and serial number. Turning to two enlisted men in full battledress he said, in German, 'This is your ward'. Orders were given to deliver me to Auswertestelle-West, the infamous interrogation centre at Oberursel, near Frankfurt am Main. In faltering English the Major briefly told me that I was being conducted to my next station by railroad. 'Your life is worth the value of one bullet. If you attempt to escape that bullet will be expended.' The manner of his delivery came neither as forceful threat nor dictatorial warning; rather as just another piece of factual information.

Moving off the airdrome in the darkness, the three of us passed slowly down the main street of a village. Not a light was shown. The village appeared to be uninhabited, no movement or sound, not a dog barked: weird. Having stumbled along in the darkness for a mile or more into open countryside, one of the guards called a stop to rest for a few minutes, whereupon he darted away into the gloom. It struck me as being a peculiar place to stop. After fifteen minutes he reappeared with a girlfriend or wife in tow. Down the country road we proceeded and in due course arrived at a one-room blacked-out railroad station. Passing through the blackout curtains we entered a waiting room crowded with men and women, all chatting noisily away. Most were civilians although a few were in military uniform. Almost immediately the conversation subsided into hushed gasps as all eyes turned my way.

Several days had now passed since my arrival in Germany and I had been unable to secure a razor or shave. As a result, a stubble beard now graced my far from pretty face. The blow on my head had blackened the right eye, displaying a respectable shiner to everyone. With rumpled hair, lacking a comb for days, there is no doubt that I had the appearance of the proverbial Chicago thug, a true 'Terror Flieger'. One of the guards unsheathed a handful of documents for inspection and stamping by some official, while I stood with the other guard and his embarrassed female companion. Although the clearance procedure took only a minute or two, these were highly uncomfortable moments for me. Trying to be nonchalant when almost everyone in the room looks directly at you, casting aspersions to the effect that shooting is too good for such a villain, doesn't help the ego. Thankfully, our party soon moved outside to the station platform where at least it was dark and isolated. This, however, was not for my benefit but so the guard could console his woman with words of endearment about not having to be gone too long. Words were quickly abandoned to a series of breath-taking kisses and fondling guaranteed to stir the blood circulation in the most indifferent imagination. All during this nocturnal love-making I was leaning against a post not three steps away trying to appear disinterested. The other guard neither spoke nor moved, apparently also trying to keep an indifferent composure.

Perhaps an hour passed before a puffing locomotive hauling two coaches pulled in. The station emptied with a rush carrying me and the guards on board. As expected, the hitherto partially filled coaches now overflowed. People elbowed each other to gain space on the hard wooden benches. Being well aware of the feelings of these people towards me, it was considered prudent not to compete and I was finally relegated to a corner on the floor. The love-struck guard managed to board the train as it started to pull out and muscling a seat near me he sat blankly staring into space for some time. His countenance gave the impression that he was the one going to prison, not I.

After midnight the wheezing train pulled into a main station which proved to be Hanover. This building showed signs of bomb damage with the occasional blown out window covered with black paper to prevent the escape of light. Inside the hall a sizable crowd of soldiers, sailors and civilians milled about attempting to make train connections. From time to time a brazen loud-speaker system blurted out the arrival or departure times of trains. It was evident that Germany moved at night during these war years. It seemed that everyone, including the women, was laden down with enormous back packs. All wore heavy winter clothing, giving the appearance of ski excursion holidaymakers starting out for some winter resort.

Among the travellers were small clusters of less well dressed men who appeared to be manual labourers. Hearing them speak in a foreign tongue I realised they must be imported workers from occupied countries. They moved about in a free, unattended manner but didn't mingle with the Germans. Knowing everyone in Germany carried a kin-card — identification card — I was surprised to find them moving around so freely, especially as this was now well past midnight. Later I learned that these people were volunteers working for the German government and for the most part were sympathetic to the Nazi cause.

My presence soon attracted considerable interest. There was no hesitancy among travellers to question guards as to who I was and what I was doing there. Despite some strong accents I could pick up most questions: 'Is he an American flier?' 'Ja; just been shot down by one of the Luftwaffe's gallant pilots somewhere near Celle.' 'He's a Colonel. Pretty young don't you think?' 'He has the shifty look of a true Terror Flieger.' 'Where is he going? To prison camp?' and so forth.

By two in the morning our south-bound train arrived. To board was again a pushing match. It was terribly crowded but after tramping through several cars the guards swung open a compartment door and the three of us entered and sat down. No doubt this was first class for there were plush covered seats and we were the only people to occupy this space. For the next day and a half I sat in comfort, if this can be called comfort. There was no non-stop run to our destination, Frankfurt am Main. Throughout this journey there was considerable jolting and jerking, backing and stalling, making me think there were tie-ups with the traffic on the line, probably as a result of Allied air attacks. Most of my time was spent napping in the corner seat, nursing my still smarting arm, reflecting on my predicament or gazing out of the window at the German countryside.

All along the route numerous military targets could be seen. Locomotives parked under camouflage nets; concentrations of tanks and vehicles among groves of trees. How often I had flown over this very territory without detecting a single suspicious sign. Now, as a victim of circumstances, before my eyes lay a veritable fighter pilot's strafing heaven. Further interesting sights unfolded as the train passed an airfield on the outskirts of Kassel. There, at the very edge of the aerodrome, two FW 190s were taxying out to take off. This was a new vantage point on Focke-Wulfs for me and the wishful thought to be flying above ready to take advantage of the situation momentarily brightened my outlook. Soon afterwards the train came to a temporary halt in Kassel freight yards where I was mildly amazed to see the large numbers of tanks, vehicles and all kinds of military equipment on railroad wagons. Not much evidence here of the Allies bombing stemming war supplies.

The train finally drew into Frankfurt, from whence my guards took me via a trolley bus trip to the gates of Auswertestelle-West. Outside what I assumed was an administrative building, stood a guard with two dishevelled men who I immediately recognised as fellow American flyers. Apart from an acknowledgement little was said as I was suspicious that they might be 'plants'. This thought no doubt played on their minds also when they saw my approach.

While waiting for one of my escort to return from inside this building, I saw, casually walking round the corner of the block, a German soldier with a fine looking German shepherd dog walking at heel on a loose chain. As I turned to look at these passers-by the dog snarled and leapt in our direction, nearly upfooting its master who, by sheer strength and a loud command, dragged the guard dog away. However, not before three American PoWs and their accompanying German guard flinched with sudden fright. The commotion and subsequent bellowing of orders brought several attendents on the run from the building. More guards appeared, weapons at the ready, no doubt concerned that this might be a PoW escape attempt. Forthwith the three of us were escorted into the reception room of this bleak hostelry and in short order directed to remove all our clothes. While several members of the German staff searched each pocket and seam for a hidden compass or magnetic needle we sat shivering and naked on a wooden bench. The thought occurred — would the next trick be the rubber truncheon or the water treatment. Having performed a minute investigation of my stinking underwear and found nothing, one of the searchers assisted me in dressing.

By the time the last zipper was closed I was told to move on to the rogues' gallery where pictures were taken. Then in walked a Luftwaffe officer (later I learned his name, Leutnant Walter Haneman). Looking the three of us over he asked in good English, 'Which of you is Zemke?' With some trepidation I said: 'I am.' With this reply he walked over and sat down on the bench next to me, asked how I felt and if I'd been treated okay. My reply was conciliatory, adding that my immediate need was to see a doctor about a sore arm and shoulder. This he assured me would be attended to although I was not convinced he meant it. Casual small talk ensued and I was asked to walk into an adjoining room with a table and several straight-backed wooden chairs. Here Haneman produced what appeared to be a Red Cross form and laid it out on the table for me to read. In the meantime he lit up a cigarette and asked if I cared for one. Knowing this was an enticement to break the social barrier, my inclination was to refuse.

The Red Cross form contained several questions in addition to name, rank and serial number, clearly more than was needed to identify a person. The Lieutenant asked me to fill it out and sign the bottom line. This I refused to do, but temptation being too great, said I'd take one of his cigarettes. For a time we argued the purpose of signing such a document, as all he had to do was notify the US government of my capture and they would notify next-of-kin. This conversation drifted on for several minutes until another interrogator entered the room. This man, a Gefreiter (Private, first class), was introduced as 'Wild Bill', although I later learned his real name was Otto Englehardt. A Canadian, rough in his speech, overly emphatic with his gestures and showing no finesse in his questioning, one immediately identified him as a bully. His command of the English language was certainly not up to that of Haneman. No doubt this interrogation technique was to see if intimidation produced faster results. Seeing that this discussion hadn't provided much information, Haneman broke it off by saying, 'If you choose not to co-operate there are other methods of gaining the information.' It was given in a tone of voice that could be conceived as a mild emphasis of the fact rather than a threat.

As the two interrogators arose, Haneman said, 'You must be very tired from your ordeal of the last few days, Colonel, so we'll show you to your new home'. Escorting me down a long corridor of solitary cells a guard stopped to sort out a selection of keys before opening a door. Each cell along the corridor was closed off by a solid door so that no visual contact with the occupant could be made. Walking inside I found a single cot, a stool and a table. The entire room had been painted white, probably whitewash. A small wire-caged bulb burned continually in the ceiling. The two barred windows had been boarded up so that all outside view was stopped. There was a small serving hatch at the bottom of the entrance door. In gruff German the guard told me to remove my clothes again and took them with him. A blanket and pillow were brought later in the evening. On the bed rested a lumpy mattress which, on examination, proved to be filled with wood shavings. Posted next to the door, a type-written sheet in English gave the house rules; all rules ended with a penalty. So I rolled out the blanket on the bed, consoling myself that a foxhole in the front lines could be worse.

Weariness brought on by two sleepless nights soon caught up with me. This night's rest should have been the best experience in a long time but it was not. Somehow the management had forgotten to turn the heat on. November in Germany is not the ideal time of the year to go to bed with a single blanket. Also, I soon discovered I was not the only occupant of the bed. The night passed between sessions of scratching and rewrapping the blanket around me to keep warm.

A heavy rap on the door gave notice that things at Auswertestelle-West were stirring again. A guard opened the door to present a large plate of cooked barley with a paper packet of sugar. What a treat. Before he departed a request was made and granted that I visit the latrine. Taking me to a washroom down the hall, the guard dallied at the door while I went through the rituals of morning toiletry. This time all procedures were drawn out as long as possible as this trip was a relief from the tight confinement of the cell. After several 'Mach Schnell!' this recreation came to an end and I was marched back. At least I'd been able to wash my hands and face, while with a bit of rag the accumulation of food debris around my teeth was scraped away. Using my fingers, I re-established the parting in my hair. Already the improvement could be felt. For breakfast the bowl of barley porridge was fine; not a morsel remained after my assault. Even the spoon was licked for fear some of the mute flavour had been missed. Still, a sizeable cavity remained in the stomach area. How quickly everyday functions, taken for granted and hardly given a thought just a few days before, now assumed overwhelming importance and obsessed the thoughts.

Now what to do with the idle time. Trying to entertain oneself in solitary confinement imposes a real problem. Humans do not practise or voluntarily submit themselves to the mastery of monotony. With me the sequence of events went something like this. First I paced the floor. Soon this wore thin as the cell was so small. Next, all the boards making up one wall were counted. This ended when all the boards in the entire room were counted. Realising there could be better things to do, I decided to sing a few songs. Frankly this was not too inspiring as the words to many had been forgotten. Reciting poetry and making up verse consumed some time. Even reciting multiplication tables helped. Tiring of these routines the next recourse was to try to nap; at least while sleeping the mind goes blank. Unhappily the fleas were not co-operative.

Mid-morning found a rattle of the keys at the door again and in walked Haneman with a guard. My clothes were returned, thoroughly dry, and I concluded they had been washed or deloused. Once I was dressed, Haneman escorted me down the corridor of closed cells to the original interrogation room where behind the desk sat Canadian 'Wild Bill'. I was asked if I had a comfortable night. I decided that it would be better to say 'Okay', knowing full well the purpose of the irrelevant question. A complaint was hardly likely to register, but I did say my arm and shoulder still pained. They expressed interest but did nothing about it. Presently a guard entered the room bearing a pot of ersatz coffee and three cups and saucers. Haneman poured the coffee, no mention being made of whether I took coffee or not. Reaching in his blouse pocket he produced a packet of cigarettes and gave me one. Here again, not offered but given, another gesture of forced congeniality. Conversation among the three of us continued in a casual manner on several non-sensitive items until the Red Cross form was again mentioned. Once more I insisted that name, rank and serial number were all that was required. The two interrogators still held that this was a standard internationally accepted form to notify belligerents of PoW capture.

During this exchange a tall, slender Luftwaffe Gefreiter entered the room. This man beamed a wide smile, strode across the room and introduced himself as Hanns Scharff. With an unassuming air of friendliness, his next words went something like this, 'Gabby and Gerald Johnson will certainly be glad to see you. Now that you're on our side all you need to do is have Don Blakeslee and Dave Schilling come and join us, then the war will be over.' This gesture, coupled with the announcement of names of close colleagues, took me a little by surprise. How did a complete stranger know that these poeple were close associates of mine. At first I professed I didn't know such individuals but Scharff only laughed at my futile attempt to hide identities and proceeded to tell me where they were and what fighter units they commanded. This interrogator struck me as being a polished actor, a salesman, who knew the techniques of his profession and applied the correct touch to produce results. Compared to the other two interrogators, Scharff's use of the English language was convincing. For the most part he did the talking and carried the conversation, often deviating to inject humour into the situation.

A little warning flag went up in my mind telling me to be extra careful with this man lest I say something of importance without realising it. Recognising a master of trivial conversation, I feared he would pop a seemingly innocent question out of the blue that could receive an innocent but helpful answer. No doubt his study of apparently inconsequencial bits of information on the organisation and operation of the 8th Air Force fighter groups formed the basis for a broader picture presented to Luftwaffe Intelligence. He knew his subject well; the names of commanders, pilots, their aerial successes and failures, stations and much more. He could recall the personal characteristics of a PoW who had passed through Auswertestelle-West long before my arrival. Subsequently I learned how his background in English and cosmopolitan traits had been acquired. As a BMW company salesman in South Africa pre-war, he had married a Scottish Squadron Leader's daughter.

My first encounter with this master left me with no indications of his seeking to extract information, indeed, hardly any sense of being interrogated. Finally, Scharff asked how I had been treated since arriving in Germany. Deciding not to mention the miserable night spent in his cooler, I complained about the lack of response to the request for a medic to look at my right shoulder and arm. He immediately ranted and raved about the incompetency of the personnel responsible for this situation. Obviously this tirade was expressed for my personal benefit as part of the normal procedure for softening up arrivals. He gave the impression of being the camp commander rather than a lowly Private 1st Class — although I already appreciated that this was no ordinary NCO. Promises were made again that these failures would be corrected. Before this meeting broke up I requested some reading material and also reaffirmed my intention to have nothing to do with the Red Cross form that the other interrogators insisted on my signing. As far as I was concerned it wouldn't matter a tinker's damn if the Allies never learned of my capture. To this Scharff said that some literature would be forthcoming and anyway the form wasn't of any great significance.

That afternoon, as the temperature in the cell began to rise, a guard pushed through the hatch an English copy of *The Life of Alfred Krupp*. Next day a razor and a bar of soap made the morning visit to the latrine washroom; a luxury to be cherished. Except for the continual gnawing feeling in the pit of the stomach, life between the four walls of the cell was almost tolerable. However, no doctor made an appearance, nor was I summoned for further interrogation and the monotony of isolated confinement began to have some effect. The mind conjures up all sort of imaginings. Having spent a most active and adventurous life delving into many activities, beside the military, to be suddenly restrained to the point of having absolutely nothing to do or no one to talk to does have a psychological effect. The inducement of mental and physical frustration was, of course, the purpose of the incarceration, with the hope that the subject would thereafter more easily succumb to questioning. In an attempt to rationalise a positive solution to the situation, the thought occurred that with hundreds of prisoners of war being captured each month, the Germans couldn't possibly retain one individual in solitary confinement for ever. Patience was the key to my predicament.

After breakfast on the third day, the guard ordered me from the cell with a brusque 'Raus! Wir gehen zum Scharff's Zimmer.' To my surprise he escorted me from the building across an open space to another wooden building. This trip from 'The Cooler' enabled me to see in daylight the composition of Auswertestelle-West, and the surroundings. Set out in rows were long wooden buildings and encompassing the camp was a double fence at least ten feet high. Along this fence were observation towers manned by guards with machine guns. Outside the barricaded perimeter more guards patrolled on foot. There was no difficulty in distinguishing where the PoWs were housed as each individual cell had a boarded and barred window. The office buildings for the Luftwaffe interrogation staff were of the same low wooden construction except that the windows of these were not barricaded, the shutters being open during daylight hours.

Scharff's office was a modest working abode containing two easy chairs, a table and some bookshelves. A picture of Hitler stared out from a frame on the wall. Scharff, in jolly mood, dismissed the guard saying, 'I have something to show you'. Lying on his desk was a sizable photo album filled with photographs of 56th Fighter Group personnel suitably captioned. The first picture to catch my eye showed Schilling, Gabreski, Christensen and myself strolling around the perimeter at Boxted. I recognised this photo as one distributed to British and US newspapers in the late summer, but how had Scharff acquired a print? Before I could ask, Scharff anticipated the question and said, 'We don't need to know much about your organisation and reputation Zemke; our sources contain plenty of information about the 56th'. I asked Scharff if he received *Stars and Stripes*, the military newspaper printed daily in London. He assured me he was a subscriber and received each edition three days after printing. 'Once in a while', he said, 'I miss a copy. I hate missing Terry and the Pirates and the Sad Sack cartoons.' As I suspected, German intelligence obtained copies via Portugal, where I had seen news stands displaying papers from countries throughout the world. It wouldn't be difficult to make a copy of any photo that appeared in *Stars and Stripes*. Before I was shown more, Scharff's secretary, a Miss Beck, came into the office from an inner door to ask if we cared for refreshments. She was pleasantly warned that Zemke could converse in German as were all those who subsequently dropped in for a look at this curious individual. No doubt this forewarning prevented any German slip of the tongue about something I wasn't to know.

During the afternoon the camp commandant, Oberleutnant Killinger, dropped in with a civilian named Schmitt. As they arrived Scharff confided that Herr Schmitt specialised in interrogating PoWs caught in the French underground system. 'Be on your toes when this man is around', he warned, as if I didn't realise that anyone here handling a German accent spelt peril. Now some serious questions popped up from time to time. In particular what were the future programmes of Generals Spaatz and Doolittle for the employment of bombers and fighters against Germany. To this the answer was simple and truthful, I saw these generals only on rare occasions. If they divulged such information to me I would have quickly been put on non-combat status in some HQ flying a desk. They were told that I had purposely not cultivated Generals more than casually for fear of finding myself assigned to some headquarters staff. The feeling prevailed that as long as I produced results in the field, the need for a competent combat leader overrode the necessity for assigning me as a staff officer. Colonels with sharp pencils were a dime a dozen; true combat leaders were a rarer commodity.

Scharff periodically reviewed his photo album of various units. There was no doubt he had accumulated a vast collection of pictures and facts on his enemies that amazed me. In one shot stood Bob Johnson leaning against his P-47 *Penrod & Sam*. Another photo showed a group of 56th boys walking down the ramp arm in arm. I beheld pictures of the operations briefing, personalities from other groups, and their aircraft, all correctly identified. Scharff even possessed a good photo taken *inside* the officers' mess at Boxted — a recent photograph at that! I could only guess that he had taken it from some PoW; although why would any pilot be carrying such a photo in a flight suit?

'Now a bit on Zemke', he said, proceeding to read from the dossier on the 56th, continuing on to the 479th, beginning where I had taken command. Then he turned to my early days, going way back to where I had been born in Montana, high school, attendance at university and then to US Army flying school. It suddenly dawned on me that such details on officers in US services were available to anyone buying the Army-Navy register from the United States Government office. Every military attaché bought a copy of this military 'Who's Who' just to keep abreast of the background potential of US military officers. Such an amount of data had now been assembled and consolidated here as an effective weapon of persuasion. The naive would be surprised and baffled by such an array of information held by the enemy and be more easily tricked into adding to this fund. Admittedly, even though I had some idea of Scharff's purpose, it was difficult to continue to feign indifference and refrain from comments that might confirm or contribute to their intelligence. Being so open about his information made me question him as to his sources. To this he always smiled and gave a dismissive reply. The session over, I was once again returned to solitary confinement. It could be concluded that all our conversations had been taped as no written notes were taken.

Later that afternoon the clomp, clomp of boots and the rattle of keys in the door made known that something was up again. Haneman and Scharff entered with a guard. The greeting was cordial. Scharff made a proposal: 'If you promise not to try to escape; give your officer's honour; we will take you for a nice walk to the dispensary at Hohe-Mark'. Not being prepared for much of an escape, I agreed; a change of scenery would be very welcome. This established, the three of us walked from the cell block to the front gate. After the interrogators signed a register the gates swung open and we followed a narrow road that wound up through a pine forest in the Taunus mountains. My leg, though still bruised, was much improved and I could now walk reasonably well. After about fifteen minutes the forest opened out and before us, on a grassy knoll, stood a three-storey brick building. Ringing a bell at the larger of the back doors brought a sister in nun's habit, who bade us enter. Climbing three flights of stairs from the vestibule brought us to an alcove which looked like a reception room. Passing through this room and into a larger room set up with tables and chairs, we came upon a number of PoW patients reading and playing cards. The patients wore white hospital pyjamas and some, additionally, grey robes. All bore evidence of combat. Some hovered around with a foot in a cast, another carried an arm at shoulder level in a traction device, a couple were hunched in wheelchairs, and there were several whose faces and hands were completely sheathed in bandages with only their noses and eyes exposed and perhaps a tuft of hair protruding from the head. One of the doors on one side of the room revealed two decks of beds where the patients slept or lay immobilised by their wounds. Another room with a drawn curtain contained an emergency operating theatre with an array of surgical equipment.

The entire place, looking clean and neat, was well heated. Exactly what functioned in the remaining portion of this large building, namely the lower floor, was never learned, except that prior to the war it had been a sanatorium run by Lutheran sisters. A lone Luftwaffe doctor seemed to be the only medical man around, although I was told an elderly civilian doctor assisted him. The nursing and orderly service was predominantly provided by mobile patients. The doctor, Hauptman Ernest Ittershagen, a man in his mid-thirties, spoke excellent English and conversed genially with everyone. It was soon obvious that he was much respected as the people in the ward all spoke highly of his dedication in performing the medical tasks at hand. He had to work with meagre facilities, an acute shortage of drugs and a lack of other supplies. His stamina was considerable in view of the never-ending stream of helpless wounded brought to him. No wonder that despite his cheeful countenance one could often detect from his remarks a cynicism about the stupidity of war. He was on call in the dispensary 24 hours a day: in fact he lived in the building.

We waited while Ittershagen, wearing a white surgical smock over his Luftwaffe uniform, finished re-dressing a patient's wound. Scharff introduced us and mentioned my arm. The doctor told me to go into the operating room and strip to the waist. The shoulder and arm, still swollen, pained if moved, particularly when rolling over in my sleep on the cell bed, which brought back consciousness with a start. While washing his hands in the sink, Ittershagen asked me how this injury had happened. Remembering Scharff was listening, I told him something must have struck me as I parachuted into Germany. 'Better learn to duck on the next occasion', was his reply. At least he had a sense of humour. The doctor pressed the shoulder and joint with one hand while grasping the forearm with the other and slowly the whole arm was manipulated and felt. Eventually he gave his diagnosis; no broken bones, but a case of extremely bad bruising. Regular exercise was recommended and given a month, all would be okay. Pointing to the sunray heater in the corner of the room he told me to try it for a half hour. Scharff and a PoW who had suffered severe facial burns put the lamp on.

While I sat with the arm soaking up the heat, this PoW introduced himself as having met me before. To my astonishment it was Captain Ken 'Snuffy' Smith of the 4th Fighter Group. Smith was one of seven who didn't return from a strafing mission back in March 1944. He was now working as a PoW medical orderly in this hospital while Ittershagen slowly grafted new skin to his face. We had first met at Debden when I had dropped in to heckle the members of the 4th Group. I hadn't recognised him because of the scar tissue on his face. Captain Smith wasted no time in finding a cup and pot of hot water from somewhere. From his pocket came a real powdered milk coffee — Nescafe. How many lumps of sugar? The treatment didn't stop here, for a packet of Camel cigarettes emerged from another pocket. What could be better; a heat lamp, a real cup of coffee and a cigarette from the first friend I had seen in Germany. When Scharff and Haneman were out of earshot we discoursed on some of his former buddies and I acquired useful information on Auswertestelle-West and the techniques used to obtain intelligence. I was to learn that Loren McCollom had been treated for burns in this same dispensary and Gabreski had also made a brief appearance before going on to some prison camp. By the time my heat lamp session was completed the patients' dinner had arrived. Haneman, Scharff and I were invited to participate. The menu consisted of a generous helping of meat, vegetables and a big red apple, a banquet compared to what I had previously eaten since arriving in Germany. That evening I walked back to Auswertestelle-West with a full stomach. In my pocket was a chocolate D-bar and three Camel cigarettes. It is amazing how a good meal and a short change in surroundings can lift a man's morale. Now, serious plans for escape again entered my mind.'

18

UNDESIRED TRAVELS

A couple of days passed without the appearance of anyone but the cell guards. No doubt the return to solitude was intended to soften up the subject. Then a clank, clank of the door found Scharff entering and I was asked if I would like to visit Hohe-Mark that afternoon. The answer was naturally 'Yes'. When we arrived Doctor Ittershagen and some PoW orderlies were changing the dressing of burned victims. Of all the wounds I've ever seen, the festering burns wounds are the most horrible. Soon after the skin is burned the body begins to exhude fluid. To prevent infection, applications of ointment and wound bandages were applied. The burned area tended to swell and nerve endings became painfully sensitive to any movement or agitation. Bandages had to be changed regularly to guard against infection and check on the healing. Their removal caused agony for the victim, while the task was not for those with a weak stomach, the smell being obnoxious. On my first visit to Hohe-Mark I had mentioned having spent a year working part-time in a hospital while attending University. Recalling this, Ittershagen asked me to lend a hand if the nauseating stench and sights were not too much. 'Hell No. I've seen worse.' I doubt if this was the case, however, but under the circumstances what other answer could I give? By dinner time at least ten burn cases had been processed. Washing up after this ordeal made me thankful that entering into captivity nothing more than a few bruises had been experienced.

Following dinner, Ittershagen asked Scharff and I if we would care to assist with a flak wound case that had just been brought in. My reply was again in the affirmative; the longer away from the cell the better. Scharff made no objection so we stayed. The part we played, together with four able-bodied PoW patients, amounted to holding down an unfortunate bomber crew member who had received wounds in the buttocks. The doctor had no anaesthetic so the man had to bear with the pain. Hitherto this sort of operation had belonged to the movies where the gallant hero was given a bullet to bite while the doctor worked. Such a portrayal bore no resemblence to what occurred here. Six rough handlers held the patient on the operating table while the doctor probed with his surgical tongs, removing several pieces of embedded shrapnel. The man, lying face down, continually screamed and shrieked. Ittershagen worked rapidly and skilfully, speaking to the patient in a quite sincere manner all the time. I had heard screams of pain and seen men jerk under applied violence before, but this case beat them all. The operation took perhaps twenty minutes yet seemed to drag on for hours. At one time a feeling of nausea began to creep over me then somehow subsided. As a fresh bandage was applied to the sobbing young man he was told the fragments of 88 mm shell had been saved for him to take back to the US after the war; some memento!

While any relief from solitary confinement was welcome, the experiences at the dispensary that afternoon were disturbing. There was plenty of time to ponder on the suffering at Hohe-Mark, for once more I was left to myself in the cell. Two days passed before the guards came in and directed me to follow. Scharff was in the outer reception room. With a smile he informed me I was heading for Wetzlar and Dulag-Luft, the distribution centre created for PoWs. He walked with me and my two armed guards to the open gates, wished me good luck and 'Auf weidersehen'. Riding the trolley car to Frankfurt station provided a good look at the destruction created by our aerial bombardment. Whole city blocks had been flattened, rubble lay everywhere. What hadn't been bombed out had been burned out.

A crowded train carried us northwards the thirty miles to Wetzlar, a small manufacturing town best noted for the makers of Leica cameras. With winter now well set in, a grey overcast sky gave the snow covered countryside a harsh, foreboding appearance. Except in the city, little life could be noted. As we travelled my mind ran over the events of the past few days. There was the satisfaction that the interrogation had been light; as an experienced group commander I had expected the third degree. What really baffled me was just what, if anything, had Hanns Scharff and his cooler crew extracted from me of military value? He never did attempt to enquire about the tactics of the fighter groups or other combat techniques. Air strategy and the future plans of aerial engagement had been raised but soon dropped. Perhaps they were convinced of my sincerity that I purposely stayed away from obtaining such information for fear of being shelved with some headquarters staff. Even so, there was a nagging worry in my mind that something had been extracted; Scharff was too wily to permit me to slip through his fingers if he thought I could supply the answers he required. Those walks to Hohe-Mark. Were they all part of the technique? Had I somehow been caught off-guard? I went over and over our conversations that I could recall yet was still none the wiser.

At Wetzlar we walked some distance from the railroad station to reach the double-wired enclosure of Dulag-Luft. Another sad array of unpainted wooden buildings with a rail spur nearby on which stood a few wooden box cars, presumably for shipment of POWs to prison camps further east. At Dulag-Luft I was pleased to find that an old fighter pilot friend of mine, from the 8th Pursuit Group days at Langley Field, was senior Allied officer. Colonel Charlie Stark had commanded a P-47 group in the Mediterranean theatre of war before going down the previous May. With a small staff of American and British POWs he now had the job of overseeing the distribution of International Red Cross supplies that came in through Switzerland. He tried to see that every prisoner reaching Dulag-Luft was fitted out with something in the way of clothing and personal requisites before moving on to a prison camp further east. This was an extremely difficult and frustrating task as there was never anything like sufficient quantities from either the Red Cross or the Germans.

I learned that as the weeks passed, so equipment from German sources had gradually diminished and for many items prisoners were now wholly dependent upon the Red Cross. The most needy cases were the bomber crews who flew in electrically heated boots to withstand the extreme cold of the high altitudes at which they flew. Their wire-filled footwear was totally unsuitable for ground use and quickly came apart. Some bomber crewmen, figuring the odds that they could end up in Germany, tied a pair of GI shoes to their parachute harness, but most arriving at Dulag-Luft had to be shod. A PoW was very lucky if he received shoes of the correct size for normal sizes were usually out of the question. Frequently he had to slop around in sizes far too large for the rest of his stay in the Reich. Some had to wear wooden clogs.

That first tour in England and the Soviet Union taught me the value of good leather boots, whether roaming around open airfields or flying an aircraft. Upon returning to the United States I bought two pairs of eight inch Russell Bird Shooter boots. These moccasin type shoes, a size large enough to accommodate two pairs of woollen socks, were comfortable hunting gear and were much cherished. One pair had fractionally spearheaded my arrival in Germany.

There was little for me to do at Wetzlar except roam the perimeter fence, meditate, or talk with other detainees. Conversation among compatriots mostly speculated on the future; just what could be expected of the permanent prison camps in eastern Germany and Poland, how would we get there, when would we go. Little was known of these destinations as the Germans permitted no inter-camp communication. The capacity of Dulag-Luft could hardly provide accommodation for more than 200 PoWs, so periodically numbers were assembled and marched to the freight cars to undertake that journey to an unknown destination. Despite my expectations, I was not scheduled for these parties and, having no assignment to any duty, time dragged by slowly.

With the Allied forces in the west approaching the German border the frequencies of air raid warnings increased. Whenever the Wetzlar sirens sounded, shutters to the windows had to be closed and everyone must be in barracks. To be caught outside opened avenues of being summarily shot. One morning the warning was given but on this occasion no one extended themselves and the windows remained partly open. Soon a number of heavy bombers could be heard coming from the south-east. The noise level increased until at last a formation of heavies could be seen, no doubt plodding their way back to their English bases. The formation wasn't large so it was concluded to have been part of a bomb wing returning from a mission deep in Germany which had somehow split off from the main forces. What a sight, B-17s high in the air; we were exhilarated. On they droned in the clear towards us. Suddenly, much to our surprise there was a swish of falling bombs. In a flash excitement gave way to fear as all of us hit the floor in an attempt to gain cover. With a mighty vroomp, vroomp, the earth quaked. Dust and debris flew into the air. The doors flew open, frames rattled and the ramshackle wooden huts shook as if they were about to collapse on us. Then came silence — except for the monotonous drone of aircraft motors moving west. Eventually the all-clear sounded. Dumbfounded, we looked out of the windows. The optical plant in Wetzlar, not more than a mile or two from the camp, was the obvious target. We expected to see ruins, instead it stood unscathed. The churned and blackened fields in between the factory and our camp showed where the bombs had struck short. What a waste of effort; but what a thrill.

December came and winter hardened while I wondered why the Germans still held me in this transit camp. The local Luftwaffe staff would or could not give an explanation. So while others came and went, I continued to occupy myself as best I could, even if a goodly amount of time was spent sleeping.

It was from sound slumbers that Charlie shook me awake around four in the morning on 11 December, 'Get up Hub, you've orders to move out. Get your things and hustle to the cook shack, then report to the headquarters office.' As my senses pushed off the veil of sleep I wondered why I'd been called so early in the day. My curiosity increased as I downed two cups of ersatz coffee and gnawed on a crust of black bread; no one else appeared to be moving. Wondering where the permanent camp to which the Germans had finally decided to send me would be, I made tracks for the administration building. There were two armed guards in the office: special escort again I figured. But I was not prepared for the shock of the destination announced by the duty officer. 'We have orders to deliver you to Auswertestelle-West, immediately'.

Back to the interrogators! Is this why I had remained at Dulag-Luft so long? A deliberate plan by Scharff and Haneman to put me on ice and weaken my resolve? What form would the grilling take this time? These and other thoughts occupied my mind as, with the two guards close by, I trudged through the snow to Wetzlar railroad station.

Around the small, dimly lit station people stood in huddled groups stamping their feet and shrugging off the early morning cold. As expected, the train was late, causing considerable grousing among the waiting passengers. Eventually dawn heralded a bleak overcast day, the kind when one would prefer to stay indoors to warm beside a fire. The prospect of further interrogation at Auswertestelle-West was not relished and for the first time I had serious intentions of escape. Not only was my arm improved, but I now had the confidence to find my way around Germany. No longer was the spoken German foreign to my ear and the sight of a uniform did not bring apprehensive feelings. To attempt a go-it-alone hike in mid-winter was out of the question. On the other hand, if some of the imported foreign labour could be contacted and an identification pass and civilian clothing obtained, with my command of German there was a good chance of success. As we waited, I listened intently to the conversations around the platform and soon picked up some men conversing in French. There was a small group of them unloading freight from a waggon. Producing one of my precious cigarettes I indicated to the guards that a light was sought and casually moved towards the French workers. What I had not appreciated was their fear of having any contact with a PoW. As soon as I started to speak they shook their heads and slithered away up the platform.

Soon after, a huffing, steaming locomotive drawing six or eight passenger cars pulled into the station. In a mad rush, the crowd surged towards the compartment doors, pushing and cursing at any resistence. The train being pretty full when it arrived, those persons trying to dismount were only pressed further into the train. With people pushing in opposite directions the doorways were completely blocked. It was almost like a brawl. My guards, failing to gain entrance through the doors, moved to a coach toilet window. One of the soldiers drew his pistol, broke the glass out, then hoisted himself in. Reaching out he hoisted me by the arms in through the window. The second guard followed, pack and all, with a heave-ho from both of us. Here was a new and strange method of boarding trains for me. Not so much the going in a closet window as breaking the glass to do it. Their orders to get me to Oberursel certainly must have had top priority. Leaving the toilet, seats were found while the unruly crowd still pushed and shoved against each other. The train crew finally resolved that everyone had got aboard or departed. With a couple of whistle blasts we were huffing and puffing on our way.

In the next hour there were several more stops where similar confusion reigned. Passengers, cursing and elbowing their way on and off. Courtesy seemed non-existent; it was every man, woman and child for himself. If no seat existed then the passenger parked his anatomy on a case or bag. This being a second or third class passenger car, it was far from commodious. One thing that was clearly out of the question on this trip was escape. A guard sat near the exit door, the other beside two German soldiers facing me. On my left, next to the aisle, perched a little dark haired German girl about ten to twelve years old. Her buxom mother and a younger sister were in the adjoining compartment. Both kids were well scrubbed and neatly attired for a visit of some importance I guessed. A certain amount of apprehension appeared on the face of my young companion when she saw 'Kriegsgefangener' stencilled on my clothes. In an effort to ease her discomfort I smiled and struck up a conversation. She was obviously astounded that I could speak German and wasn't a demon who would eat her. We talked about her school, that I had a little son back in America, and other such matters relative to a child's world. At first shy, she quickly gained confidence and proved highly entertaining. My guards observed this exchange with some amusement.

As the train chugged along at a snail's pace through the mountain valleys north of Frankfurt, the sky began to lift and breaks in the cloud allowed the sun to shine through and brighten the day. From my position facing the rear of the train not a great deal of the scenery could be observed as we wound along, so I continued to practise my German on the little girl. Occasionally there was a need to stretch out my legs and alter my position on the uncomfortable seat. I was in the process of doing just this when the blissfulness of the moment erupted into carnage. Before my eyes splintered holes appeared in the wood panel opposite with a deafening whip-like crack. The little girl who had been beside me fell across my extended legs, the top of her head a bloody pulp. One of the soldiers opposite pitched forward, a bullet through his middle. People screamed and struggled to escape as, with a violent jolt, the train came to a halt. Knowing full well what was happening my first reaction was to try and seek protection on the floor, a reflex action rather than thought provoked movement. At this instant an explosion ripped into the side of the carriage sending the window glass flying and causing a partial collapse of the structure. Self preservation knows no courtesy; with a bound I was out into the aisle and through a door on the opposite side of the car. The track lay on top of a small embankment and with no more than two strides I was down it and prostrate behind some large boulders. The roar of aircraft, bursts of machine-gun fire and exploding bombs filled my ears; a fighter-bomber attack. Having meted out this sort of punishment, I was now on the receiving end! My guards had left me in the confusion. The ideal opportunity to escape. I looked behind me and was dismayed to find a sheer rock face stretching away in both directions.

The railroad was squeezed between a river and a mountain at this point, the foot of the mountain no doubt having been blasted away during construction. There was no way I could scale that rock face. After the next strafing run I looked up to see two flights of red-nosed P-47s circling around, not the 56th, but probably some outfit of the Allied 1st Tactical Air Force whose aircraft mostly used scarlet as a force identifying mark. Because of the partially protected position where the train had been caught, the fighters' firing passes could only be accomplished through very steep dives and at long range. Nevertheless, the boiler of the locomotive had been hit and a column of steam now wafted up some 500 feet. I felt I could survive the firing passes as each P-47 took it in turn to sweep down on the train but the 500 pound bombs they were dispensing were another matter, even though so far they had struck far from their mark. Now basic humanity asserted itself as my senses responded to the screams of the frightened and moans of the wounded and dying. Only a few seconds had elapsed between the shock of the attack and my accelerated exit from the car. The distraught mother of the two girls was up there crouching beside the train, pleading for someone to save her two children.

Seeing another P-47 was about to make an approach, I rushed up the embankment and grasping the woman by the arms unceremoniously dragged her down to the safety of the rocks. Sprinting back, the terrified younger sister was retrieved just before the next fusilade of bullets smashed into the train and ricocheted over the rocks. The hysterical woman kept crying out for her older daughter and attempting to get up. Pulling her down I said firmly, 'Mother, your daughter is dead. For your own safety lie still.' Such was her state of mind she still tried to go back to the train and I had to lie on her to keep her down when the next aircraft began its firing run.

While other passengers tried to console the woman, more dashes were made back to the wrecked cars to help extract wounded or those too petrified to move. A German soldier assisted; uniform, status and nationality no longer counted in this dire situation. Having used up their ammunition and bombs or decided this train was sufficiently wrecked, the Thunderbolt section finally departed the scene.

People began to emerge from hiding places and soldiers attended to the wounded and dying in the shattered railcars. Both my guards had disappeared and were not among the casualties in my proximity. Now, as I stood beside the train, I was conscious of a change of attitude among the passengers; their fear and panic gave way to anger and hatred. As the perpetrators of the deed were flown away their attention focused on the 'Terror Flieger' in their midst with 'Kriegsgefangener' emblazoned on his jacket. Threats were made and I saw two men pick up stones. Soon a small crowd of cursing and gesticulating civilians surrounded me. One man had a length of splintered wood and from what he said he was just about to use it. Realising the gravity of my situation my mind sought desperately for the best move to make. Suffice it to say there were few options. To cringe before an unruly mob would probably unleash the impending violence. Faced with a steep cliff on one side and a battered train and river on the other, the only outlet to escape remained up or down the railroad track. Too many passengers stood along the track for me to attempt to run, and if I did, some aggrieved soldier would probably shoot me on the pretext of my trying to escape. Stymied, I waited for the first blow; not frightened but outraged that I was to finish as a lynching victim after all my other close brushes with extinction.

At this precise moment a tall German Werhmacht Leutnant appeared from behind the crowd, drew his pistol and with a sharp command addressed my oppressors; 'Anyone harming this prisoner of war will be shot'. Then directing a few soldiers who had been onlookers to surround me for protection, the Leutnant said I was to follow him up the track. Earlier I had seen this officer directing rescue efforts further along the train. Perhaps he had noted my similar actions. At any rate, his timely presentation came not an instant too soon. The party escorted me up the railroad to where a narrow bridge spanned the river. This we crossed to follow a path across an open meadow to a farmhouse. The farmer and his family met us, the Leutnant asking to use a room to house this PoW and some other people from the train. Leaving me in the front room of the farmhouse with a couple of soldiers, the Leutnant departed.

Perhaps an hour passed before he returned, and with him was one of the original guards who had picked me up at Wetzlar earlier in the day, and a very attractive female. Dressed in a three-quarter length dark mink coat and chic knee-length black boots, this comely German woman was the most striking example of femininity thus far encountered during my wanderings in Germany. She had styled shoulder length brown hair and wore cosmetics subtly applied. The way she walked and spoke indicated that she came from a class of society accustomed to being served and pampered. From the ingratiating way she was greeted by the farmer's wife and others I suspected connections with someone of high status. No doubt she had been briefed about the PoW as I saw no surprise on her face when she entered the room. This attractive creature became the centre of attention for the family and soldiers, pampering which she appeared to expect. With her admirers, she remained near the fire across the room at some distance from me. The chatter overheard gave me no clue to her identity so I resolved to attempt to strike up a conversation if the opportunity arose.

Eventually, this gorgeous young lady did move nearer to where I stood. Before I could say anything she killed the desire by giving me a riveting look filled with hate. The axiom still prevailed that 'Terror Fliegers' kept their distance. While the others conversed, during the next few hours I stood looking out of the window or sat with my eyes on the wall thinking about recent experiences. I could well understand the feelings of these Germans and their loathing of all I represented as an American flier. To them the strafing had been a barbaric act inflicted on a civilian train with the killing of 'innocent' civilians — like the child who sat beside me. To the pilots of those P-47s it was an enemy train supporting the German war effort and could be carrying military personnel or war workers, if not now, tonight or tomorrow. No sane pilot would choose to strafe civilians, but the facts were that in this conflict involving a nation's whole economy, the military and civil populations and installations were inseparably entwined. In this total war the women and children of Germany were as much in the front line as those of Britain, Russia and the many occupied countries. Already, even before this incident, I had seen more hatred and threats of violence expressed by 'innocent' civilians than by any war sickened combatant.

From the window I saw several ambulances appear and medical attendents assist the wounded. Because access to the track was so restricted the casualties had to be carried down the track on stretchers and then over the footbridge. Another locomotive arrived, eventually pulling the train away. By noon the entire scene had cleared as evidently no bombs had hit the rails. I wondered why we still remained in the farmhouse. At last, at about 3:30 pm a grey staff car drew up to the farmhouse. The vehicle gave the impression of having been in every engagement from Dunkirk to Stalingrad, such was its worn and battered state. However, it was the driver who caused more interest in that he did little to uphold the name of the Aryan race, being Mickey Mouse sized, cross-eyed and of doubtful intelligence.

Looking at the staff car and driver I thought, 'Here we go again, another adventure with destiny!' The day was fading fast but not yet over. Although the car had been ordered up for the transportation of myself and the Luftwaffe guard, with two seats vacant, the Leutnant who had rescued me from the mob prevailed upon my guard to let him and the fair lady occupy the remaining space. After some discussion my Luftwaffe guard rode in the front with the driver while the mink coated beauty of the fair fragrance sat in the back between the Leutnant and myself. A somewhat restricted but cosy arrangement to say the least; not that I enjoyed the situation as my female companion never looked my way or said a word to me. Admittedly, I cannot have been a pleasant sight with my pants and jacket spattered with dried blood and mud, particularly my pants. I squirmed back and tried to rearrange my legs to hide this reminder of the recent dire situation.

We spun along at a respectable 35 mph. Past small farmsteads and spreads of conifer forest. There was some satisfaction being in a warm car looking at attractive countryside even though I was apprehensive about returning to Oberusel. After about a half hour on the road, nearing the outskirts of Frankfurt, the Leutnant suddenly shouted to the driver: 'Jabo, Jabo. Get off the road.' This shout so unnerved our driver that he cranked the wheel with a violent jerk to the right. Before we really knew what was happening the car hurtled off the road, turned over on its side, to slide twenty to thirty yards down an embankment before coming to a halt. Fortunately the car had toppled over onto the driver's side, opposite where I sat. As a result the three of us in the back wound up in one heap; the Leutnant at the bottom, the delectable lady next and the repugnant PoW on top. There followed a mad scramble to untangle our anatomies and make a dash for the closest cover. To get out, the door on my side had to be opened and pushed up. Naturally, I had to step on someone to gain a footing for the exodus, the object being to get out as fast as possible. As it turned out, the P-38 fighters had not spotted us and cruised on.

Extracting the girl became a pleasure, ruffled as she was, she stood up and held her composure as before. Next came assistance to my previous rescuer. Those of us in the back seat were not hurt except for a few bruises, some of which were undoubtedly due to the placing of my trusty boots. Those in the front had not fared so well. The Luftwaffe guard cracked his head against the windshield hard enough to leave a shattered impression on the glass. The driver sustained the greatest injury when he was thrown against the driving wheel and bumped along the door on his side. We finally extracted him from the further dilapidated staff car, smoking its last gasp. Perhaps the driver was fortunate to have sustained some physical injury as the wrath of the German officer was unrelenting at this point. His rage was such that the driver's sentence could have been a bullet. At least I could confirm another crippled staff car to the Allied fighters — without a shot being fired!

Nearby lay a small village and with the assistance of the Luftwaffe guard the injured driver was carried to the local guesthouse while the rest of us walked. In due time my guard rounded up another lift to Frankfurt in an automobile. Before departing I threw a half-hearted salute at the Leutnant, though not a word was spoken. Somehow I felt some semblance of mutual respect between the two of us although we were hardened enemies. With regard to the wearer of the mink coat and shiny black boots, a tinge of a smile was cast in her direction. Her icy countenance mellowed a little for a return nod was given. Who knows, if this day was typical for the German wife in wartime, there could be little to smile about.

Passage to Frankfurt and by the trolleycar to Oberursel proved uneventful and well after dark the two of us wearily trod through the gates of Auswertestelle-West. A reservation in the same pesky solitary cell found the lock closing behind me. Stretching on the same flea-ridden bunk, sleep was soon found. Thus ended a day I would never forget.

Early the next morning a knock on the door and a turning of the key found Hanns Scharff and a couple of his sullen armed guards standing before me. With his usual smile Scharff said, 'You certainly had some unusual experiences yesterday. You are extremely fortunate to be here.' Evidently word had already gotten round. 'Why was I brought back here?' was my immediate question. Scharff's reply was more extraordinary than anything I could have imagined. 'Your people in America wrote a nice article about you going down in *Time* magazine the other day. This has been picked up by the red stripe panters in Berlin and now they want to see you. They are the officers from the German general staff, the OKW. You are to be taken to the Opel hunting lodge in the Taunus mountains to await their arrival.' Was this some joke or interrogation ploy? What on earth would the OKW want from a mere combat colonel. Scharff didn't know or wasn't inclined to tell me. What really made me mad was the thought that this twist in events rested on unwanted publicity. I had enough problems without my own side adding to them. Another example of American vanity, they had to have their heroes.

After breakfast a staff vehicle picked me up with Scharff and a Kapitan Horst Barth. A short drive from Oberursel into the mountains north of Frankfurt brought us to a modest villa surrounded by thick forest. It was the hunting lodge of George von Opel who headed the German auto manufacturing firm of that name. Though not lavish, the facility was far from austere. On its interior walls hung the preserved heads of European and African animals, and even an American elk. I assumed Opel had been an international hunter and that these were trophies he had brought back from around the world. Evidently the lodge was available to the Oberursel interrogators for special purposes. I noticed an ample military presence patrolling the area. After warning me not to try to escape, my escorts departed, leaving me to wander round the lodge looking at the collection that von Opel had acquired. Eventually settling into an over-stuffed chair in the library, I was later approached by an elderly man who seemed to be in charge of the household staff. Pushing my luck I requested permission to take a hot bath and have my clothes washed. The steward complied and told me to make myself at home. The ring of grime around the bath was removed before I slipped into a borrowed bath robe and the remainder of the day was spent lounging in the library. Dinner was served to me alone in the large dining room, a tasty three course meal on fine Rosenthall china. The contrast in day to day living that I now encountered touched the extremes. Last evening I had gone without dinner after a long and arduous day and the night had been spent in a flea infested cell on a straw mattress. This evening saw the other end of the spectrum, dining in splendour in warm surroundings, with retirement to a nice bedroom with clean sheets and feather quilts.

Not until after lunch next day did the officers in the red striped pants make their appearance. With them Gefreiter Scharff and Kapitan Barth reappeared. It amazed me to see a Private 1st Class present in such a gathering of rank. This individual's sociability among superiors seemed quite accepted. He laughed and joked with all of them, but I never saw or heard him provoke a point of argument. A wily master of dialogue, even among his own country-men. When finally all had arrived, there must have been seven or eight officers and one civilian. All the officers wore full uniform with regalia and Iron Crosses. As some spoke no English the conversations for the most part were carried on in German. As expected, they had been told by Scharff that I could speak their mother tongue. Having not the slightest idea why these high ranking officers should seek to talk with me, I had decided that the best course was to take an assertive stance and tell them how they were losing the war. There would be no point in arguing so the intention was to convey my firm conviction as to the Allied victory. I realised I must be on my guard and evade any serious discussion of tactics.

Fortunately, with some manoeuvring, the topic of conversation mainly concerned the hunting trophies that decorated the walls of the spacious living room. Having participated in hunting for most of my life, this collection could have only tantalised the imagination of the most avid sportsman. The baron had spent a lifetime, and no doubt a fortune, accumulating this display. Dinner, served in several courses, was set with silver on white linen. A fine selection of wines were served in elegant crystal and, I assumed, came from the baron's cellar. During the course of the lengthy meal the conversation became less constrained with a considerable number of jokes being passed by the Germans. In other circumstances, in peacetime or among friends, I could have thoroughly enjoyed the entire affair. The meal was superb and I took advantage of the opportunity to fill out that last wrinkle of my emaciated stomach. Following dinner, the entire party retired to the lodge main living room where more bottles of light wine found their way.

Immediately, the conversation directed at me became more serious. How did I think the war was going? In replying I told them that in all honesty and truth the Allies were literally grinding the Wehrmacht and the German nation into the ground. The devastation I had seen in flights over much of Germany would be added to daily. The ground lines might be static during the winter months but the air assault would continue and subject them to ever-increasing punishment. In the air it was evident that the training and quality of the first-line Luftwaffe fighter units had diminished appreciably. There were many days when I had led my fighters and never seen a German aircraft. Feeling there was no reason why the message should not be driven home, I went on to say that the German units now seldom showed the fighting tenacity of a year previous. The American manufacturing juggernaut was now shifting into high gear whereas

German war production and transportation were being pounded daily. Their demise was a foregone conclusion.

Here the German officers retorted that they had secret weapons coming that would annihilate their opponents. With the Me 262 and other jet fighters, the day would come when such superior performance would prevail. In my case, having fought several battles with Me 262 without consequence, a retort was not difficult. Even with the superior performance of the aircraft, the overwhelming numbers of Allied fighters could trap the jets in the air and on the ground before any degree of effectiveness could be achieved. The discussion came to a stalemate with neither side conceding a point. Actually, I felt that each officer present may have agreed with me but wouldn't express his doubts for fear of alienating himself with his fellow officers. Despite my deliberate audacity, in no way had the debate become heated.

The conversation then turned to Communism and the Eastern Front. The topic was raised by one officer saying whole Russian units were giving up to come over to the German side. I suspected I was being provoked into commenting on the Red Army and Communism from my first hand experience. A few Russian units may have changed sides in the early days of the war but when Mother Russia was attacked the vast majority of her people defended her with all conceivable effort. Strangely, the fact that I'd been stationed in the Soviet Union was not brought out at all by anyone in the room. It was at this point that one of the senior officers made the most extraordinary proposition. Would I head a volunteer fighter organisation to combat the Communists? The combat would be exclusively restricted to the Eastern Front. The pay — in gold — was the equivalent of a thousand dollars a month plus ample allowance for mess, uniform and quarters. So this was the reason for their interest in me. Did these intelligent men really think I would consider such a far-fetched proposal? My answer was quick and emphatic: 'Hell No!' This did not deter them from further attempts at persuasion, insisting I would be fighting Communism which they were now opposing for the western Allies. Even if disenchanted with one's own side, did they seriously expect anyone to change allegiance at this stage in the war; it would have been suicide. The subject was ultimately dropped but not before they made much of trying to draw out my views on the possibility of enticing individual western soldiers to fight against the Russians. No wonder Germany was in such a mess if its general staff officers put their faith in such naive schemes. As tunics were shed and ties loosened the pressure on me subsided and some drifted away to hold their own conversations and imbibe liberally of the wines. Perhaps it was military heresy for command officers of any nation to concede approaching defeat. All I could say to their cause was the famous old expression: 'You don't miss the water until the well runs dry'.

Now I was approached by the civilian, von Collande, who spoke fluent English and said he was a playwright and movie director currently working on documentaries for the government. This handsome, outgoing individual with long wavy hair and blue eyes, made me another proposition. He said he was in the midst of turning out a documentary on the Allied air operations and needed a technical adviser to render him assistance. With my background as a group commander of a combat unit I would be ideal. Here too there would be an ample salary with a certain amount of freedom and special privileges. Von Collande's reassuring manner and eloquence in the English language enhanced his salesmanship. He reviewed the type of movie production while I politely listened. My refusal to help in any way drew suggestions that it could do no harm to better my own position now as my country would have no use for me once this war was over. My reply was to the effect that if anyone was foolish enough to accept his offer they would be mapping out a brief future. Realising his request would have to be attempted on someone else, further conversation on this topic reverted to the back burner.

By now the hour was late and, hoping I could duck out of further conversations, I requested that I be allowed to retire. As the whole affair had now dwindled to personal stories and private conversations between the officers, permission was granted. Crawling into bed that evening I lay awake trying to rationalise some of the aspects raised at this meeting. Did they really believe they could turn me traitor? Or was it to try and make propaganda; for I suspected von Collande worked for Goebbels' department. Or again, did Scharff and company set the whole thing up to try and extract intelligence from me. Then perhaps it was no more than an excuse for OKW officers to relax in the country. I never did learn the truth.

Arising next morning I found a fine breakfast waiting, in which the red stripe officers took part. I was then informed by Barth and Scharff that if I gave my parole as an officer and gentleman I could depart that day with a special escort to Stalag Luft I at Barth; my permanent prison camp. It was explained that if I didn't choose to give my parole for the trip, then I would be sent to the Dulag-Luft at Wetzlar to await the assembly of another PoW train. My choice was immediately to accept the more comfortable means of travel. Not having met anyone who could brief me on PoW camps, I knew nothing about the life and conditions that prevailed. I had no desire to spend more uncertain days in Dulag-Luft so the decision was taken to get moving and find what was in store at the end of the line. The OKW officers departed and lunchtime passed without any sign of escort. The lodge servants went about their task of cleaning up facilities while the armed guards patrolled the grounds.

Later in the afternoon a tall Luftwaffe Leutnant drove up in a small staff car to introduce himself as my escort. He asked if I had my things ready, making me smile. Except for my home-made cap tucked in my belt, my sole possessions were the clothes I wore. With no need for delay, we departed from the Frankfurt-am-Main railroad station. For me it was a blessing to be travelling at night. At least there would be no strafing from Allied fighter aircraft. For the first time on my German travels the compartment was warm, perhaps it was a first class carriage. A corner seat was acquired in which I leaned back and a fitful sleep gave some relief from the boredom.

As dawn broke the train moved into the railroad station in Hanover. Once again there was a long wait for our connection. My guard intended to seek refreshments but this idea was abandoned with the wail of the air raid sirens. In orderly fashion the passengers and station attendants moved underground into the well marked shelters, Luftschutzkeller, to await an all-clear signal. Inside the illumination was good, but with insufficient seating accommodation many people were forced to sit on the floor. Time was passed staring at the walls, looking at the groups or individuals and listening intently for the drumming of heavy bomber motors. Eventually the rumble of heavy anti-aircraft fire could be heard. I wondered where the bombers were going. Berlin perhaps. The rate of ack-ack fire increased and the noise grew louder. Some excitement and concern became apparent as everyone looked at the ceiling with anxiety. Then the faint drone of aircraft engines penetrated through the shelter entrance. A chill went through me; the bombers wouldn't fly over a city like this unless they were going to bomb it!

Instinctively we crouched waiting helplessly for the onslaught. With a thunderous crash the first bombs struck and with them came the terrifying realisation that the railroad yards and station must be the target. The shelter shook from near impacts but people did not become alarmed until the lights went off, leaving the place in darkness. However, shortly thereafter, standby lights flicked on and restored some confidence. The thick concrete withstood the rain of high explosives as the assault continued. Though shielded from direct blast effects the noise and concussions affected the ears and caused sharp pains in my head. Dust and dirt rose from every corner and crack and filled the air. Then came a lull. Having no way to look from the bomb shelter I could only anticipate that more bombs would come, knowing that our bombers attacked by spaced group or combat wing formations.

When escorting high over the bombers I had often watched as wave after wave went over a target that quickly became covered by a column of smoke and dust that might rise 10-15,000 feet in the air. I wondered how could people survive, little thinking that one day I would find out the hard way. Again the shelter shook and concussions assailed the ears. Would that direct hit come? Every soul in that place must have had the same dread thought. After stretching my luck so far in this war, how ironic it would be to die in a bunker bombed by my own flying pals. Wave after wave of bombers passed; it seemed the pounding would never cease. Hanover was, of course, the major railroad terminal for north Germany with extensive marshalling yards stretching for several miles. A major target in the campaign to cripple enemy communications. But did they have to pick the very hour Mrs Zemke's little Hoo-bart was in town! This ordeal of frightening suspense must have lasted well over half an hour. Eventually the muffled drone of aircraft engines faded away and the guns ceased to fire. The all-clear signal proclaimed that our lives had been spared.

Wearily people walked up the long stretch from the bunker to behold a spectacle of devastation and fire. The main station building lay in ruins, walls collapsed and roof gone, the wooden sections splintered or burning. Twisted rails and upturned cars littered the area. The pungent smell of detonated explosive hung in the air. Fire-fighting crews were already in action although the task looked hopeless. At a later date I learned that over 300 B-17s had dropped more than 900 tons of bombs on this area.

My guard spoke to several station attendants and was advised to walk out down the line to where another train might be caught. Striking out along the tracks became a laborious task. For the first few miles wrecked railroad cars, signals and equipment lay strewn everywhere among the bomb craters, continually impeding our progress. Soon after leaving the ruins of the smouldering station we were joined by a troop of German soldiers carrying full packs, rifles, gas masks and steel helmets. There were perhaps fifteen or sixteen of these chaps who had been caught in the bombing of the station. My officer guard fell in with this lot and told me to join the line. As we marched past other little groups wending their way along the track, there was obvious surprise to see one PoW with such escort; they must have thought I was a mighty important hombre!

It was a clear, crisp wintery day with an inch or two of snow on the ground and when we rested I sat by myself, dedicated to silence, observing the situation. By late afternoon we had walked well outside Hanover city limits, behind us above the scene of destruction, smoke still billowed well up into the sky. Eventually, on rounding a curve in the track, we at last beheld a wheezing loco and passenger train standing near a small village. At its station my guard showed his papers at the booth and soon we were resting in a first class railroad carriage. Personally, I didn't relish resting aboard a stationary train any place in Germany. As straggling passengers arrived on foot from Hanover the train filled to more than capacity. After about an hour it slowly pulled out, still leaving a sizeable throng waiting on the little station. Most of that night the train jogged along making long hauls between stops. A fitful series of naps, then waking occasionally to stretch out, occupied the time. During the journey I learned that my escort had been a lawyer by trade and I suspected he was not enthusiastic about being in the military.

It must have been well past midnight when we arrived in Berlin, another blacked-out city huddled in snow. In the eerie hooded lights of the large station hall signs of past bombing attacks showed. Once on the platform my officer guard hesitated not a moment to find a restaurant and in short order both of us sat at a small table gobbling up a generous plate of stew supplemented with the usual coarse black bread and margarine. Ration coupons but no money appeared to change hands and I concluded the sustenance was a benefit provided by the Third Reich. Towards the end of the savoury meal the air raid sirens began to wail. My guard rose instantly saying we'd better seek out an air-raid shelter. Hunger not yet sated, I finished the stew with a gulp, and ramming the remainder of the bread in my jacket, followed. It had become a personal axiom that if killed it would be with a full stomach.

A cellar air-raid bunker was not hard to find, and crouching against the wall nibbling bread it was not long before the rumble of distant guns indicated the German capital was the bombers' objective. So now it was the RAF. I was beginning to think the Allies were out to get Zemke in view of what had happened during the past few days. However, this must have been an RAF Mosquito nuisance raid, for although the anti-aircraft guns hammered with great intensity and regularity, the explosions we heard were distant and not as violent as the Hanover raid. Eventually, after an hour, the all-clear sounded and we filed quietly from the bunker like a congregation departing a Sunday service, to find the station as we had left it.

A passenger train heading north to Stettin on the Baltic, carried us away from Berlin in the wakening hours of a new day. We were running in fairly open lands between low rolling hills and scattered pine forest, cold and foreboding countryside. At Stettin a small passenger freight train was boarded to follow a western route, along the Baltic coast, and late that afternoon we arrived at our destination, Barth. Disembarking from the rail cars, it was not difficult to obtain directions to the prison camp. We tramped through the darkened town in the ebbing day and along a gravel road. As we left the built-up area, in the far distance a sprawl of low buildings with high guard towers could be made out in the gloom. Despite the foreboding appearance, my spirits were uplifted with the thought that in a short while I'd be among friends and people of my own kind. I had enough experience of travelling in Germany to last me a lifetime.

19

AN APPRECIATION

When the gates of Stalag Luft 1 closed behind Colonel Hubert Zemke on 16 December 1944, his was to be no typical mundane tale of military incarceration. Prisoner experience opened a new and very different chapter in his colourful wartime career, for Hub suddenly found himself the Senior Allied Officer of a camp that eventually numbered some nine thousand souls. Once more that flare for leadership shone bright in the course of extraordinary events with surprising outcomes. Before eventually returning to his homeland, Hub was yet again to find himself in tight corners; while a display of initiative sparked one of the early incidents in the Cold War. But all that is another story.

In retirement, Hubert Zemke, as befits his outlook, has a habit of dismissing his achievements in life with a joke. Others who have known him accord him substantial honours, in particular recognition as probably the most successful American fighter leader of the Second World War. This the subject contests, not through modesty but because he does not believe it to be true. He insists that the successes in air fighting were due to the quality of whole organisations and not to one man. Given recorded facts, what then is a fair assessment of his wartime contribution?

To begin with there are written pronouncements that the 8th Air Force commanders considered Hubert Zemke their foremost fighter leader and that General Kepner, as head of VIIIth Fighter Command, viewed him as his best group commander. Without question it was Zemke's 56th Fighter Group that showed what could be done to take the fight to the Luftwaffe and lead the way. Its score of enemy aircraft destroyed in air combat was unsurpassed by any other American fighter group fighting in Europe, and it also had the best ratio of enemy aircraft destroyed to own losses — eight to one.

While many achievements credited to air power in the Second World War may be debatable, all reputable studies acknowledge that the gaining of air superiority in enemy air space and maintaining this domination until the end of hostilities was a decisive factor in achieving victory. Initially, this air superiority was largely due to the endeavours of VIIIth Fighter Command units, albeit that their original mission was to provide protection for the American day bombers. For single-engine, single-seat fighter aircraft to eventually take the air war into the heart of the German homeland and win the day would have been considered a preposterous proposition in 1940 yet it was a reality four years later. Much was due to technical advances but all finally depended upon the men in fighter cockpits. There was no substitute for the determination to win and that became the hallmark of the 56th Group and eventually the whole of VIIIth and IXth Fighter Commands.

Whether or not the 56th would have risen to such heights if Zemke had not been its original master and, in turn, influencing the outcome of the whole fighter campaign, can only be speculative. The generation of young Americans who took to the air in the Second World War produced many fine leaders and it is reasonable to suppose the end result would have been the same. However, to what extent did the success of VIIIth Fighter Command depend on 'The Wolfpack' pacesetters? Not only by the challenge of example and fighting spirit, but through influence of tactics developed and adopted by the Command? A fair assessment would give this to be substantial. And to what extent was the 56th's success due to Zemke? The opinions of many who served with him may be swayed by emotion but it is fact that his brand of aggressive leadership, demanding air discipline and team participation, might not have been forthcoming from anyone else in the group. He deliberately sacrificed popularity to guide the group the way he believed it should go and this provided the environment in which the tenacious go-getting fighter pilots like Gabreski, Bob and Gerry Johnson, Mahurin, Schilling and the rest could flourish. On such conjecture Hubert Zemke can stand as an exceptional fighter leader.

His personal record as a fighter pilot was also among the best. He was responsible for bringing down at least nineteen enemy aircraft and, in the dangerous task of ground strafing, eleven aircraft, more than fifty locomotives and innumerable other ground targets had succumbed to his fire and ordnance. Despite this prowess he admitted to being no more than an average pilot and not mujch of a shot; he misjudged and made mistakes. Such frank acknowledgement of his own shortcomings and fallibility extended to other spheres, notably the detested staff work for which he insisted he was ill suited.

This personal honesty was part of Hub's strength. He endeavoured to think hard, long and honestly about important matters before making decisions. He believed you made your own luck. With his extraordinary record of narrow escapes even he could not deny that good fortune played a part now and again. Rather he meant that whatever part luck or fate eventually played, it was still dependent on the indiviual's ability to size up the situation and a determination to master it. The philosophy of the boxing ring was carried into a fighter cockpit and the command of a fighting group. This was Hub Zemke's hallmark, a stubborn determination to succeed; the prime constituent of good leadership.

That Hubert Zemke was the greatest American fighter leader of the Second World War is a sweeping statement that might find favour in popular folklore but not with true historians. What can be said and supported is that if in history a name is needed to represent the success of the American fighter pilots of the Second World War, there is no better candidate than Hubert Zemke.

As a frustrated forester it is Hub's wish that when the time comes his ashes are to be interred beneath a towering sequoia in the Sierra Nevada mountains separating Nevada from California. While his mortal remains may lie in the forest that he loved so dearly, for those who have known Hubert Zemke, either personally or through the medium of the written word, his presence is elsewhere. Far away, high above the land of his forefathers, where whisps of cirrus form and fade in the frigid blue, the spirit of Hubert Zemke forever soars: 'This is Yardstick. Follow Me.'

INDEX